Subterranean Britain

SECOND WORLD WAR SECRET BUNKERS

Subterranean Britain

SECOND WORLD WAR SECRET BUNKERS

Nick McCamley

FOLLY BOOKS

First published in Great Britain in 2010 by Folly Books Ltd

Second edition published 2014

A catalogue record for this book is available from the British Library.

ISBN 978-0-9928554-2-0

Published by Folly Books Ltd
Monkton Farleigh
BA15 2QP
www.follybooks.co.uk

Designed and typeset by Vicky *(left)*

Printed and bound in India by Replika Press Pvt Ltd

Jacket and introductory photographs
Front jacket: No.6 District, Tunnel Quarry
Facing title page: 'A' Loop, RAF Fauld
Facing page 1: Sgt Major Kennedy, RE, surveying Monkton Farleigh Quarry in 1937

PREFACE

This book is the culmination of almost forty-five years of research, some of it decidedly desultory in nature and some – particularly when my previous publisher indicated worrying signs of hypertensive stress at my lackadaisical approach to printing deadlines (my manuscripts were often more than a year late in delivery) – rather more frenetic. This is the book that I wanted all my previous books to be; in it I hope to transfer to the reader some of the visceral excitement I experienced when I first physically discovered, investigated, (often with some trepidation and at personal risk), and later researched the recorded history of the underground structures detailed within.

The genesis of this book was a chance comment made by a friend at sixth-form college in 1967. He mentioned that he had discovered while on a cycle ride near Bath the previous weekend a huge and disturbingly deserted army camp, littered with railway lines, strange buildings and many secret corners. It was, he said, just like a set from *The Avengers*; one expected to turn a corner and discover a bowler-hatted Patrick Macnee driving down the road in a vintage Bentley, with the sound of an old door creaking ominously in the distance and tumbleweed rolling lazily down the pavement. The camp was at Monkton Farleigh and the following Saturday my friend Graham and I decided to investigate it ourselves.

The site proved even more fantastic than the description we had been given. In the middle was a building that appeared to be a boiler house; it had a tall chimney and emerging from its roof and walls were a number of large pipes, two feet or so in diameter, that ran out across the surrounding fields in all directions, through hedgerows and woodland, over bridges and under culverts, before plunging down vertical concrete-lined shafts, approximately one hundred feet deep and twelve feet in diameter. Having investigated the boiler house and pipes, our attention turned to a long, low, sinister building, windowless, and fronted by four huge steel doors, welded shut, that obviously gave on to lorry loading bays within. By means not entirely ethical, we managed to gain access to the building via a small pedestrian door and found ourselves confronted by near total darkness. Striking matches for light, we made out two wide rubber conveyor belts running the full length of the building. At the end of the building the belts seemed to disappear through a hole in the wall, partially secured by hinged rubber flaps about two feet square. Inquisitive, we pushed aside the rubber flaps and climbed through. Instantly, we were both plummeting downhill in utter darkness at an alarming rate. On the far side of the hole the conveyor belts dipped at an angle of forty-five degrees and plunged underground; condensation had made the rubber extraordinarily slippery and we could get no grip to retard our lightning descent.

Bruised, battered, disorientated and stranded one hundred feet underground, we picked ourselves up and assessed our situation. Lighting the last of our matches before it spluttered into darkness, we observed the dim outlines of tunnels radiating before us. Being semi-experienced cavers we were aware of the rudimentary 'left-hand-rule', which states that when you are lost underground, if you reach out to the left-hand wall and continue to follow it, you will eventually arrive at your way out. Putting theory into practice I reached out and immediately felt what appeared to be a steel box with knobs on, located on the wall. Assuming they might be switches of some type, I turned one and lights suddenly blazed in a corridor ahead of me. Turning another, a further hundred yards of corridor was brightly illuminated. Having turned all sixteen switches we were confronted with a long straight corridor that seemed to converge to a vanishing point very far away. We walked the length of this corridor for a distance of a quarter of a mile or so until we came to another passageway containing a double line of narrow-gauge railway tracks. More and more passages branched off of this and soon we were hopelessly lost. Most of the tunnels contained conveyor belts and we discovered that push buttons mounted beside the belts at intervals of about a hundred feet would start the belts in motion or stop them, depending upon whether the buttons were red or white. When in motion the belts travelled a little faster than walking pace, so for the next six or seven hours we explored the rest of the underground complex in comfort by sitting on the moving belts, stopping them for a look around when anything took our attention. On our journey we found a huge underground generating station, air-conditioning plants with fans twice our height in diameter, offices and workshops, and acre upon acre of empty storage space.

At sixteen years of age we had no conception of exactly what it was that we had found, but it was simply and absolutely overawing and that sensation alone provided sufficient satisfaction. Later, we learned that what we had explored was Monkton Farleigh sub-depot No.3 of the Corsham Central Ammunition Depot and that it was the largest underground ammunition depot in the world. Building had begun in 1937 in preparation for the Second World War and it had finally been decommissioned just weeks before we found it in 1967.

Years later, in 1984, my wife and I were fortunate enough to acquire the depot, by then heavily vandalized and in very poor condition, with a view to restoring the site and opening it to the public as a heritage venture. Our possession of the quarry seemed to open many doors that before were securely closed. We received a great deal of co-operation from the Ministry of Defence at Corsham and elsewhere, previously secret documents were made available to us, access was allowed to a number of other underground sites in the Corsham area, and arrangements were made for us to visit Tunnel and Spring quarries to recover equipment for the restoration of Monkton Farleigh Quarry.

One day in the summer of 1985, shortly after the restoration process had begun, an elderly but very sprightly gentleman turned up unexpectedly at the mine. He explained that his name was Fred Allen and that from 1936 he had been in charge of the construction of not just Monkton Farleigh Quarry but of all the government quarries in north Wiltshire. In his pocket he had a wonderful, water-coloured plan of our quarry which, he explained, was prepared during the building of the depot. He went on to tell us that during his working life at Corsham, up until his retirement in 1966, he had scrupulously retained all the documents, plans and photographs pertaining to his work at Corsham in order that the history of the project should not be lost through neglect. Contact with Eric Bryant of the Air Ministry Works Directorate, with whom Mr Allen co-operated regarding temporary RAF storage facilities in the Corsham area, resulted in the accumulation of more documents and photographs of historical significance. He told us that he had all this material – maps, plans, contracts, correspondence and boxes full of glass-plate negatives – packed in tea chests at home and that, if we wished, we could make copies of it all. The next day we leased an industrial photocopier, drove it around to Fred's house and spent the following thirty-six hours copying all he could dig out from storage. Shortly before his death in 2003 (at the age of 96) Fred gave me many of the original documents that we had copied eighteen years earlier. Then, in 2009, I was contacted by Fred's son, David, who explained that he had discovered many more documents and drawings and all of his father's wartime diaries and notebooks – none of which I had seen before – and that if I could make use of them I could have them. This book would have been impossible without the contributions from Fred and David Allen and to them I offer heartfelt thanks.

Thanks must go out, also, to the small group of volunteer helpers at Monkton Farleigh Quarry – most of them teenagers at the time but all now approaching (or, like me, well into) middle age – whose enquiring minds were stimulated by their work there and whose interest in Britain's subterranean infrastructure has expanded rather than waned with the passage of time. Amongst this group of friends, all of whom have contributed to the photographs collected for this book in one way or another, I must give special acknowledgment, in no particular order of merit, to Derek Hawkins, Mark Rivron, Bradley Wyatt, Bob Scammell, Peter Yarbrough, Bruce Maskery and Sam Catalani. I must also thank my long suffering wife, Vicky, not only for her photographic skills, but for sharing my enthusiasm for this, my life-long work.

Special thanks are due to Nick Catford who has most generously provided many of the photographs for this book. Of particular note are his stunning images of Rhydymwyn, Longbridge, Drakelow, Trecwn, Dean Hill, Portland and Llanberis together with some brilliant photographs of Farleigh Down Sidings taken in the mid-1980s when, for me, things other than photography took precedence at Monkton Farleigh Mine.

Finally, I have to offer a very special thanks to Bradley Wyatt and Paul Hurren for the misery they must have endured in obtaining the absolutely unique images of Clubhouse Quarry seen in chapter 6, and also to Bruce Maskery for helping to arrange the trip that made those photographs possible.

Nick McCamley
Monkton Farleigh
August 2014

CONTENTS

		Page
1	*INTRODUCTION*	1
2	*CAD CORSHAM: Quarry conversion; Ridge Quarry, Eastlays, Tunnel Quarry and Monkton Farleigh Quarry*	14
3	*UNDERGROUND FACTORIES: Spring Quarry and Olga Lehmann's murals, Limpley Stoke Quarry, Westwood Quarry, Drakelow, Longbridge and Rhydymwyn Shorts of Rochester, Plessey Tunnels, Henley on Thames, Warren Row*	134
4	*ADMIRALTY STORAGE: Bradford-on-Avon, Pickwick & Elm Park, Copenacre, Trecwn and Dean Hill*	217
5	*RAF BOMB STORES: Chilmark, Llanberis, Harpur Hill, Grange Cavern and Fauld*	240
6	*VAULTS & REPOSITORIES: Westwood Quarry, Manod, and Clubhouse Quarry*	275
7	*PORTLAND COMMAND BUNKER*	298
	BIBLIOGRAPHY	302

Chapter 1

INTRODUCTION

By the summer of 1934 the British government and the military strategists upon whom it relied were convinced that another major European war was inevitable. How long its gestation period might be was difficult to foresee but the general consensus was that the continent would once again be engulfed in a conflict with Germany within the next four to ten years.

Assessments of German air power, later proved to be wildly pessimistic, indicated that within hours of the declaration of war the skies over London would blacken with German bombers, the capital would be annihilated by a storm of high-explosive bombs, incendiaries and poison gas, the seat of government would be destroyed, and that would be the End of England. On a slightly more optimistic note, however, the analysts calculated that, whilst the Luftwaffe might possess an overwhelmingly powerful bomber force, the aircraft were severely fettered by their limited range of action. London and the home counties might be indefensibly vulnerable to aerial bombardment but the rest of the country would remain, for a while at least, virtually immune.

Based upon these assumptions the Chiefs of Staff of the armed services and heads of numerous government departments began, towards the end of 1934, to make secret arrangements for the evacuation of key departments, state institutions and military establishments to safe locations beyond the range of the German bombers. Amongst the military the War Office was the most overtly proactive in its planning. In many ways its key storage depots for army ammunition were the most vulnerable; huge stockpiles, much of it reserve and obsolete stock dating from the First World War, were held in surface storage sheds at Woolwich Arsenal and at Bramley near Basingstoke, both of which were within range of the German bombers. Once the nature of the threat was fully assessed the staff of the Master General of Ordnance drew up an outline evacuation scheme. A notional line was drawn from the Wash to the Solent and the whole of the country to the west and north of that line was deemed safe. To be doubly sure the War Office decided upon a 'belt-and-braces' approach; not only would their alternative storage facilities be within the safety zone but they would also be built underground. Initial discussions with the Treasury somewhat deflated the War Office scheme when its representatives were told that the cost of excavating a vast, new network of underground tunnels would be prohibitively expensive and, given the nation's straitened financial situation, could not be countenanced. With remarkable rapidity the plans were revised and, before the year's end, teams of Royal Engineers officers were dispatched to the remoter regions of the country tasked with finding suitable existing underground locations that might, at reasonably modest cost, be adapted for ammunition storage.

Over the ensuing six months virtually every cave, quarry and abandoned mine in Britain was examined and reported upon. The sites visited included salt mines in Cheshire, limestone and gypsum quarries in Derbyshire and Cumberland, slate quarries in North Wales, disused railway tunnels throughout the whole of Britain and, most significantly, oolitic limestone quarries in north Wiltshire. Most were immediately dismissed as unsuitable due to dampness, geological instability, remoteness from transport links or the difficulty of obtaining sufficient labour locally to undertake the task of conversion. Twenty or so sites were singled out for further attention but none, except for the Wiltshire stone quarries, appeared particularly promising.

Attention soon focussed upon the vast subterranean network of worked-out and abandoned stone quarries in the vicinity of Corsham in Wiltshire. At depths of between eighty and one hundred feet below the surface building stone of the highest quality – probably, indeed, the best building stone in the world – had been intensively quarried for more than a century. In the late 1870s most of the Wiltshire quarry owners had combined to form the Bath Stone Firms Ltd, and some years later a further amalgamation led to the formation of the Bath & Portland Stone Company which held a virtual monopoly over the supply of oolitic limestone for building purposes. At the time of the Royal Engineers' visit, however, the Bath & Portland company was in trouble. Although there was still stone left in its quarries the reserves were running out and that which was left was generally of slightly lower quality and was more difficult to extract. With Britain entering the worst recession the economy had ever experienced the building industry was in decline and consequently the market for building stone was quickly contracting. The company faced other problems too. Stone quarrying in Wiltshire was a highly conservative and labour intensive industry. For over a century working men in the Wiltshire countryside faced only two career choices – they could work on the land as farm labourers or under it as quarrymen. Historically, there was always a surplus of labour so wages were low and there was no incentive to mechanize. The most startling feature of the underground quarries in the early 1930s was that the tools and techniques being used to extract stone were the same tools and techniques that were being used when Queen Victoria ascended to the throne. By the middle of the decade, however, things were changing. Wage rates generally were rising and, with the government's belated re-armament programme stimulating manufacturing industries, there was suddenly more competition for labour. All of these factors threatened the viability of the Bath & Portland Stone Company which found itself saddled with rapidly increasing labour costs, falling demand and the dead-weight overhead costs of a dozen or more unproductive quarries. Thus, when the directors were approached by the War Office with tentative enquiries about the prospective purchase of some of their freehold quarries at commercial rates they were overjoyed.

Within the War Office there were men who were already aware of the potential value of the Corsham quarries, for under their aegis during the First World War, Ridge Quarry, a small underground working approximately six acres in extent situated near the village of Neston, had been temporarily occupied on behalf of the Ministry of Munitions for the storage of high-explosives for which no suitable accommodation could be found at Woolwich Arsenal. In January 1935 the War Office was given permission to make surveys of all the Bath & Portland quarries in the Corsham area and, based upon the result of these surveys, Ridge Quarry and the much larger, fifty-acre Tunnel Quarry just to the north of Brunel's Box railway tunnel, were purchased on 15 August for the sum of £35,000. A few months later Eastlays Quarry at Gastard was acquired, followed by Monkton Farleigh Quarry in March 1937. These four quarries jointly encompassed an area of approximately 150 acres and were later to become 'Central Ammunition Depot Corsham', the history of which will be illustrated in the following chapter.

A year or so after the War Office initiated its quest for underground accommodation the Air Ministry began a similar search. In 1934 the RAF was essentially a force of wooden biplane fighters and light, short-range bombers designed principally for army support duties. It was not until the series of expansion programmes, with their emphasis on fast, metal-skinned monoplane fighters and heavy bombers, got under way in 1930s that the Air Ministry realized that it had no secure storage sites for the munitions that would arm its new range of aircraft. By the summer of 1936 bombs in huge quantities were rolling out of British factories, swelling the tide of similar weapons imported from the United States that were trundling on trains from the ports en route to the RAF's only, and hopelessly inefficient,

Nº	Name	Location	Type	Probable Area (Sq. Ft.)	Average Headroom (Ft.)	Width of Galleries (Ft.)	Acces
	Scottish Area						
1.	Middleton	Nr. Gorebridge. Midlothian	Limestone Workings.	75,000	15 to 20	Probably about 20(ft)	Readily avai
2.	Mine Nº 1 Philpstoun.	Nr. Linlithgow. West Lothian	Shale Mine.	Extensive, but restricted size could be enlarged	Probably 6-9 ft.	Probably about 8-10 ft	Bad. Hutc 10' × 8'6" × 63 or gradient,
3.	Thornton Hall.	7½ miles S.E. of Glasgow	Limestone Workings.	No detailed report, but understood			
4	Murrayshill.	Nr. Cambusbarron 1½ miles S.W. of Stirling	Limestone Workings	750,000	7-8 ft.	about 25 ft.	2 entranc
5	Scotland Street Tunnel	Edinburgh-(Waverley Sta)	Disused Railway Tunnel	38,000. unoccupied.	16 ft. to crown of arch.	24 ft.	Available.
6	Burdie House	5 miles S of Edinburgh	Limestone Workings	150,000	10-30 ft.	Not stated.	5 entranc
7.	Cocklakes	6 miles from Carlisle	Gypsum Mine	435,600	8-18 ft.	20 ft.	1 inclined s
	Newcastle Area						
8.	Coatham Stob	Eaglescliffe. Nr. Stockton Co. Durham.	Limestone and Sandstone workings	20,000	20-30 ft.	24 ft.	Bad. Tunn side of ope
	Leeds Area.						
9.	Brunswick Tunnel.	Harrogate.	Disused Railway Tunnel	25,000	17'6" to crown of arch.	25 ft.	Not state
	Cumberland Area						
10.	Elterwater Quarry	12 miles from Windermere	Slate Workings	30,000	24 ft ?	24 to 90 ft.?	2 entranc
11.	Acorn Bank & Houtsay Area.	Temple Sowerby Nr. Penrith	Extensive Gypsum Mines	?	?	?	?
12.	Kirkby Thore-Stamphill	Stamphill. Nr. Penrith.	Extensive Galleries	?	3 × 300 ft. galleries. ?		
	North Wales Area.						
13	Grange Quarries	Holywell.		4,000			
14	Prince Llewellyn Quarry	Dolwyddelan	Slate Quarry ?	23,000			Tunnel to of 3 Chamb
	Birmingham Area						
15.	Dudley Limestone Quarry.	Dudley. Nr. Birmingham.	Limestone Quarry.	400,000	?	?	Access to o group only canal, one
	Derbyshire Area.						
16.	Disused Railway Tunnel	Buxton, Burbage.	Mineral Railway Tunnel	36,000	20 ft. (max)	14 to 20 ft.	By old track Burbage Vil Nr. main Bu
	South Wales Area.						
17.	Railway Tunnel.	Nr. centre of Pontardawe	Railway Tunnel.	4,000	11 ft.	11 ft.	Not diffic small brid
18.	Llanfair Slate Quarries	Merrioneth.	Slate Quarries	17,000	8 to 70 ft.	?	2 adits 1 blocked
19.	Aberllefenni Slate Quarries	Merrioneth.	Slate Quarries	(16,900 see sketch)	60 to 200 ft.	30-60 ft.	1 Tunnel co with narrow track 1 Tunnel dire existing
20.	Bath Stone Quarries	(See separate	report.)				

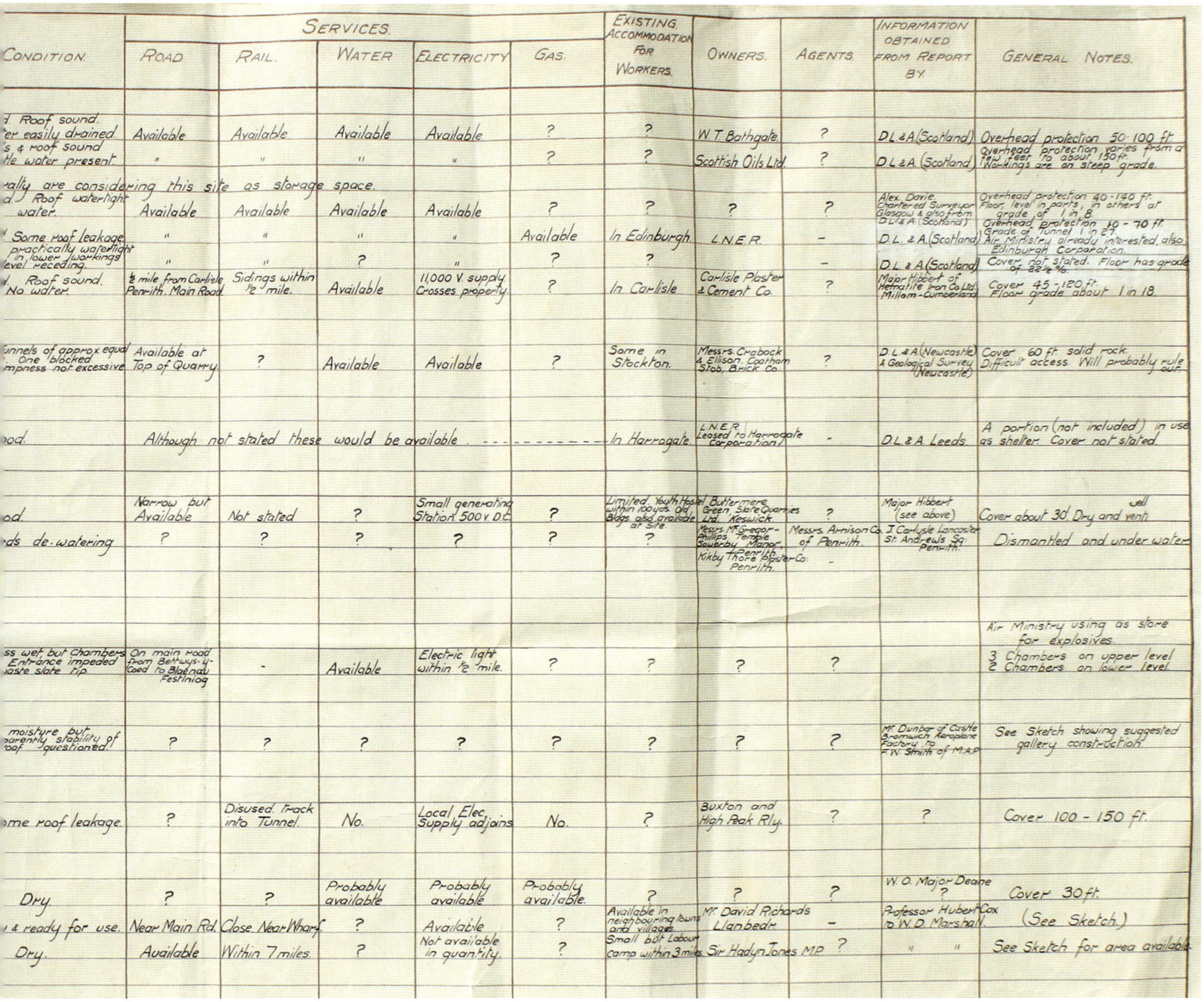

Condition	Services: Road	Rail	Water	Electricity	Gas	Existing Accommodation for Workers	Owners	Agents	Information obtained from Report by	General Notes
…d. Roof sound. …er easily drained.	Available	Available	Available	Available	?	?	W.T. Bathgate.	?	D.L. & A. (Scotland)	Overhead protection 50-100 ft
…s & roof sound …tle water present	"	"	"	"	?	?	Scottish Oils Ltd	?	D.L. & A. (Scotland)	Overhead protection varies from a few feet to about 150 ft. Workings are on steep grade.
…ally are considering this site as storage space.										
…d. Roof watertight …water.	Available	Available	Available	Available	?	?	?	?	Alex. Davie. Chartered Surveyor Glasgow & also from D.L. & A. (Scotland)	Overhead protection 40-140 ft. Floor level in parts, in others at grade of 1 in 8
… Some roof leakage.	"	"	"	"	Available	In Edinburgh.	L.N.E.R.	-	D.L. & A. (Scotland)	Overhead protection 10-70 ft. Grade of Tunnel 1 in 27. Air Ministry already interested, also Edinburgh Corporation.
practically watertight in lower workings …level receding.	"	"	?	"	?	?		-	D.L. & A. (Scotland)	Cover not stated. Floor has grade of 22½%.
… Roof sound. No water.	½ mile from Carlisle Penrith. Main Road	Sidings within ½ mile.	Available	11,000 V. supply Crosses property.	?	In Carlisle	Carlisle Plaster & Cement Co.	?	Major Hibbert of Hematite Iron Co Ltd Millom-Cumberland	Cover 45-120 ft. Floor grade about 1 in 18.
…unnels of approx equal … One blocked …mpness not excessive	Available at Top of Quarry	?	Available	Available	?	Some in Stockton.	Messrs. Craback & Ellison. Coatham Stob, Brick Co.	?	D.L. & A. (Newcastle) & Geological Survey (Newcastle)	Cover 60 ft. solid rock. Difficult access. Will probably rule out.
…ood.	Although not stated these would be available - - - - - - - - - - - -					In Harrogate.	L.N.E.R. Leased to Harrogate Corporation.	-	D.L. & A. Leeds	A portion (not included) in use as shelter. Cover not stated.
…od.	Narrow but Available	Not stated	?	Small generating Station 500 V. D.C.	?	Limited. Youth Hostel within 100 yds. Old Bldgs. also available at Site.	Buttermere Green Slate Quarries Ltd. Keswick	?	Major Hibbert (see above)	Cover about 30'. Dry and well venti…
…ds de-watering	?	?	?	?	?	?	Messrs. McGregor-Phillips. Temple Sowerby Manor, Penrith.	Messrs. Arnison Co. of Penrith.	J. Carlyle Lancaster St. Andrews Sq. Penrith.	Dismantled and under water
							Kikby Thore Plaster Co. Penrith.	-		
…ss wet, but Chambers … Entrance impeded …aste slate tip.	On main road from Bettws-y-Coed to Blaenau Festiniog	-	Available	Electric light within ½ mile.	?	?	?	?		Air Ministry using as store for explosives. 3 Chambers on upper level 2 Chambers on lower level
…moisture but …parently stability of …oof questioned.	?	?	?	?	?	?	?	?	Mr Dunbar of Castle Bromwich Aeroplane Factory to F.W. Smith of M.A.P.	See Sketch showing suggested gallery construction
…me roof leakage.	?	Disused track into Tunnel.	No.	Local Elec. Supply adjoins	No.	?	Buxton and High Peak Rly.	?	?	Cover 100-150 ft.
Dry.	?	?	Probably available	Probably available	Probably available.	?	?	?	W.O. Major Deane ?	Cover 30 ft.
…& ready for use.	Near Main Rd.	Close. Near Wharf.	?	Available	?	Available in neighbouring towns and villages.	Mr David Richards Llanbedr	-	Professor Hubert Cox to W.D. Marshall.	(See Sketch.)
Dry.	Available	Within 7 miles	?	Not available in quantity.	?	Small but Labour camp within 3 miles	Sir Hadyn Jones MP	?	" "	See Sketch for area available.

Left: The original schedule of underground sites examined by War Office surveyors in 1935. The Corsham area was subject to a separate survey and its schedule of locations is shown overleaf.

armament storage depot at Altrincham in Cheshire, which had been designed solely for the maintenance of small-arms ammunition. At this point the Air Ministry Works Department, entrusted with the task of locating underground storage capacity for its burgeoning stockpile of bombs, was disconcerted to find that all the best sites had already been snapped up by the War Office. As an interim emergency measure the War Office was persuaded in 1936 to hand over the majority of Ridge Quarry, then nearing completion, to the RAF and in the following year permission was also obtained to occupy part of the Eastlays depot at Corsham.

Meanwhile the search for their own dedicated underground capacity continued. Eventually five sites were secured, none of which were ideal and three of which proved to be catastrophic failures. Initially three old mine workings were identified: Chilmark Quarry near Wilton in Wiltshire that had provided stone for the construction of Salisbury Cathedral, Linley Caverns near Brownhill in Staffordshire that a century earlier had provided building stone for Birmingham but which, since late Victorian times, had intermittently functioned as a tourist attraction, and the Fauld gypsum mine near Burton-on-Trent in Staffordshire. The Chilmark depot was the least unsuccessful of the Air Ministry ventures underground. Despite the fact that it was subject to frequent and unexpected roof falls

1	2	3	4	5	6	7			8
NO.	NAME OF QUARRY	TOTAL QUARRIED AREA (EXCLUDING PILLARS)	FLOOR AREA FULLY DEVELOPED (SEE NOTE A)	FLOOR AREA CLEARED (SEE NOTE B)	BALANCE OF QUARRIED AREA - UNDEVELOPED (SEE NOTE C)	PRESENT OCCUPATION DEPT.	AREA	USER	PRESENT TITLE
1	SPRING	A 3,343,948 = 77 acres	2,271,200	E. 468,300	604,448	M.O.S. ADMIRALTY P.O.	1,476,280 772,208 22,712	STORAGE DO. T.E.	R.
1A	SANDS	A 138,234	-	E. 59,320	78,914	-	-	-	R
2	HAYESWOOD	E. 493680	-	E 227,190	266,490	-	-	-	-
3	WESTWOOD	E. 719,270	148,969	E. 268,742	301,559	M.O.S. (ENFIELD) BRITISH MUSEUM	113,749 35,220	FACTORY NIL	R. PT. 336,447
4	COPENACRE	E 514,260	288,619	E 42,600	283,041	ADMIRALTY	288,619	STORAGE	R
5	TRAVELLERS REST	A 20,042	-	A 20,042	-	~~ADMIRALTY~~	20,042	~~NIL~~	~~R~~
6	RIDGE PARK	E 183,000	-	-	-	~~MINISTRY~~	DE[illegible] UNKNOWN		R
7	ELM PARK	A ~~93,567~~ 66,500	-	A ~~93,567~~ 66,500	-		-	-	-
8	BROWNS AREA	A 43,000	43,000	-	-	AIR MINISTRY	43,000	TEL - COMM.	R
9	GROUNDSTONE	E. 46,290	-	E 31,600	14,690	W.D.	46,290	AIR SINK	R.
10	PICKWICK	E 81,675	-	E 81,675	-	~~ADMIRALTY~~	81,675	~~NIL~~	~~R~~
11	BROCKLEES	E 40,000	-	E 40,000	-	~~ADMIRALTY~~	40,000	~~NIL~~	R
12	TUNNEL	E 1,633,500	-	-	-	W.D.	DETAILS UNKNOWN		C.
13	RIDGE	E 203,000	-	-	-	W.D.	DO		C.
14	EASTLAYS	E. 871,200	-	-	-	W.D.	DO.		C.
15	MONKTON FARLEIGH	E. 1,633,500	-	-	-	W.D.	DO.		C.
16	MONKS PARK	A ~~763,700~~ 519,600	-	E ~~190,925~~ 109,500	~~572,775~~ 410,100	-	-	-	-
17	PARK LANE	E. 548,800	-	-	548,800	-	-	-	-
18	BETHELL	E. 120,000	-	E 100,000	20,000	-	-	-	-
19	CLUB HOUSE	E 17,000		-	17,000	-	-	-	-
20 21	CLIFT AND BROWNS No. 4.	E. 3,335,500	-	-	3,335,500	-	-	-	-
22	KINGSDOWN	E. 116,670	-	-	116,670	-	-	-	-
23	HOLLY BUSH	E. 6,000	-	-	6,000	-	-	-	-
24	WESTWELLS	E. 101,000	-	-	101,000	-	-	-	-
25	BREWERS YARD	E 34,000	-	-	34,000	-	-	-	-
		15,100,826	2,751,788	1,623,951	6,200,887				

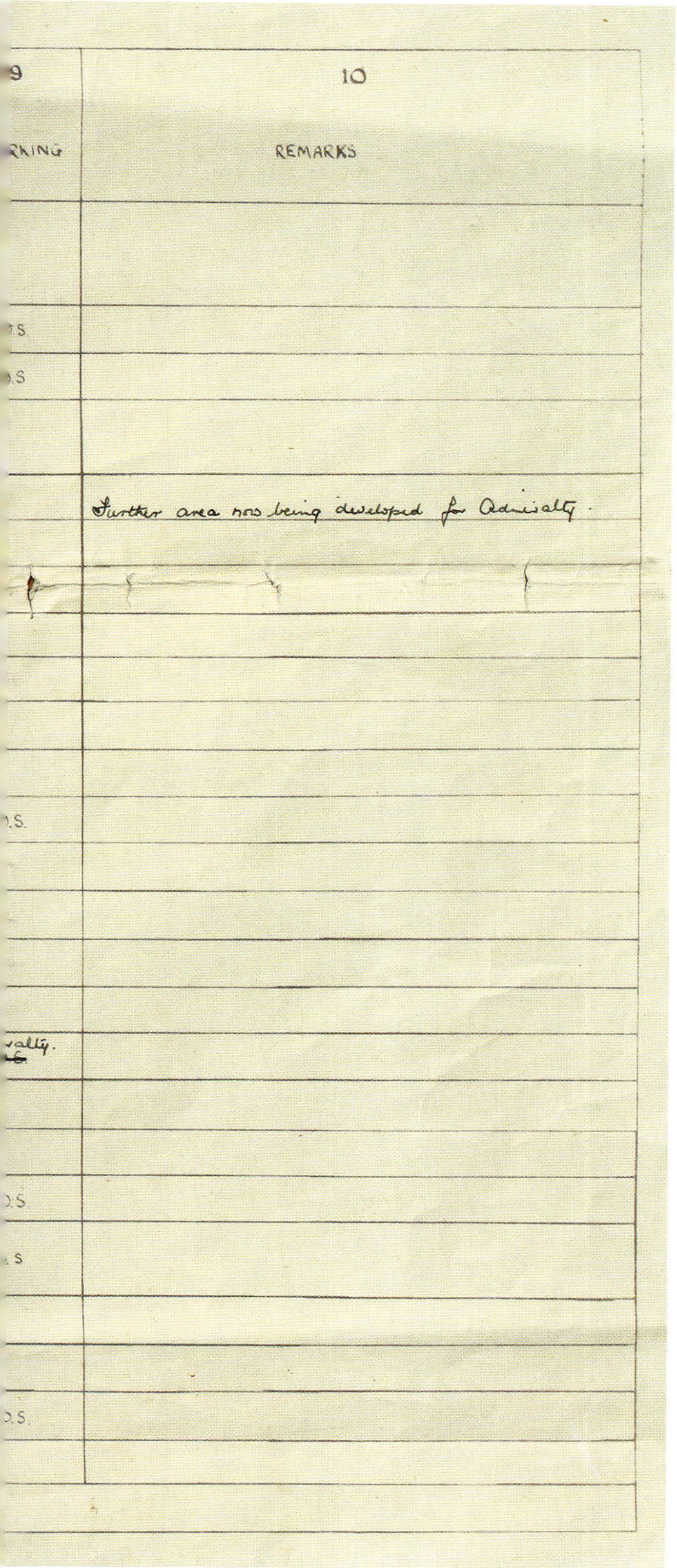

Left: The original, auxiliary schedule of underground sites in the Corsham area inspected by the Royal Engineers, showing the estimated space available for government use and the prospective occupiers.

throughout its life it survived the Second World War intact and remained in RAF service until the early 1990s. Linley caverns proved disastrous; intermittent flooding of the lower levels and frequent roof falls in the upper galleries led to its abandonment even before construction was complete. Fauld mine was developed into an enormous, fifty-acre underground storage depot rivalling in scale the immense army depots beneath Corsham. The mine at Fauld became the principal RAF storage depot and home to the RAF's Master Provisioning Officer and staff who were responsible for the overall logistics of keeping airfields throughout Britain supplied with weapons. It functioned efficiently and without incident until 27 November 1944 when careless handling of a high-explosive bomb resulted in the simultaneous detonation of some 4,000 tons of high-explosives deep underground. The explosion was the largest non-nuclear detonation the world has ever seen. Castle Hayes Farm, situated directly above the seat of the blast, evaporated, other adjacent farms were almost completely destroyed and there was widespread damage in surrounding towns and villages. A dam supplying water to a nearby plasterboard works was breached resulting in the flooding of the factory by a deluge of mud and the loss of dozens of lives. The resultant crater, one hundred feet deep and almost a quarter of a mile in diameter, remains as a monument to those who died in the blast and is clearly visible in satellite imagery today.

Long before the occurrences of the disasters that dogged their subterranean adventures the Air Ministry, finding themselves beaten by the War Office in the race to acquire suitable abandoned underground real estate, decided to take a different approach and build instead their own 'artificial' underground bomb stores. In the summer of 1938 an extensive open quarry at Harpur Hill near Buxton was purchased from Imperial Chemical Industries Ltd. The former limestone quarry – worked to provide not building stone or aggregate but raw material for a number of chemical processes – was almost one hundred feet deep and had good rail access. A single-storey reinforced concrete structure consisting of a series of parallel arched tunnels, with their walls pierced at regular intervals to allow free access across the width of the depot, was built in the bottom of the quarry and when completed was overlain with forty feet of loose rock debris to give additional protection against aerial bombardment. Due to the sloping nature of the quarry floor it was found that a lower, second level could be incorporated into the design of the bomb store for part of its length. When the depot became operational this lower area was used to store chemical weapons.

Just a month before the outbreak of war a slate quarry at Llanberis in North Wales, similar in dimension to the limestone quarry at Harpur Hill, was acquired and developed in a similar manner, except that the extraordinary depth of the quarry at

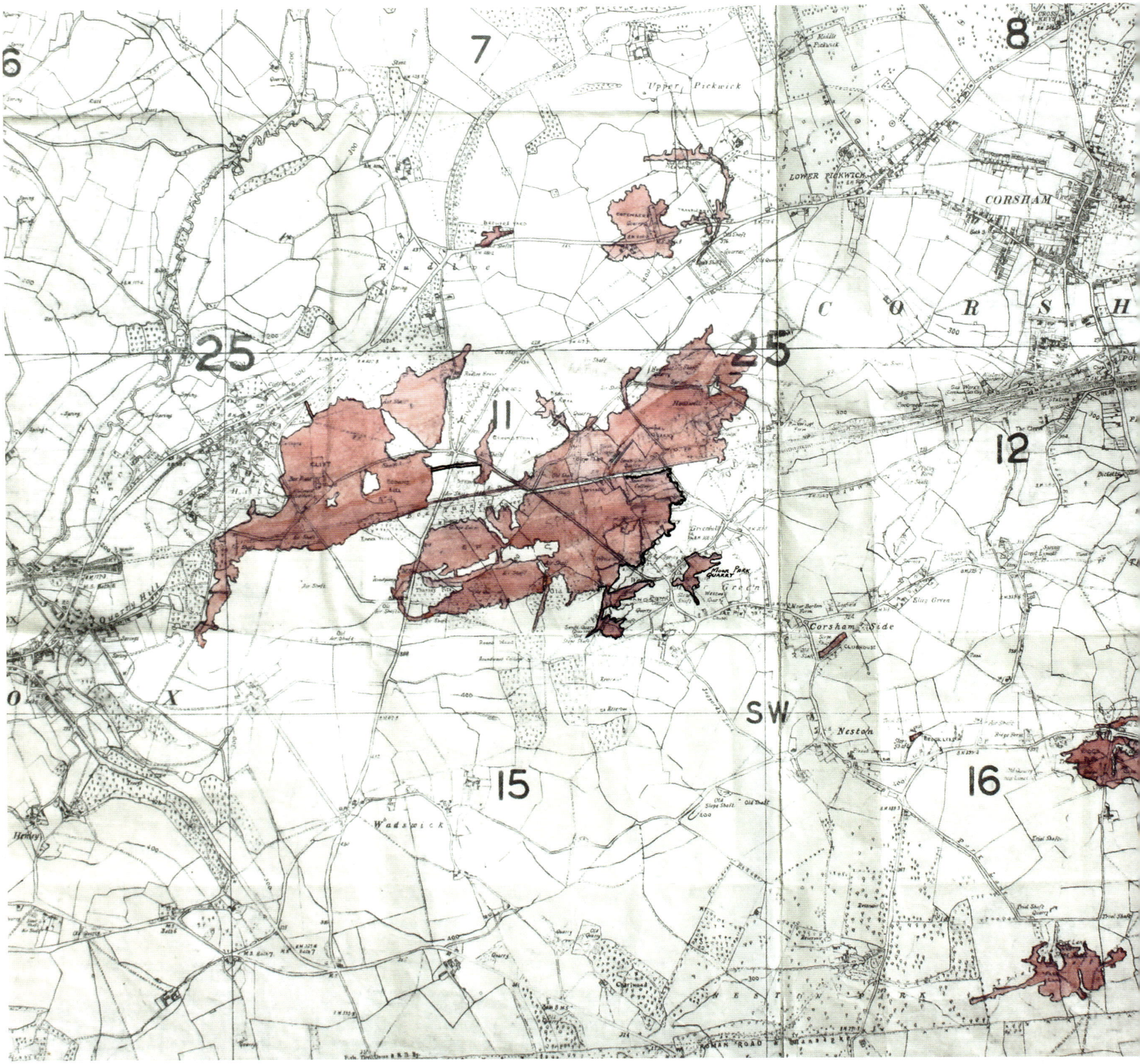
7
8
6
Upper Pickwick
LOWER PICKWICK
CORSHAM
C O R S H
25
25
11
12
Moor Park Quarry
Corsham Side
SW
Neston
15
16
Wadswick
X
Quarry Hill
Henley

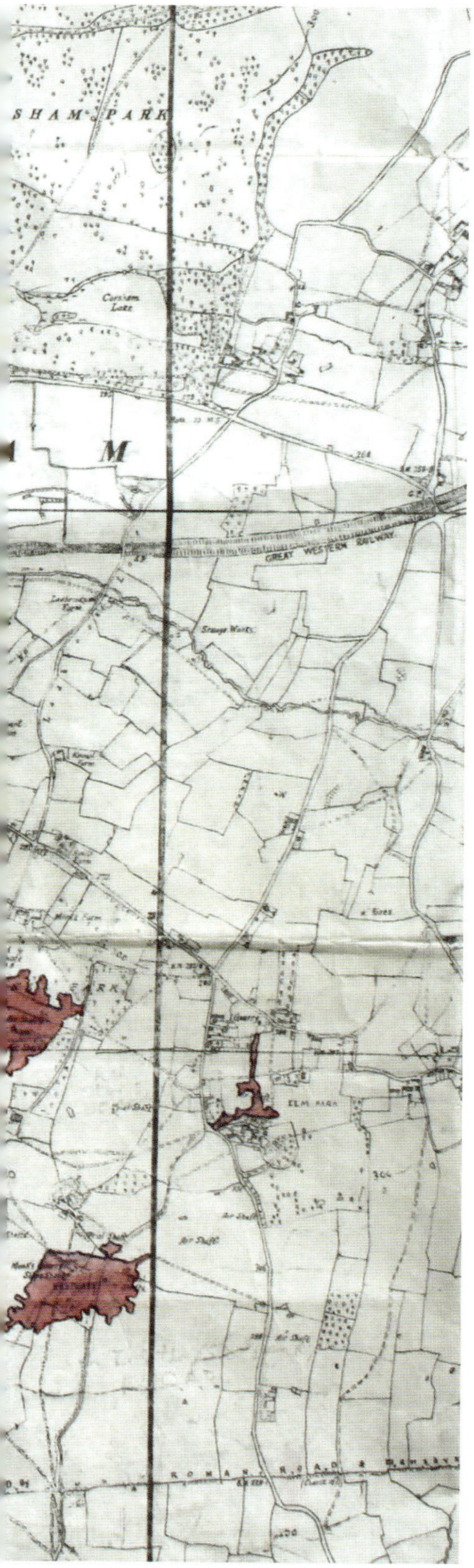

Left: This plan, prepared during the War Office tour of inspection in 1934, shows all the quarries in the Corsham area (except Monkton Farleigh, which is further to the south-west) that were visited and roughly surveyed at that time. Some, which were of no interest to the War Office, were later requisitioned by the Admiralty and the Ministry of Aircraft Production. Clubhouse Quarry was requisitioned by the Ministry of Works on behalf of the De La Rue security printing company for the storage of bank notes, printed for a number of mid-European countries, that could not be delivered due to German occupation.

Llanberis allowed a double-level underground structure to be built. At both locations tunnels into the hillside enabled standard-gauge ammunition trains to enter deep into the depots in order to tranship their cargos at secure underground loading platforms.

Unfortunately, due to a combination of faulty design, poor quality materials and inexperienced labour, both depots were fatally flawed. On 25 January 1942, only six months after coming into service, two thirds of the Llanberis depot collapsed within seconds under the weight of the overlying backfill, burying a train that was unloading at the time and trapping 14,000 tons of high-explosive bombs. An examination of the Harpur Hill site revealed disturbingly ominous cracks developing in the structure there also, so an emergency evacuation of all stocks was ordered. Many of the bombs previously stored in or destined for the Harpur Hill and Llanberis depots were diverted to Corsham where additional space was set aside in the War Office reserve depots. Although this was ostensibly a temporary arrangement the RAF remained in occupation of much of the Eastlays site at Corsham throughout the war. Meanwhile, recovery work at Llanberis continued for more than a year before the final buried bomb was rescued and the debris cleared from the site. The surviving sections of the tunnels at Llanberis were reinforced and much remedial work undertaken at Harpur Hill but the Air Ministry had lost confidence in the structural stability of both depots. The tunnels at Llanberis were never re-occupied and Harpur Hill was subsequently used to store only unfilled bomb casings and obsolete weapons pending disposal. The full story of the RAF central reserve depots can be found in chapter five.

While the Army and Air Force were scrambling to acquire the seemingly sparse amount of underground space available on commercial terms, the Admiralty remained obstinately aloof. With some justification they argued that the weight and physical size of most naval ammunition was such that handling it underground, and particularly retrieval via inclined access shafts like those at the army ammunition depots at Corsham, would render such a storage solution unfeasible. Their preference was to retain the limited surface storage capacity they already had with additional accommodation for the excess in floating hulks, supplemented by a huge number of railway wagons parked indefinitely in railway sidings in close proximity to the naval dockyards. In 1938 the Admiralty stance underwent a rapid reversal and the concept of underground storage was suddenly embraced with great enthusiasm. Plans were prepared for two massively-engineered and monumentally expensive tunnelled storage facilities at Dean Hill, south of Salisbury in Wiltshire and at Trecwn in west Wales. To overcome the difficulties previously identified with underground storage the two new Admiralty depots were designed as a series of short, horizontal concrete-lined tunnels bored herringbone-fashion into hillsides. At Dean Hill the tunnels were in two closely spaced groups along a chalk hillside while at Trecwn the two groups were burrowed into opposite sides of a narrow valley. A complex network of narrow-gauge railways connected the individual storage tunnels to standard-gauge interchange sidings.

With war now looming inevitably on the near horizon, and with reserve stocks of ammunition increasing at an alarming rate, the Admiralty reluctantly decided in October 1938, at the time of the Munich crisis, that they would have to adopt some sort of existing underground storage, at least as a temporary measure until Trecwn and Dean Hill were completed and commissioned, in order to release some of the railway wagons that were seriously congesting the sidings at Portsmouth and elsewhere. By that time, however, there was little available and they were compelled to take up a number of small, inconvenient and in many ways unsuitable quarries; one at Beer in south Devon and three – Brockleaze, Traveller's Rest and Elm Park quarries – at Corsham. Custody of the latter quarry was a matter of some contention between the Air Ministry, who claimed to have discovered it first with a view to using it as a lubricating oil store, and the Admiralty who eventually found themselves in grudgingly disputed possession. The story of all the Admiralty depots is the subject of chapter four.

The Fall of France and its consequences

An important feature of the series of underground acquisitions made by various government departments during the 1930s is that they were all undertaken in peacetime and under conventional commercial terms. When Monkton Farleigh Quarry, the last of the Corsham quarries, was purchased by the War Office in 1937 and land acquired for the Admiralty's Trecwn complex in 1938, it appeared at the time that Britain's subterranean military adventures were complete.

Similarly, the plans of another highly secretive and very important government organization, the Museums and Galleries Air Raids Precautions Committee, appeared to have been put into operation smoothly. Its task was to evacuate all the pictures and other artefacts in the London museums and galleries to places of safety for the duration of the war. To this end the committee had entered into secret negotiations with the owners of remote country houses throughout the 'safe' area of the country who were willing, as a patriotic endeavour, to take custody of the treasures until the conflict was over. A list of forty properties, known as the National Register, was drawn up early in 1935 and each was allocated a particular museum or gallery from which it would receive at least a proportion of the contents. Artefacts from the Victoria & Albert Museum, for example, were allocated to Montacute House in Somerset, pictures from the National Gallery to Penrhyn Castle and other properties in North Wales, the contents of the British Museum to Boughton House in Northamptonshire and Skipton Castle in Yorkshire, pictures from the Tate Gallery to 'Old Quarries' at Avening in Gloucestershire, to 'Hellens' at Much Marcle and to Eastington Hall nearby. Preparations were made for the evacuation years in advance; a special LMS train, for example, was kept constantly in steam at Camden goods yard from the summer of 1935, waiting for the day that it would be called upon to whisk the contents of the National Gallery northwards to Penrhyn beyond the shield of the Snowdon mountains.

When the evacuation happened, just hours before the declaration of war, all went smoothly and within just a few days every picture and artefact reached its allocated destination safely. Nothing was lost and nothing damaged. For a few months the scheme had all the appearances of success, but in the early spring of 1940 it all broke down in chaos. The owners of the country houses, already hard pressed by rising taxation and falling rents, discovered that the Treasury expected them to foot the bills for the extra fuel required to maintain reasonable environmental conditions for the artefacts in their care, to finance the structural alterations and repairs required and to pay for the necessary security measures. Most of the larger institutions wished to maintain their peacetime procedures during the period of evacuation. The business of new acquisitions, restoration and cataloguing would go on more or less as normal, but to accomplish this it was necessary that key members of staff should be evacuated along with the pictures and pots. To their horror, the property owners found that the museum and gallery trustees expected these staff members to be treated as country house guests – as if on a weekend retreat – that free accommodation should be provided for them and that the family servants should wait upon them.

Tensions at the country houses was reaching the point of rebellion in the early Spring of 1940, but the tipping-point came with the Fall of France in June. Previously, as we have seen, German bombers flying from homeland airfields could reach only the tip of England but now, in possession of French airfields all along the channel coast, the Luftwaffe could range over the whole of Britain. Skies over the previously safe areas west and north of the Wash-Solent line were opened to the enemy and all the previously secure provincial country houses vulnerable to attack. The Treasury, which was in overall control of the museum evacuation plan, realized that swift and unpalatable action was required. From the inception of the scheme in 1934 the Treasury had been opposed to underground storage for the art treasures and antiquities on both financial and political grounds. Financially, they were aware that the limited funding available for war preparations was better spent upon material required for the armed services politically, there was a feeling that it would be dangerous, in the words of a government official, to "spend money protecting elitist trifles when we have announced that there will be no provision of deep level air raid shelters for the population of London." There was now little option but to go underground and a frantic search began for suitable accommodation. The problem was that other government departments, too, were now seeking subterranean capacity on an unprecedented scale. Chief amongst these was the Ministry of Aircraft Production, under the abrasive leadership of Lord Beaverbrook, with ambitions to transfer the entire British aircraft industry into an immense network of underground factories.

Eventually two more or less suitable locations were found. Following painstaking investigation and negotiation by Brigadier H Temple-Richards, the senior civil engineer at the Ministry of Works Defence Architect's Department, an enormous and terribly wet underground slate quarry was discovered at Manod in the Snowdon mountains. This was subsequently adapted with much ingenuity to house the 2,000 pictures from the National Gallery that had previously sheltered at Penrhyn Castle and elsewhere in North Wales.

Meanwhile, in Wiltshire, parts of Westwood Quarry near Bradford-on-Avon was acquired by the Museums and Galleries Air Raids Precautions Committee and, by the summer of 1942, had been converted into a vast underground repository to house all the treasures from the British Museum, the Victoria & Albert Museum, the National Portrait Gallery, Science Museum, Imperial War Museum, British and Bodleian libraries and some forty other of London's museums, galleries and archives all of which had, earlier in the war, been distributed widely under the country house scheme. The extraordinary story of the art treasure repositories is told in chapter Chapter 6.

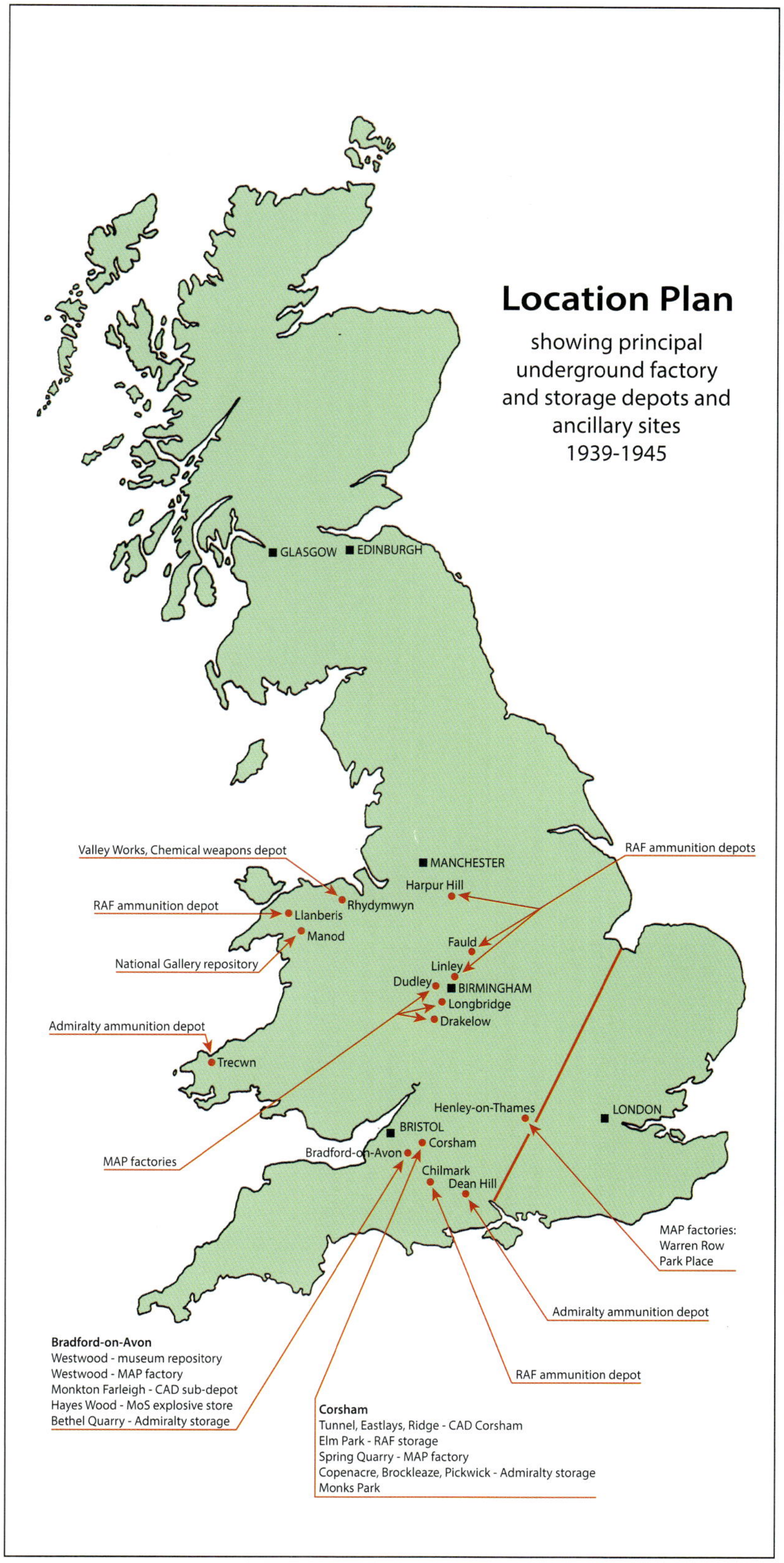

Right: Boucher's *Sunrise*, hastily evacuated on a coal lorry from an upper-floor gallery of the Wallace Collection in Manchester Square, just north of London's Oxford Street, on 2 September 1939. The picture is *en route* to Balls Park, its resting place under the 1934 Museums and Galleries Air Raids Precautions dispersal plan.

The underground factories

The threat to Britain's art treasures in the wake of the French capitulation was as nothing compared to that which faced Britain's survival as a nation. All of the RAF's defensive airfields in southern England were now open to German aerial bombardment and it was expected that the full weight of the Luftwaffe would be hurled against them. Once the RAF's airfields and its fighter force were destroyed Germany would be in command of British airspace and the war would be lost.

The viability of Fighter Command as a defensive force depended upon three elements: pilots, aircraft and airfields. Experience had shown that the Air Ministry Works Department was remarkably adept at getting airfields up and running after they had sustained even serious bomb damage, but the loss of pilots and aircraft were more intractable problems. Replacement pilots took some time to train but there was a constant stream of young men going through the process and, anyway, the loss of an aeroplane did not always also mean the loss of a pilot. Lost aircraft, however, required a skilled workforce, scarce and valuable material resources and a finite amount of time to replace, and needed extensive and immobile premises in which to manufacture them. It was assumed that the Luftwaffe attacks would be targeted against both the airfields and the aeroplane factories, for if the factories were destroyed then the RAF would be unable to replace the aircraft that were destroyed.

Immediate steps were taken to safeguard the aircraft manufacturing facilities. During the height of the Battle of Britain measures were already being taken to disperse elements of the most important aircraft factories from the industrial cities to remote country locations. Fears that Germany would turn her attacks from the airfields, where stiff opposition had been felt, to London and the industrial cities were justified by the commencement of the London blitz in September 1940. The vulnerability of the aircraft industry was highlighted when the Bristol Aeroplane Company's engine plant at Filton near Bristol was attacked on the nights of 25th and 27th September and 160 workers killed.

Clearly, an enhanced programme of dispersal was an urgent necessity but the Minister of Aircraft Production, Lord Beaverbrook, thought this inadequate and in October 1940 issued an edict to the effect that within six months underground accommodation would have to be found for the entire British aircraft industry. The response from the Treasury and the Ministry of Works was not encouraging. Beaverbrook was told that there was insufficient existing underground space capable of adaptation to house more than a tiny fraction of the surface factory accommodation, that there was no money to finance the construction of new, purpose-built tunnels and that, even if there was sufficient money and sufficient resources and labour, the excavation alone would take three years to complete. Over the following month Beaverbrook's plan was rolled back to the point where, towards the end of November, it was decided that only the aircraft engine factories should be transferred underground. Further rationalization, at the insistence of the Treasury, resulted in the scheme being restricted only to the Filton engine plant of the Bristol Aeroplane Company.

Once again the search was concentrated in the Corsham area. Four quarries were identified as suitable although all four were still being actively worked by the Bath & Portland company, though on a very limited scale. The four locations were Spring Quarry, a huge and rambling labyrinth of tunnels extending over 3,300,000 square feet, Westwood Quarry (of which we have earlier heard mention) some 250,000 square feet in extent, and two smaller quarries at Limpley Stoke and Monks Park. The process of acquisition was in sharp contrast to that employed by the War Office in the mid-1930s. On 5 December 1940 the regional requisitioning officer made a peremptory call upon the offices of the Bath & Portland Stone Company with a requisition order for all four quarries which were to be transferred to government control that day. Labourers working in the quarries were laid-off with one day's notice and told not to return to work the following day.

It was intended that all four quarries should be handed over to the Bristol Aeroplane Company; Spring, Westwood and Monks Park quarries would be used for production while Limpley Stoke would become a warehouse to house a buffer stock of completed engines in excess of those for immediate consumption by the airframe manufacturers. Unfortunately the scheme began to unravel after the first day. Custody of Monks Park quarry was contested by the Admiralty who claimed to have made a prior request for its requisition, the argument continuing for several months with inconclusive result. At one point a third party, the Birmingham Small Arms Company also staked a claim but then withdrew. Eventually all the contestants lost interest and the quarry was forgotten about until the 1950s when the Admiralty finally occupied it for general storage. Meanwhile the Bristol Aeroplane Company, which had been supportive of the underground factory scheme in its initial stages, suddenly lost enthusiasm and had to be bullied and cajoled into maintaining its participation. Eventually the company agreed to occupy rather less than half of the area allocated to it in Spring Quarry, leaving the Ministry of Aircraft Production with the problem of finding other tenants for the remaining sections which had been acquired and converted at great expense. The Birmingham Small Arms Company took up a small part of the quarry which was developed as a gun barrel factory, and Parnall Ltd and Dowty agreed to occupy the remainder in which to build, respectively, gun turrets and undercarriage assemblies for Stirling bombers. Both companies subsequently reneged on their agreements and much of Spring Quarry remained unoccupied throughout the war. Ultimately the Spring Quarry project proved to be a shambolic white elephant; construction, which should have been completed within six months, was still unfinished at the end of the war and the factory, despite the £30,000,000 spent on it (against an initial estimate of just £100,000) produced just a negligible number of engines.

It was soon apparent that there would never be enough surplus engines to warrant the retention of Limpley Stoke Quarry, which was subsequently disposed of to the Ministry of Supply who used it, most successfully, to store tens of thousands of tons of high-explosives destined eventually for shell filling factories at Usk, Bridgend and elsewhere in south Wales.

The Royal Enfield Company of Redditch, famous before the war (and after) for its range of very British motorcycles, was persuaded to develop a new production facility in Westwood Quarry near Bradford-on-Avon in Wiltshire. We have already seen that while development of the underground factory was in progress a section of the quarry was transferred to the Museums and Galleries Air Raid Precautions Committee for use as a secure repository for art treasures. Once completed, the factory produced a wide range of esoteric precision instruments for the Ministry of Supply including No.3 anti-aircraft predictors, bomb sights, gun sights and gun sight stabilizers and vane-oil motors.

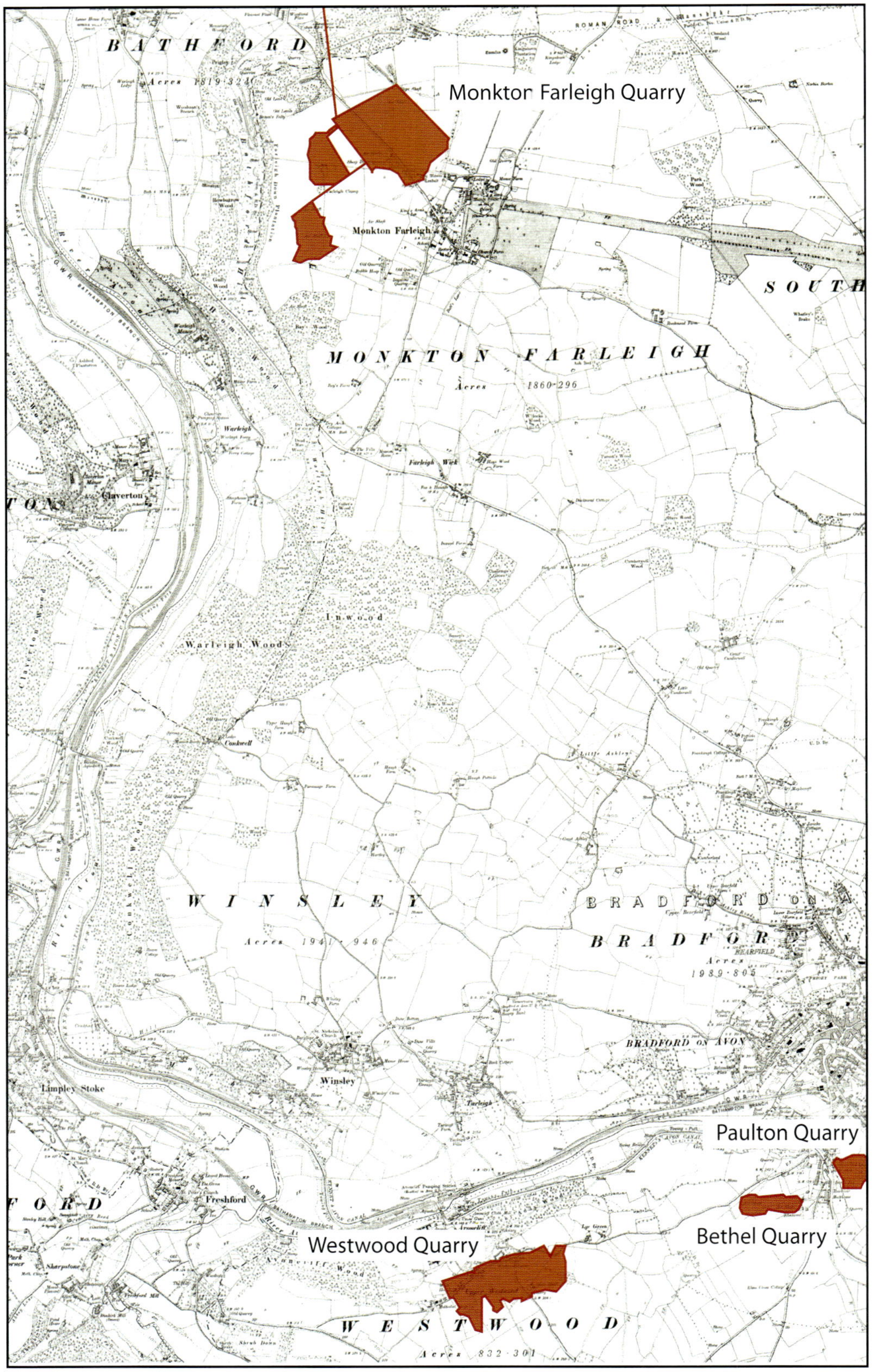

Although the Ministry of Aircraft Production's technical advisors had argued against the construction of purpose-built underground factories on the grounds of cost and the time required for excavation and building, two such factories were eventually built in the Midlands. The first, consisting of a modest network of interconnecting tunnels, was built beneath a hillside behind the Austin Motor Company's Longbridge plant near Birmingham, while the second, built into a sandstone hillside on the Blakeshill estate at Drakelow near Kidderminster, consisted of a rather more sophisticated system –four 1,000-foot long parallel tunnels intersected at regular intervals by cross passages which functioned as workshops, machine shops, stores etc. The Drakelow factory was operated on behalf of the Ministry of Aircraft Production by the Rover Car Company and produced components for Rolls Royce aero engines and sleeve valves for the Bristol Hercules air-cooled radial engine. Another Black Country project, to convert the limestone caverns below Dudley Castle into an underground factory, was beset by sudden roof falls and catastrophic collapses and was abandoned before completion.

Four other small underground factories were constructed as a result of private initiative. Two, operated under the direction of the Hanworth-based engineering firm of Sir George Godfrey & Partners, were built in chalk hillsides at Warren Row and Park Place near Henley-on-Thames. Construction of these sites was undertaken by Gordon Carrington & Co Ltd, a local building contractor. A similar small factory was established in chalk cliffs behind the Short Brothers engineering works at Rochester in Kent. The last of this group of factories, all of which were built close to or actually within the danger area, was established by the Plessey Company in an uncompleted section of the Central Line tube tunnel near Gants Hill in east London. The underground factories are the subject of Chapter 3.

The Admiralty has second thoughts

The Admiralty's attitude towards underground storage (we have seen already that they were markedly inimical to the concept when the other services were fighting each other for underground capacity in the 1930s) underwent a radical reappraisal in January 1941 after their main Fleet Air Arm stores at Coventry and Woolston were destroyed during air raids. By this time Corsham was a major development area with every service department and a number of primary defence equipment contractors represented there, so it was not surprising that the Admiralty, seeking secure storage, turned its attention there also. It was quickly discovered that Copenacre Quarry, one of the series of working quarries initially requisitioned by the Ministry of Aircraft Production some months earlier but subsequently released, was available. The quarry was immediately requisitioned by the Admiralty and plans prepared on the most lavish scale for its conversion. Elaborate heating, ventilation and transportation equipment installed and massively proportioned, grossly over-engineered shaft-head buildings erected on the surface. Two long disused quarries at Bradford-on-Avon – Bethel Quarry and Paulton Quarry, both of which had been utilized during the inter-war years as underground mushroom farms – were also requisitioned by the Admiralty at this time.

After the war the Admiralty consolidated its interests at Corsham; the Bradford-on-Avon quarries and the small and inefficient Traveller's Rest and Brockleaze quarries were discarded but Monks Park and the greater part of Spring Quarry were added to its portfolio and survived, along with Copenacre, as the central stores for naval electronic and other specialist equipment throughout the Cold War, finally closing in 1997.

Chemical weapons

A particularly sinister system of tunnels was constructed at Rhydymwyn near Mold in North Wales to accommodate the nation's stockpile of mustard gas. Chemical weapons were never viewed with great enthusiasm by the armed services; the chief protagonists of such weapons were the chemical companies who would profit by their manufacture and the scientists whose reputations to some extent depended upon their adoption. The military men knew that chemical weapons were, as tactical weapons, useless and had no role on the battlefield. This had been obvious since the First World War. They did, however, have a valuable deterrent role and for this reason large-scale production plants for the manufacture of mustard gas and its various precursors and derivatives were set up in the Runcorn area under the management of Imperial Chemical Industries Ltd, which acted as agent for the Ministry of Supply. Under pressure from the scientific and industrial lobbies, the government steadily increased output of chemical warfare agents to the point at which bulk storage became a critical issue. It became apparent that filled mustard gas bombs had a finite and relatively short shelf life. After just a few months, sedimentation and chemical decomposition started, the active agents became increasingly unpredictable and the thin metal bomb-cases began to corrode. Production of chemical agents was halted and bulk storage, with bombs filled only when required, was investigated as a partial solution and, indeed, had been considered advantageous even before the problem of degeneration was recognized. Retaining bulk storage at the factories was not feasible; they were all located within the Liverpool-Manchester industrial complex, many of them close to dense residential areas, and the risk of widespread contamination should a tank be ruptured due to enemy action was too great.

Planning for the production facilities began in 1937 and by the end of the following year most of the factories at Randle, Rocksavage, Wade, Royd Mill and Springfield were well under way and consideration was being given to the storage problems outlined above. A search was initiated for a suitable site, underground, remote enough from the factories but sufficiently close to allow easy transportation from factory to storage, and, if possible, with adjoining land upon which a filling factory and an additional mustard gas production facility could be built. Of the five locations subsequently identified, a site in the Alyn valley at Rhydymwyn was selected. A steep limestone hillside rose to the north of the river at this point and the flat floor of the valley seemed ideal for the construction of the requisite factory and filling plant. Elsewhere in the valley the Halkyn United Mining Company had quarried limestone from underground galleries for decades and their expertise was called upon by the Ministry of Supply to excavate storage chambers into the hillside adjacent to the factory site. Three tunnels, 150 feet apart, were driven into the escarpment and connected by four lateral passages each 535 feet long to form storage chambers. Later, two of these lateral tunnels were extended when it was decided to store filled bombs as well as bulk mustard gas at the site. The tunnels and the surviving remnants of the factory are illustrated in Chapter 3.

Chapter 2

CAD CORSHAM

Conversion of old quarry workings into sophisticated storage facilities

Initially, the War Office requirement for underground ammunition storage had been quite modest and it was assumed that the six acres available at Ridge Quarry would be sufficient. Almost immediately, however, it was realized that much more extensive accommodation would be required so in August 1935 an agreement was reached with the Bath & Portland Stone Company to purchase both Ridge Quarry and the fifty-acre Tunnel Quarry. Within a few months this too proved insufficient and a further quarry at Eastlays near Gastard was acquired in May 1936. The strengthened plans for the air defence of Great Britain outlined in the early months of 1937 called for much larger reserves of anti-aircraft ammunition than had been earlier anticipated and to meet the storage requirements for this stockpile a further quarry at Monkton Farleigh was purchased in March 1937.

Conversion work at both Ridge and Tunnel quarries began simultaneously. The first stage in the process of development was to remove the huge volume of waste stone and debris that had accumulated underground as a result of many decades of quarrying activity. At Tunnel Quarry alone some two million tons of waste stone 'backfill' had to be cleared, a task which took the initial workforce of 12,000 labourers over four years to complete. This task, although overseen at the planning level by a small team of Royal Engineers, was undertaken by a civilian labour force under the administration of a civilian works directorate. Assembly of this workforce was a prodigious affair and was an overt exercise in social engineering organized by the Ministry of Labour. It was decided that unemployed men from the distressed areas of north-east England should be offered employment on the War Office project; transport to Wiltshire would be subsidised by the government and lodgings for every man would be found with a family somewhere within a radius of twenty miles of the works. The concept of containing all these men within the close confines of a labour camp – the usual method of personnel management previously used on large civil engineering projects – was specifically excluded. The high ambition of the War Office was that these men, many of whom had never been in employment, should gradually be weaned into the disciplines of work and that they would become integrated into the culture of the south-west of England. Eventually, it was hoped, they would bring their families down from Durham or Tyneside and start new lives for themselves in Somerset and Wiltshire. At its peak the scheme involved in excess of 25,000 men.

Once the waste stone had been removed the floor throughout the quarries were levelled, the rough roof support pillars left by the quarrymen were strengthened and steel girders put in place to reinforce the overhead cover where necessary. Concrete division walls were built in order to create within each quarry a series of regular, self-contained storage magazines each approximately five acres in extent. Ventilation systems and, later, highly complex air-conditioning plants, were installed in order to maintain satisfactory environmental conditions underground. Vertical lift shafts and smoothly graded inclined shafts were constructed to facilitate ammunition movements and, in total, some twenty miles of conveyor belts put in place and several miles of narrow-gauge railways laid. Tens of thousands of spark-, flame- and explosion-proof electric light fittings were installed and, at the three major sites – Tunnel, Eastlays and Monkton Farleigh – huge standby power stations built underground.

Right: The original cross-sectional survey of rock strata at Tunnel Quarry. Note the different depths of the worked stone at the west and east ends of the quarry. To the west the stone has been worked for a depth of almost thirty feet and here the quarry floor was built up with waste stone in order to achieve the optimum ceiling height of eleven feet in the magazine areas as required by the War Office. At the east end the original quarry headings were less than seven feet in height and it was necessary during the conversion process to cut away the floor to achieve the required clearance.

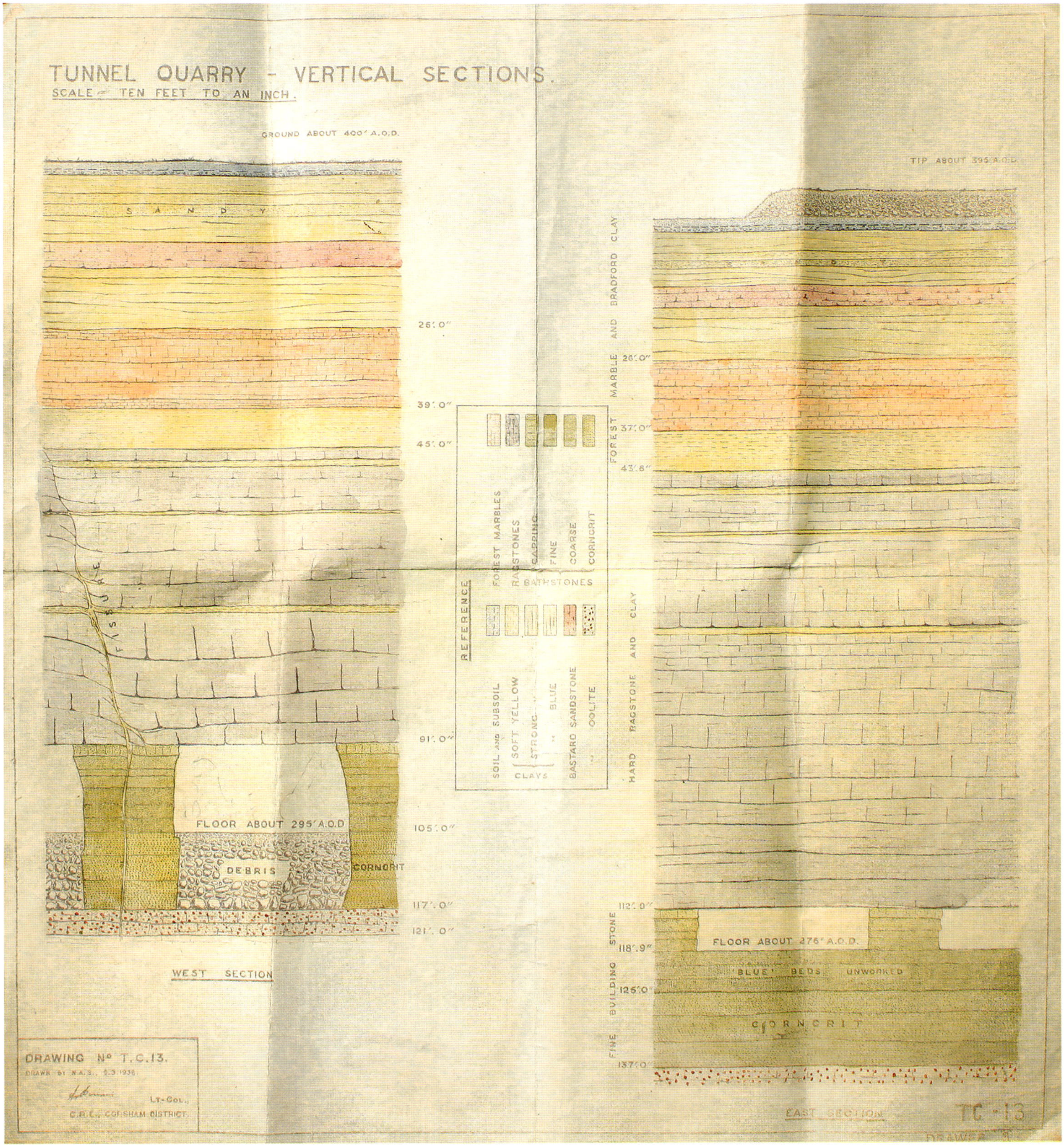
TUNNEL QUARRY - VERTICAL SECTIONS.
SCALE - TEN FEET TO AN INCH.
GROUND ABOUT 400' A.O.D.
SANDY
26'.0"
39'.0"
45'.0"
FISSURE
91'.0"
FLOOR ABOUT 295' A.O.D
105'.0"
DEBRIS
CORNGRIT
117'.0"
121'.0"
WEST SECTION
REFERENCE
SOIL AND SUBSOIL
SOFT YELLOW
STRONG
BLUE
CLAYS
BASTARD SANDSTONE
OOLITE
FOREST MARBLES
RAGSTONES
CAPPING
FINE
COARSE
CORNGRIT
BATHSTONES
FOREST MARBLE AND BRADFORD CLAY
HARD RAGSTONE AND CLAY
FINE BUILDING STONE
TIP ABOUT 395' A.O.D.
26'.0"
37'.0"
43'.6"
112'.0"
118'.9"
125'.0"
137'.0"
FLOOR ABOUT 276' A.O.D.
'BLUE' BEDS UNWORKED
CORNGRIT
EAST SECTION
TC-13
DRAWING Nº T.C.13.
LT-COL.,
C.R.E., CORSHAM DISTRICT.

Above: Although virtually all the underground workings in the Corsham area were acquired by one government department or another between 1935 and 1942, not all that was purchased or requisitioned underwent conversion. Large sections were eventually abandoned following a detailed survey because they were too damp or the stone was too faulted, the overhead cover inadequate or the structure too unstable. This photograph illustrates a typical example of abandoned workings as they are today and offer, perhaps, some idea of the task faced by the War Office. Note the huge amounts of waste stone packed between the supporting pillars, all of which had to be removed before conversion could begin.

Above: "Well, I've got a right job on here and no mistake!" Faced with what appears an impossible task, a workman stands, armed only with a spade, seemingly lost in a sea of stone. It had been hoped to use mechanical excavators to clear much of the backfill but, once work began, it became apparent that in most areas the support pillars were much closer together and the whole quarry generally more congested than anticipated, making access for large machinery impossible.

Above: Since the 1860s a side tunnel adjacent to the eastern portal of the main line tunnel at Box led to an underground stone loading platform within Huddswell quarry. The heading was very deep at this point so, to avoid a steep approach gradient, the quarrying company had raised the floor level of the quarry by infilling the void with waste for a depth of twenty feet. The War Office subsequently realigned this underground siding for its own use but, on account of the greater weight of its ammunition trains, wished to lay its rails on the solid bedrock, compensating for the extra depth by lengthening the approach gradient. Here we can see how waste stone from the floor was removed: men on trestles passed it, one shovel-full at a time, from platform to platform until the man at the top threw it into the railway truck just visible in the background. Elsewhere in the quarry millions of tons of rubble were moved using this technique.

Right: The initial clearance was completed by manual labour only, but once a few roadways had been cleared through the rubble it was possible to lay narrow-gauge rails, after which the process was greatly accelerated. Eventually, fifty-four diminutive five-ton Ruston Hornsby diesel locomotives and 500 skip trucks were employed underground at Tunnel Quarry alone.

Left: It was found necessary to extend some areas of quarry and to make new connections to render the workings more suitable for ammunition storage. The War Office introduced a number of coal-cutting machines into the quarries with great success. The 'Samson' coal-cutter was the most successful of these and was, indeed, so successful that in the 1950s, when a few of the quarries were de-requisitioned and the Bath & Portland Stone Company was able to restart quarrying, they purchased a number of these machines from the War Office. It says much for the reliability, longevity and efficiency of the Samson that several of the War Office machines, supplied in 1936, are still in active use today.

Above left: A Hardiax arc shearer in operation. Several of these machines were used at Monkton Farleigh where the irregular distribution of support pillars made the employment of the larger Samson impossible.

Above right: A typical machine-cut passageway with a large concrete mixer in the background.

Left: The Royal Engineers were faced with a particularly tricky problem at the west end of the underground railway station at Tunnel Quarry where substantial roof reinforcement was required to span a wide corridor on its approach to the platforms. A concrete skew arch was erected using scrap rails recovered from the Bath tramway system, bent to shape to form the core reinforcing elements. This photograph shows the reinforcement in place together with the wooden centering and the bottom shuttering for the arch. The six-inch pipes in the foreground were used to carry wet concrete over considerable distances from a central concrete mixing plant.

Above left: Where the roof was unstable substantial steel beams were inserted, supported by reinforced concrete pillars or, as illustrated here, by vertical girders carried by concrete footings set in the floor.

Above right: Frequently the roof support pillars were reinforced by encasing them in concrete 'corsets'. The pillar is surrounded by removable steel shuttering attached to an angle-iron frame; concrete is poured in and after each layer has set the panels are raised up to the next level and the process repeated.

Right: Steel reinforcing was added to the shuttered concrete to increase the strength of the corsets. Two pillars encased in steelwork can be seen in the background while to the left is a partially concreted example.

Above: Construction almost completed. All the pillars on the right-hand side of the passageway have been encased in concrete corsets, steel beams inserted to support the roof and permanent electric light fittings installed. The conduit carrying the lighting cables can be seen attached to the right-hand wall. The cables hanging loose on the left-hand side are for the contractors' temporary lighting and will soon be removed.

The floor has been levelled with crushed and graded limestone which has been produced on-site from quarry waste in an underground crushing plant. Interestingly, all the concrete used underground was of a novel type using crushed Bath stone of various grades, also produced in the underground plant, as aggregate rather than the harder gravel used in conventional concrete.

Right: It was intended to level the floors with a consolidated Bath stone finish, but it was soon realised that this would give rise to unacceptable levels of dust. Conventional tarmac using gravel aggregate was ruled out due to the risk of sparks generated by metal objects striking particles of gravel. The solution was to lay a five-inch covering of Colas (a substance similar to tarmac but using coal chippings in place of gravel as aggregate) over the entire floor area. This photograph shows a five-ton Barford road-roller applying the final finish to the Colas floor in Tunnel Quarry.

Left: A view of one of the storage bays adjacent to a district haulageway shortly after completion but before it was handed over to the RAOC. Note the overhead rope haulage system (later replaced throughout the mine by belt conveyors) and the small, cast-iron turntables. The wagon in the background is loaded with drums of white cementatious paint used to cover the walls and ceilings of the mine to improve visibility and also to help hold back moisture in the rock and prevent dust.

RIDGE QUARRY

Construction work began at Ridge Quarry in July 1936 and was scheduled for completion by the end of December, by which time it was to be ready to receive the first consignment of RAF bombs destined for storage there. Although a War Office depot and nominally a constituent part of Central Ammunition Depot Corsham, the quarry was handed over, first in part and later as a whole, to the Air Ministry on a supposedly temporary basis. As the Air Ministry's own storage schemes collapsed in disarray as the war progressed, 'temporary' became permanent and Ridge Quarry remained in RAF hands until its closure in 1950.

The requirement to complete the tasks of building and fitting out within six months meant, inevitably, that the engineering works undertaken at Ridge Quarry would be on a modest scale and the facilities provided minimal. Shortly before the arrangement with the Air Ministry was finalized a more comprehensive programme of works had been put in hand but was subsequently abandoned. A start was made on reinforcing the stone support pillars with concrete but this was stopped after no more than one-twentieth of the work was completed when it was realized that it could not be finished within the specified time, that sufficient resources were not economically available and that concentrating labour on this task was delaying more vital work. Unlike the other depots that comprised CAD Corsham, Ridge Quarry was not provided with forced air ventilation or heating, it did not have a dedicated power station (although it did share an emergency electricity supply with the nearby Eastlays depot), and it was never fitted with a permanent, conduit-enclosed electric lighting system.

The one great advantage possessed by Ridge Quarry was that it had been used for explosives storage by the Ministry of Munitions during the latter part of the First World War. The quarry was cleared of debris at that time and the floors levelled. Rails had been laid in the main slope shaft and were still in place in 1936 although the steam winding engine in the surface transit shed and all the narrow-gauge Decauville track underground had been removed at the end

Left: The only known wartime view of Ridge Quarry, showing a lorry-load of bombs arriving at No.1 loading platform.

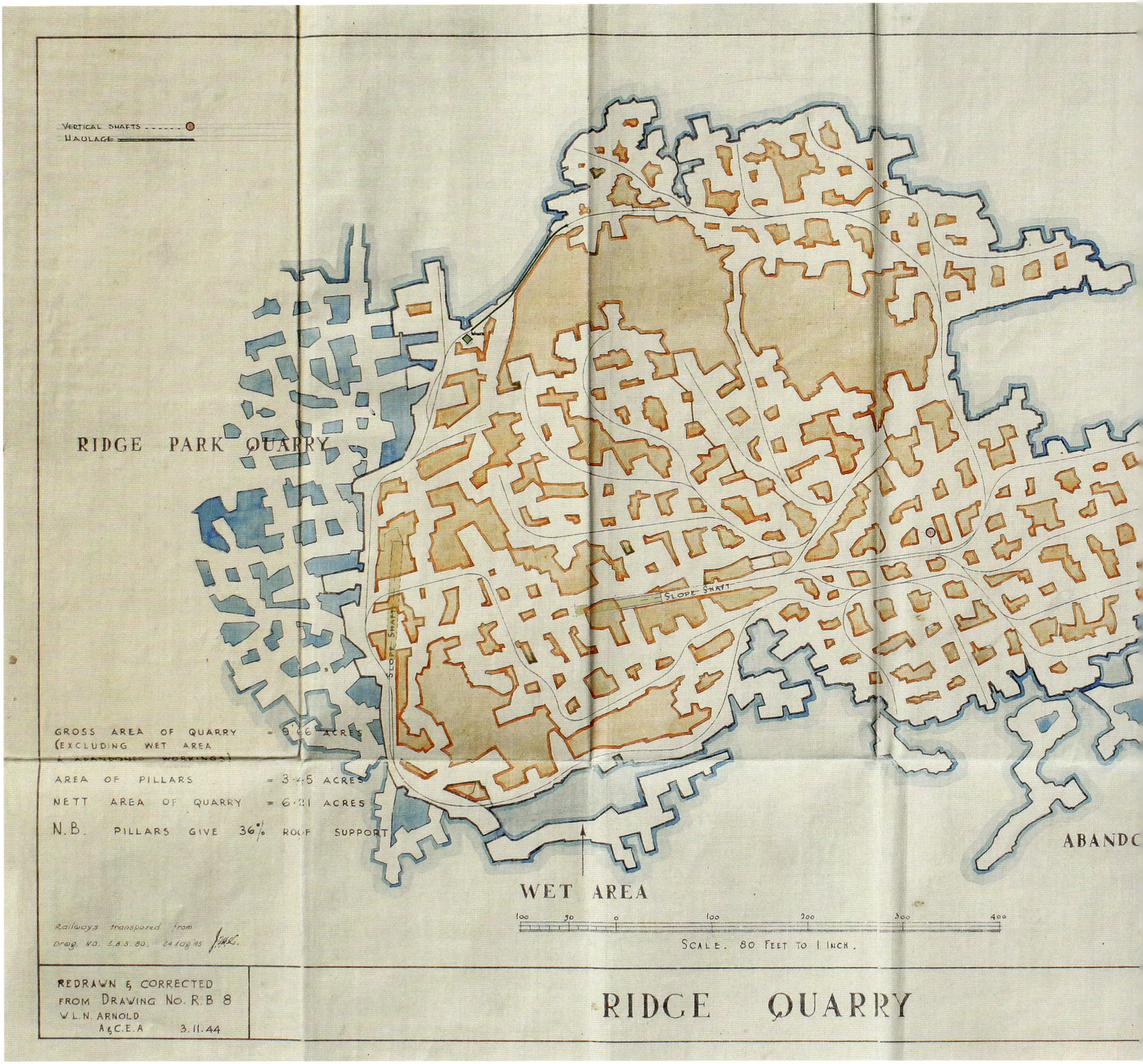
VERTICAL SHAFTS
HAULAGE
RIDGE PARK QUARRY
SLOPE SHAFT
SLOPE SHAFT
GROSS AREA OF QUARRY = 9·66 ACRES
(EXCLUDING WET AREA
AREA OF PILLARS = 3·45 ACRES
NETT AREA OF QUARRY = 6·21 ACRES
N.B. PILLARS GIVE 36% ROOF SUPPORT
WET AREA
ABANDO
100 50 0 100 200 300 400
SCALE. 80 FEET TO 1 INCH.
Railways transposed from
Drwg. No. S.B.S. 80. 24 Aug '45
REDRAWN & CORRECTED
FROM DRAWING No. R.B 8
W.L.N. ARNOLD
A&C.E.A 3.11.44
RIDGE QUARRY

of the war. All that was required of the War Office in 1936 was to relay a couple of thousand yards of temporary track, reinstate the winding engine, erect a few division walls and offices underground and install a pretty primitive lighting system with electric cables strung from hooks let into the quarry roof. In order to increase the maximum throughput of ammunition a ventilation shaft situated in the middle of the quarry was adapted for haulage by the installation of a simple, double-cage lift running in timber guides.

In 1942, at the request of the Air Ministry, the capacity of Ridge Quarry was substantially increased by the re-opening of a long-disused slope shaft at the west end of the quarry that gave convenient access to further areas of underground workings. Due to the presence of a geological fault that runs through the quarry these extended workings are at a level some twenty feet below the main area, so a pair of inclined passages were bored to connect the two parts of the quarry. Winches were installed at the head of each underground incline, powered by small steam engines adapted to run on compressed air, the air being provided by two compressors on the surface. The passageway linking the 'new' inclined shaft to the existing workings ran through an area of treacherous ground and the engineering in this area is noticeably heavier than in other areas of the quarry, with many substantial concrete walls and large steel girders supporting the roof.

Storage conditions at Ridge Quarry were barely adequate and the weapons stored there – mainly obsolete bombs of American manufacture delivered early in the war – deteriorated dangerously. All were finally removed during a delicate operation in 1949; the following year the Air Ministry terminated its occupation and the site reverted to War Office control. Ridge was never used again although it was kept on minimal care and maintenance until 1964 when the Army, too, abandoned the site. The quarry was eventually sold under terms of pre-emption in 1975 to the Neston Estate from whom it had been purchased in 1935. Soon after, rails and many of the roof support girders underground were recovered for scrap, leaving some areas of the quarry in a precarious state. Most of the surface features were demolished including the lift-top building and the transit shed at the head of the main inclined shaft. Debris from the demolition was bulldozed into the shafts and there is now no evidence of their location on the surface. The loading platform at the top of the new or No.2 slope shaft of 1942 survives at the time of writing, and the slope shaft is still visible and was, until recently, open and accessible.

Left: Fred Allen's original, hand-coloured drawing of Ridge Quarry, showing the overall layout and arrangement of railway lines.

Left: No.2 loading platform at Ridge Quarry. This is the only surviving surface feature of the sub-depot as both No.1 platform and the lift-head building were demolished in the early 1970s.

Below left: A view from the loading platform towards the top of the slope shaft. In recent years large blocks of stone have been placed over the top of the incline in an effort to deter the inquisitive.

Below right: Looking east from the top of the incline into the loading bay. Note the narrow-gauge railway track. Trucks were hauled up the incline by a steam winch positioned at the far end of the platform.

Left: Looking down the No.2 inclined shaft into Ridge Quarry. Very little additional work was done to adapt the existing quarry shaft for military use. The rails on the incline were removed for scrap in the 1970s.

Above: The red painted sign gives directions to bay M1; this is one of a number of distinctive relics of the occupation of the quarry by the Ministry of Munitions during the First World War.

Left: The bottom of No.2 incline shaft. Note the steelwork supporting the roof at this point. A large steel girder once rested on the circular concrete pillar in the centre of the photograph and spanned the gap between it and the right-hand wall. This was removed for scrap in 1974. Miraculously, the roof above has remained secure.

Above: The bottom of No.1 slope shaft at Ridge Quarry. The surface loading bay at the head of this shaft was demolished soon after closure and debris from the surrounding buildings bulldozed into the shaft. There is now no evidence of its location on the surface. The bay to the right of the shaft once housed the quarry foreman's office and a small electrical switchroom controlling lighting throughout the depot.

Left: The base of the vertical lift shaft at Ridge. The surface buildings here, and a nearby compressor house, were also demolished and pushed down the shaft when the depot closed. The lift was a crude, twin-cage affair running in wooden guides, the remains of which can be seen amongst the rubble.

Right: A view from half-way up the western incline between the upper and lower levels of the quarry. The concrete block structure in the centre background housed the winch which hauled wagons up the incline. This was powered by compressed air delivered from compressors on the surface and one of the steel loops that formerly supported the air supply pipe can be seen attached to the quarry ceiling.

Left: Near the top of the eastern underground incline. Unlike the incline shown in the view above, this was not an original feature of the quarry and was cut by the Royal Engineers in order to make movements between the two levels more flexible.

Above: The marks left by the machine used to cut the eastern incline are very obvious in this view. This proved an extraordinarily difficult passage to photograph and the ghostly images are shadows of the photographer vainly attempting to illuminate the scene.

The uncompleted area of Ridge Quarry

Right: The boundary between the concreted and unconverted areas with a heavily corbelled concrete pillar in the foreground.

Left: An example of unfinished concrete-work showing the various stages of construction.

Right: The degree to which this section of Ridge Quarry was over-engineered is obvious in this photograph where much useful floor space has been sacrificed for the construction of new walls and pillars.

Below: This unfinished pillar in the 'concrete' section of Ridge Quarry illustrated the various processes involved. The rough pillar has first been trimmed, then surrounded in reinforcing steelwork and finally encased in shuttered concrete.

Above: An interesting general view of the quarry. Note the carving on the corner pillar beneath the 'Exit' sign. There were once many carvings in the quarry but most have been defaced. The large concrete block in the foreground is the foundation for a compressed air winch used for rope-hauling wagons on the narrow-gauge railway system. The haulage rope was guided around corners by means of vertical capstans, the square concrete support for one of which is visible in the right centre ground. The steel hoop attached to the ceiling supported the compressed air pipeline.

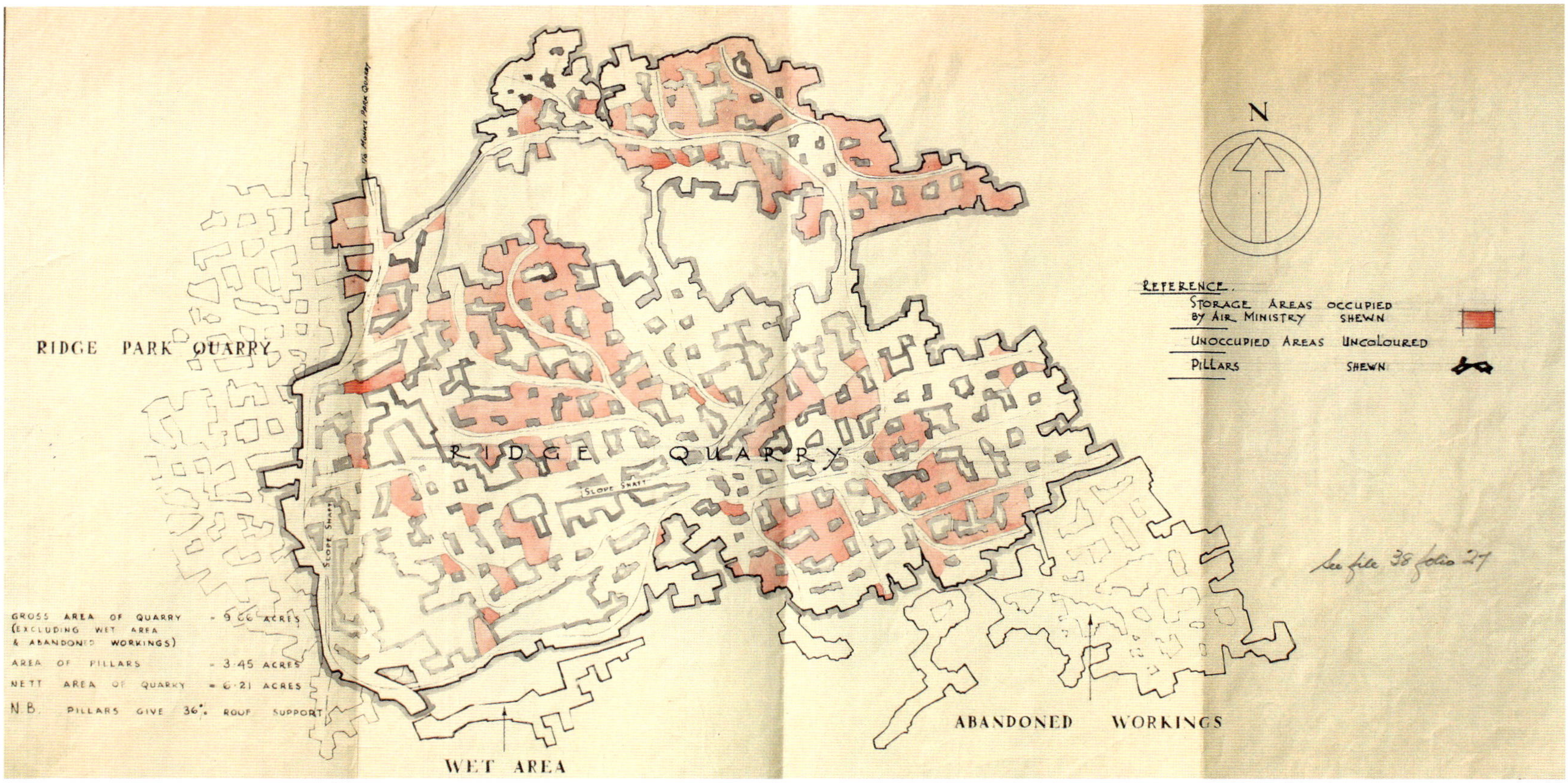

Above: At the end of the Second World War Ridge Quarry was heavily stocked with obsolete bombs, mostly of American manufacture, supplied during the early days of the conflict. By the end of 1944 the Air Ministry was making plans to dispose of these surplus weapons but officers on site were concerned that the bombs had degenerated to a condition such that moving them would be distinctly dangerous. This plan, prepared in August 1945, shows the storage locations of the suspect bombs. All were eventually removed, transported by rail to Barry Docks and dumped in the Irish Sea.

Left: Some years after the depot closed ownership of the quarry reverted to the Neston Estate with whom the Bath & Portland Stone Company still had an unexpired period of lease still running. Having no immediate need of the stone reserves the quarrying company simply recovered the remaining steelwork in the workings for sale as scrap. In this photograph it is possible to see where rolled steel mining arches have been removed, leaving the brick infill hanging precariously from the roof.

In the early 1980s Sir John Fuller, owner of the Neston Estate, made it known that he had no further intention of exploiting the stone reserves beneath his land. In recent years, however, the estate's policy has changed with the re-opening of nearby Park Lane Quarry and the resumption of stone extraction on a fairly large scale.

EASTLAYS

With the administration of Ridge Quarry transferred to the Air Ministry, the organization of CAD Corsham was restructured. Ridge became a satellite of the much larger Eastlays depot which was under construction nearby. Physically, and for operational purposes, the three main quarries which comprised the Central Ammunition Depot – Eastlays, Tunnel Quarry and Monkton Farleigh – were divided into a series of twenty-five separate storage magazines or 'districts' each of approximately five acres in extent and numbered consecutively. Districts 1-11 were to be at Tunnel Quarry, 12-20 at Monkton Farleigh and 21-25 at Eastlays. Confusingly, the depots themselves were given a number sequence that did not correspond to the district numbering sequence. Hence Tunnel Quarry was classified as Sub-depot No.1 with Districts 1-11, but Eastlays, nominated Sub-depot No.2 contained Districts 21-25. Sub-depot No.3 at Monkton Farleigh was home to Districts 12-20. There is no rational explanation of this numbering system; it reflects neither the order in which the quarries were purchased, built or brought into service. There is a further slight complication that District No.1 at Tunnel Quarry does not exist because the area in which it was to have been built was abandoned as unsafe after construction had begun, and District No.13 at Monkton Farleigh is absent solely for reasons of superstition.

Work started on the conversion of Eastlays in July 1936 but progress was at first held back by the urgent need to complete the preparation of Ridge Quarry for the RAF. Thereafter, the escalating storage requirements of the RAF caused constant changes to be made to the design of the Eastlays depot. Although conceived as a primary element of the army's central ammunition supply chain, Eastlays, in fact, did not play a role in this organization until the very end of the Second World War when it was used as the principal reception point for surplus ammunition returned from the various theatres of war.

Before its acquisition by the War Office, Eastlays Quarry was a rambling network of headings and working faces severely congested by waste stone debris. The only access was via an awkwardly placed, narrow and very steep inclined shaft that dropped into the middle of the workings. The War Office engineers realized from the outset that this shaft would not be suitable for ammunition movements in the completed depot so one of their first tasks was to arrange for two new, more favourably graded inclines to be sunk at each end of the quarry. Once the debris had been cleared it was found that the pillars supporting the roof had been dangerously undercut by the quarrymen in an attempt to extract the last easily accessible stone from underground, and that as a consequence the whole quarry was somewhat unstable. In order to stabilize the structure the War Office was compelled to build very extensive concrete walls and pillars, making Eastlays by far the most heavily engineered of the Corsham quarries.

Work progressed from west to east and even before District No.21 at the far west of the depot was completed in August 1939, arrangements had been made with the Ministry of Supply for it to be used for the storage of bulk TNT destined for the new bomb filling factories then under construction. In May 1940, District No.22, the next to be completed, was also transferred to the Ministry of Supply for the storage of 40,000 tons of cordite. By the end of the month the two completed districts were issuing in excess of 2,000 tons of high-explosives to the filling factories each week. District No.23, completed in October 1940, was very quickly filled with bulk TNT and in December the recently completed Districts 24 and 25 were handed over to the RAF for the storage of bomb and small-arms ammunition.

To handle receipts and issues of bulk explosives, which was delivered in small packages, the original War Office electric belt conveyor was retained in No.1 slope shaft. At the east end of the depot, No.2 shaft, which fed the bomb stores in Districts 24 and 25, was fitted with a winch and narrow-gauge rails to handle the heavier weapons stored there. Underground, the Air Ministry provided Ransom Rapier battery electric trucks for movements within the magazines.

The storage of cordite and TNT underground presented problems that had not been envisaged when the original scheme for the Corsham depots was drawn up. The underground depots were designed for use in wartime, and solely for the storage of field service ammunition – bullets, mortars and artillery projectiles – all of which were sturdy, weather-proof items that could withstand a degree of mishandling. Moreover, because the depots were designed as essentially temporary wartime exigencies, it was expected that the materials stored underground would turn over very quickly, the quarries acting as no more than transit depots between armament factory and battlefield. Cordite and TNT, however, are sensitive, unstable substances liable to degradation if atmospheric conditions are not maintained within a limited range of temperature and humidity. It was necessary, for the safe storage of propellants and high-explosives, to equip Districts 21, 22 and 23 with sophisticated air-conditioning, heating and ventilation apparatus to ensure the necessary conditions were maintained. The plant installed at Eastlays was massive in scale and was at the time of its construction one of the most complex in the western hemisphere.

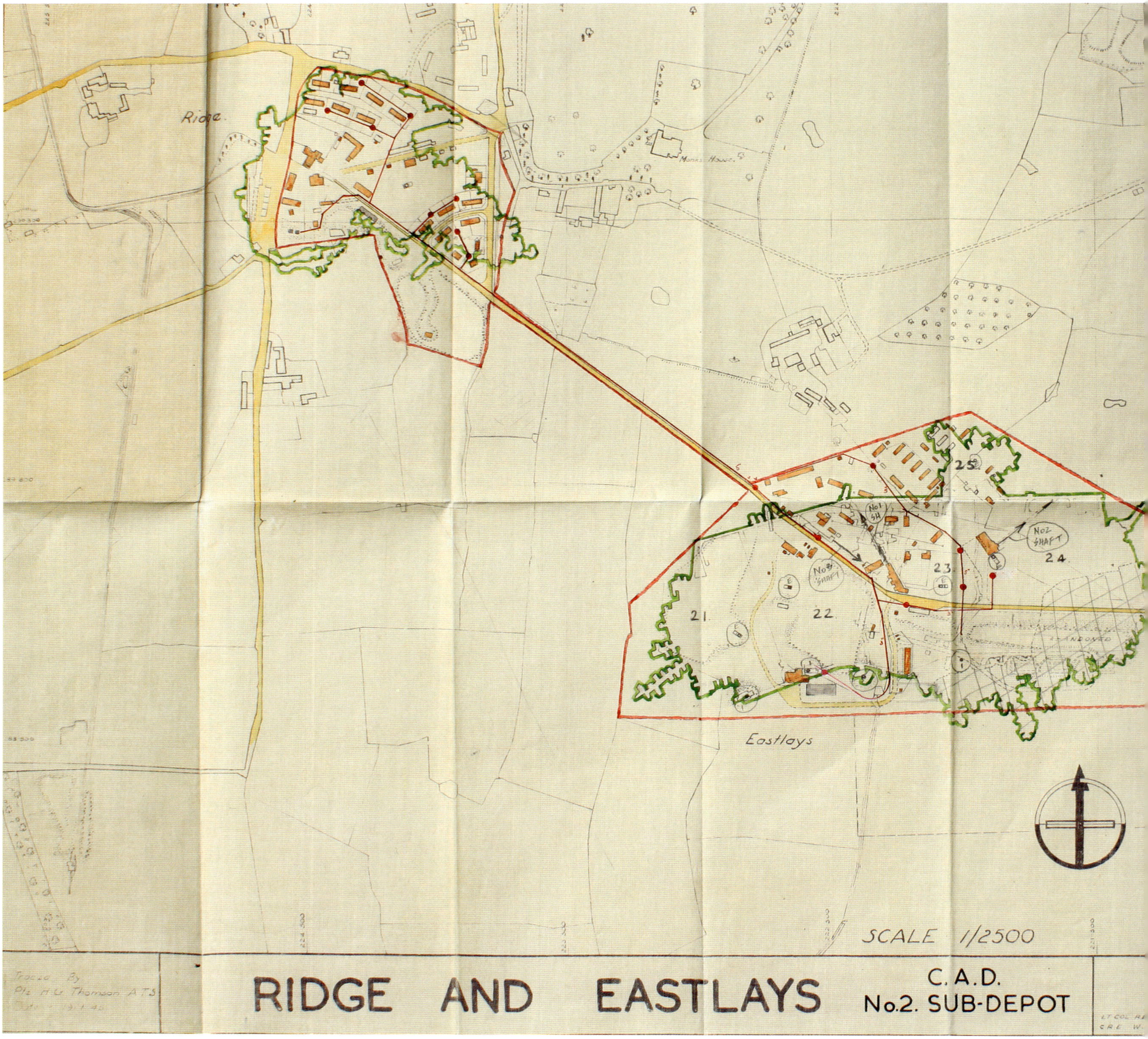

Above: Plan of the Ridge-Eastlays complex showing the underground areas, outlined in green, superimposed on the surface features.

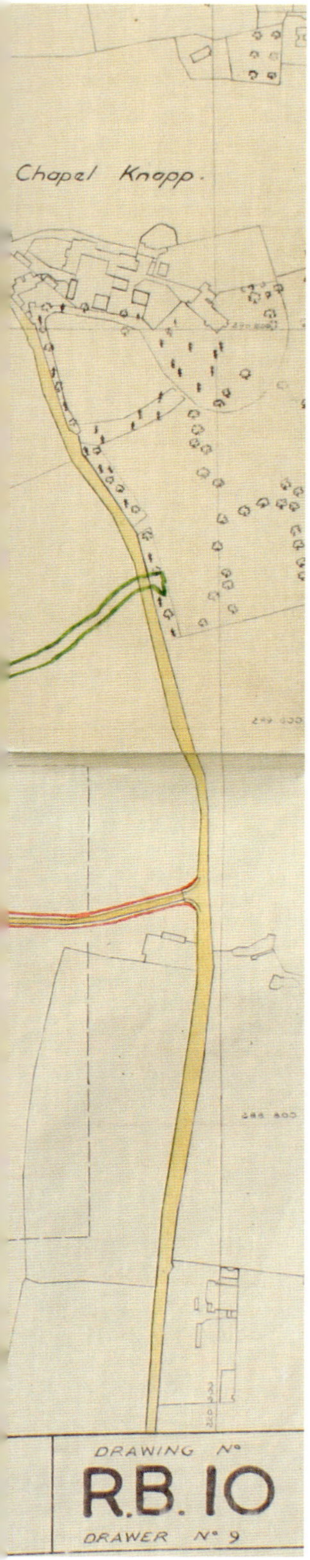

Above: Although known as No.2 shaft, this was the main entrance to Eastlays Quarry and housed the narrow-gauge haulage system used by the RAF to transport large bombs to and from the underground storage areas. The monolithic nature of the building is somewhat lost in this recent photograph as it is partially hidden behind the green corrugated steel extension erected by the wine storage company that now operates the site.

Below: The intimidating shaft-top building above the engineers' service incline at Eastlays Quarry. Wagons were drawn up this very steeply graded shaft by a winch at the left-hand end of the open platform visible in the photograph. The Germanic camouflage is not of wartime vintage but dates from 1983 when episodes of the BBC drama *The Fourth Arm* were filmed at Eastlays.

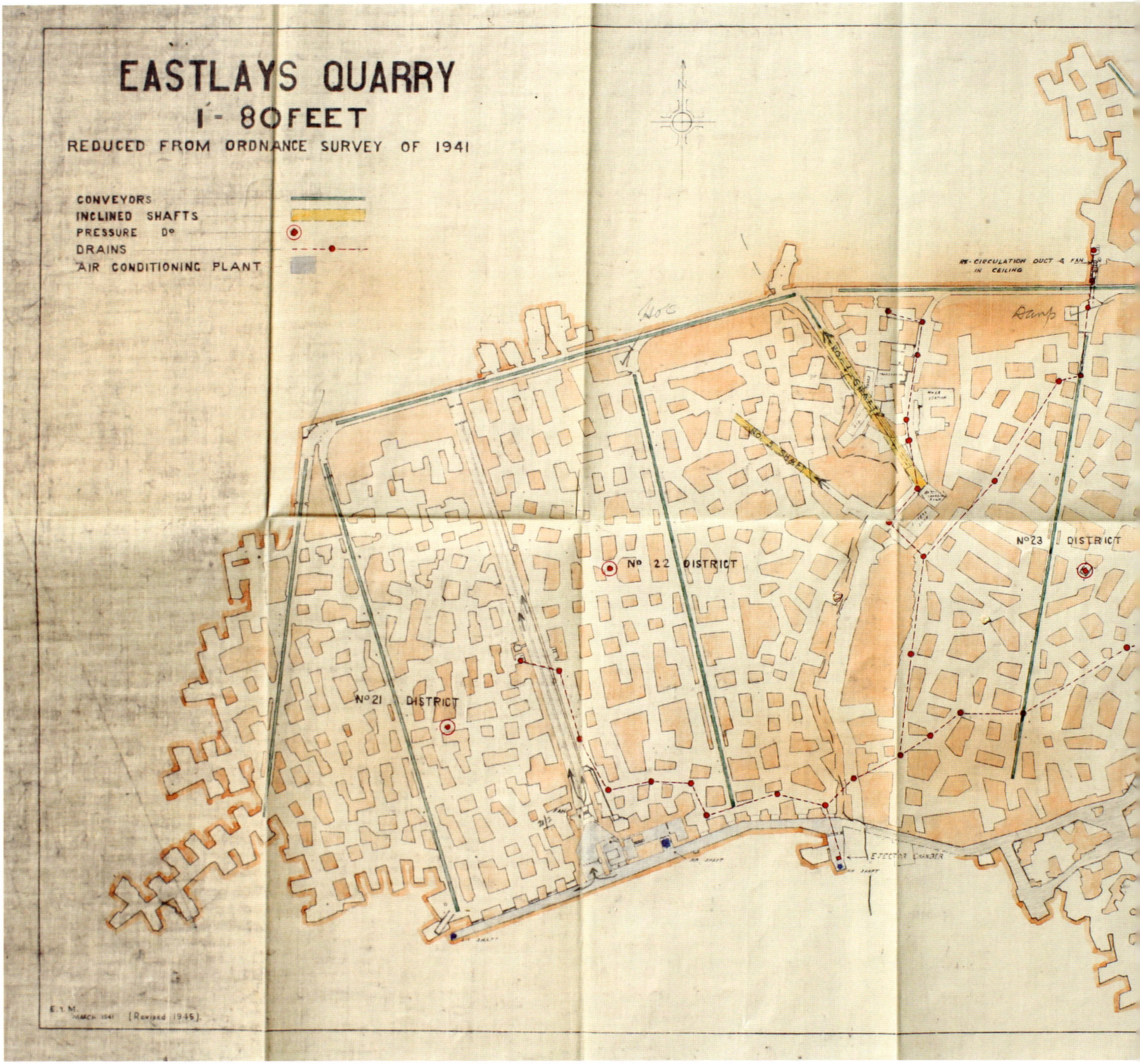
EASTLAYS QUARRY
1'- 80 FEET
REDUCED FROM ORDNANCE SURVEY OF 1941
CONVEYORS
INCLINED SHAFTS
PRESSURE Do
DRAINS
AIR CONDITIONING PLANT
N
RE-CIRCULATION DUCT & FAN IN CEILING
Ramp
No 21 DISTRICT
No 22 DISTRICT
No 23 DISTRICT
EJECTOR CHAMBER
E.Y.M. MARCH 1941 [Revised 1945]

Above: A view from the bottom of the Royal Engineers' slope shaft with the charging room for the batteries for the depot's fleet of electric trucks in the background. The passage to the left leads to the generating station and switchroom.
Below: Taken from the same location, this is a view up the Royal Engineers' slope shaft. The steel girders hinged from the roof are Warwick Beams, part of an interlocked system working together with the beam seen in the photograph above to prevent the risk of wagons running away on the slope.

Right: Unlike the other Corsham ammunition depots which standardized on Ruston Hornsby 5VLB diesel driven generators in their underground emergency power stations, Eastlays was provided with a much more sophisticated Blackstone Brush 8M9P eight-cylinder horizontally opposed, supercharged power unit. This engine still survives in good condition in the depot which is currently used as a wine store.

Left: A driver's end view of the Blackstone Brush generator set. The black-cased instrument in the centre of the stainless steel panel is the engine tachometer with a large glazed oil-level indicator below. The brown pipes carry lubricating oil. There is a manually operated in-line oil filter visible in the right-hand pipeline. Below the two maker's plates are a pair of engine-driven cylinder lubricators, the feed pipes to the four cylinders on each side can be seen emerging from the top of each pump. Engines like these are started by injecting compressed air into one of the cylinders; the brass handle on a polished steel circular mounting to the left of the central console is the main air-start lever.

Above: Low-voltage switchgear in the powerhouse at Eastlays. The instrument pillar in the background is a synchronising column, used to ensure that when there is a switchover between the mains supply and the standby generator set, the cycles of the alternating current are in phase and at a broadly similar voltage.

The heavily populated panel in the centre of this view carries control and monitoring instruments for the generator while the right-hand panel is a bus-coupler. The instruments along the bottom of these panels are earth-leakage and over-current safety trips.

Below: Due to the hazardous nature of the material stored in the Corsham depots all the switchgear for the lights in the storage areas was of a flameproof, colliery pattern and was located outside the magazines in the ventilation corridors that ran between the storage districts. This is one of the main isolators for the lights in No.22 District. Notice how the switch lever on the right of the case is mechanically interlocked with cams which ensure that the covers cannot be removed unless the electricity supply is isolated. The square section galvanised trunking on the left is a modern addition put in by the wine storage company that has occupied the site since 1985.

Left: Conditions for the long-term storage of cordite and TNT must be constrained within tight limits of temperature and humidity in order to prevent rapid decomposition or decay. This is most important in the case of cordite propellant because, although it may appear outwardly to be in good condition, if it has absorbed even small amounts of atmospheric moisture then its burn rate will be affected and thus the ballistic properties of the bullet or shell it is propelling will become unpredictable. For this reason the districts at Eastlays in which propellants and high-explosives were stored were air-conditioned from their inception.

These huge underground areas, each some five acres in extent, were heated and dehumidified by a large air-conditioning plant and boiler house on the surface. Steam for heating was provided by a rather ancient pair of marine boilers, removed from a French destroyer that had the ill luck to be moored in a British port at the time of the French capitulation. These boilers also provided steam for a Bellis & Morcom compound steam engine, seen here, which acted as prime mover for the depot's refrigeration plant.

Right: The steam engine seen here drove a large ammonia compressor which produced by means of condensers and evaporators, a supply of chilled water which was used to dehumidify air circulating underground by passing it through chilled water air washers. The air-conditioning cycle is, at first sight, somewhat counter-intuitive. Air from the surface, which in summer may be very humid and thus have a high water vapour content, is blown through a curtain of cold water which – one would be excused from assuming – might make it even wetter. What, in fact, happens is that the very cold water spray rapidly cools the air, the cooled air is incapable of holding water vapour so all the moisture in it condenses out leaving, on the output side of the air washer, a current of very cold but very dry air. This then passes through a radiator which raises its temperature and renders it capable of abstracting moisture from its surrounding. The air, now partially saturated with moisture abstracted from the underground environment, is extracted to the surface and the cycle is repeated.

Over 40,000 tons of TNT and a slightly smaller quantity of cordite propellant were stored in Districts 21, 22 and 23 on behalf of the Ministry of Supply. All of this was destined for shell and bomb filling factories at Bridgend, Glascoed and Hereford. Some of the stock was of British manufacture – cordite, for example, was supplied by the rather anonymously named British Manufacturing and Research Company of Grantham – but large quantities were imported from Canada and the United States. High-explosives were imported from the United States in the years before the Lend-Lease agreement despite America's neutrality by means of a dubious commercial fiction whereby the British government established and financed explosives factories that were actually operated by established American explosives manufacturers. Profits were retained by the American parents but the goods could be exported to belligerent Britain because, in a rather shadowy sort of way, they were the produce of a British company. The photographs below shows boxes of TNT from these sources, marked up as the products of the Atlas Powder Company and the Tennessee Powder Company.

Right & below left: A delivery of American manufactured 1,000lb and 250lb bombs being stacked in No.24 District at Eastlays. These are amongst the first Lend-Lease consignments to arrive in Great Britain and this series of photographs was taken for publicity purposes in the United States press. Bombs were transported underground on a winch-hauled narrow-gauge railway system in No.2 slope shaft and moved to their specified location in either No.24 or 25 District on trailers hauled by diminutive Ransome Rapier electric tractors.

Below right: Stocktaking in the bomb store, just to be sure that nothing 'fell off the back of a lorry' whilst in transit.

The four-ton electric winch at the head of No.2 slope shaft was fitted with an interlock mechanism designed to ensure that wagons could not be accidentally jolted over the edge of the incline if the brake of the haulage engine was disengaged. The system could not, however, prevent disaster if a wagon or wagons became detached from the rope whilst descending the shaft or – worse still – if the winch operator inadvertently forgot to attach the hook before pushing wagons onto the incline.

This is exactly what happened on Monday, 8 May 1944. Three trucks loaded with twelve 500lb bombs became detached at the top of the shaft, hurtled down the incline, scraped around the right-angle bend at the bottom – sparks flying – and smashed through the reinforced blast doors into No.24 District. Surprisingly, there was no injury, no explosion, and no bombs were seriously damaged although the district doors were buckled beyond repair.

Above: A panoramic view of the Eastlays compound from the east, taken in 1985. The main structures visible, from left to right, are: compressor house for sewage ejectors, ablution block, blast wall surrounding ammunition repair workshop and, on the hilltop, the aircraft lookout post.

Below: Stockpile of abandoned reinforced concrete roof-support pillars hidden amongst the trees to the right of the picture above.

Below: The blast wall of the ammunition repair w Nissen hut compressor house in the background.

Below: Aircraft spotters' lookout post on the highest part of the waste stone mounds surrounding the Eastlays depot.

with

Above: By the time this rather poor photograph was taken in 1984 the wooden-framed loading platform building at No.1 entrance had completely collapsed, leaving just the concrete portal of the inclined shaft visible in the undergrowth.

Above: Fine wines have replaced bombs as the staple item stored in Eastlays. This view shows wagons loaded with wine boxes at the bottom of No.2 shaft. *Below:* Thirty years later the scene around No.1 entrance is unrecognisable with a modern four-bay loading platform built at the head of the shaft.

Above: Although still extant, the massively constructed reinforced concrete loading platform above No.2 shaft is now completely enclosed by a range of more recent steel-clad extensions erected by the wine storage company that now occupies the site.

TUNNEL QUARRY

Tunnel Quarry was the largest and operationally most flexible of the sub-depots that made up CAD Corsham. The flexibility was due to the characteristics of the old quarry workings within which it was constructed. To the north of the site Huddswell Quarry had been worked via a pair of vertical winding shafts, while the southern section of the quarry adjacent to Box railway tunnel had the advantage of being served by a railway branch line that entered into the heart of the workings. A steep incline, No.7 shaft, also penetrated the quarry from the surface; this shaft was used during construction but was blocked and abandoned in 1941. The Huddswell lift shafts, on the other hand, were refurbished and fitted with locally fabricated lift cages to transport large artillery shells. The lifts were powered for the first couple of years by an improvised steam winch until replaced by a permanent installation of 30 cwt Herbert Morris double-cage lifts in December 1940.

Underground, the stone-loading platform was replaced by an impressive double-platform underground station connected to the extremities of the storage areas by eleven miles of conveyor belts. The underground station was brought into service in October 1939. Meanwhile, on the surface directly above the station, work was advancing on the construction of the Main Surface Loading Platform or MSLP. This building, partially buried into the hillside, consisted of four lorry loading bays that fed, via short conveyors, into a hexagonal rear chamber from which radiated four inclined shafts descending into distant areas of the quarry. The MSLP became operational towards the end of 1941.

Tunnel Quarry is part of a network of workings encompassing more than 100 acres of underground space. Tunnel Quarry is to the north of the Box railway tunnel and Spring Quarry to the south. At the eastern end of the workings the railway tunnel and the quarry workings are at the same level, but as one travels to the west the inclination of the stone strata rises while the tunnel dips so that a little beyond the western extremity of the underground station the railway is below the quarry workings. The GWR was concerned that, over the length of tunnel where railway and ammunition depot were on the same level, precautions were taken to ensure that an accidental explosion in the depot would not pose a risk to their tunnel. To ensure safety a twenty-foot thick concrete barrier was erected along the whole length of the southern extremity of the depot.

Tunnel Quarry was conceived as a completely self-contained bomb proof structure with all its vital facilities safely concealed beneath one hundred feet of rock. Just north of the underground station the Royal Engineers built a locomotive shed where the three War Office standard-gauge diesel locomotives were stabled and serviced; close by was an underground powerhouse containing two Ruston 5VLB diesel generating sets; a little to the west was an office complex housing all the administrative facilities that one would normally expect to find on a conventional army depot including a telephone exchange, while further to the west there were barracks for 300 men. The latter fell into disuse in 1942 when the threat from German bombing had become insignificant.

Adequate ventilation of the depot was a problem that taxed the ingenuity of the Royal Engineers for many years. At first it was hoped that natural ventilation, aided by an induction fan sucking air from the surface, would suffice. Whilst this system kept the air below ground relatively fresh it did little to improve the high humidity and consequent condensation in the magazines. The second stage of the ventilation scheme involved the erection of a 160-inch diameter fan – the largest fan in any of the Corsham quarries – at the far west end of the depot at which point it drew in air via Brewer's Drift and the Wind Tunnel from the old quarry workings on the perimeter of the depot. The hope was that, in its transit from outside the quarries to the fan through half-a-mile or more of subterranean passageways, air drawn into the depot would deposit most of its water content in the old workings before reaching the fan. This system, too, failed to live up to its expectations.

The third stage was something of an experiment. A small boiler was set up underground providing steam that heated radiators placed in the inlet air ducts for No.2 District. Air was blown into the district through the radiators by means of a dedicated fan and extracted by a second fan placed at the top of the district's outlet shaft. Sufficiently adequate conditions were produced by this pilot installation to encourage the War Office to prepare plans for a large-scale heating system for the whole depot. Steam for this system would be provided by a boiler house situated in a surface compound north of the MSLP. Difficulties in obtaining both labour and materials delayed completion of this project until the winter of 1944.

Opposite: The main railway entrance to Tunnel Quarry in 1948. The entrance is in the deep cutting at the east end of Box Tunnel. The portal of the main line tunnel can be seen to the left with the small entrance to the ammunition depot on the right. One of the War Office standard-gauge Ruston Hornsby diesel locomotives is drawing an ammunition train into the depot.

PROHIBITED AREA
ENGINES MUST NOT PASS THIS BOARD

CORSHAM. TUNNEL QUARRY.
CENTRAL AMMUNITION DEPOT.
REFERENCE
Quarry Face
Incline Shafts
Upcast Air Shafts
Other Shafts
Airways
Railways
Conveyors
Rope Haulage
BROWNS
QUARRY
BARRACK
AREA
BOX TUNNEL
G.W.R.
TUNNEL
FAN

When the CAD scheme was first proposed it was assumed that the maximum daily issue of ammunition would be no more than 2,000 tons. The underground platforms and the MSLP were each designed to cope with this capacity, with the MSLP intended as a reserve capacity in the event of a breakdown of the railway system. Throughout the early war years these maximum figures were never attained; practice showed that the most efficient means of supplying the field army was to ship ammunition direct from ordnance factory to port for onward dispatch to the theatre of war, completely bypassing the reserve depots. When it was necessary to hold stock for short periods of time this was generally undertaken at surface ammunition depots having basic facilities or by the use of temporary roadside dumps. Thus, the reserve depots tended gradually to accumulate stocks of slow-moving and obsolete ammunition. Things changed, however, during the preparations for D-Day when huge volumes of ammunition of all types started to arrive at Corsham. Turnover of fresh stocks during April and May 1944 amounted to 32,000 tons, while 10,500 tons were issued during the last week of June with comparable quantities shipped during the weeks thereafter.

Although planned as a temporary wartime expedient, CAD Corsham was later reclassified as a permanent depot and continued to function for almost twenty years after the end of the Second World War, with regular supplies being made to British units in the Far and Middle East and to forces engaged in the Korean War. The end finally came on 4 December 1962 when, as a consequence of the defence review of that year, the depot was finally closed. It has, however, for almost fifty years remained in the hands of the Ministry of Defence under care and maintenance.

Left: Fred Allen's original hand-coloured survey of Tunnel Quarry, drawn shortly after construction was completed. At the far left-hand edge can be seen Brewer's Drift, the passageway linking the ammunition depot with the extensive old mine workings beneath the village of Box, through which ventilation air was drawn into the storage depot. To the right is South West Control, originally intended to be No.1 storage district but instead occupied by the RAF as a communication's centre. The long heading to the north of this area leads to Brown's Quarry, which during the Second World War housed the Operations Room for No.10 Group, RAF Fighter Command. Slightly to the east is the underground barrack area beyond which are the main storage districts. Huddswell Drift, containing a narrow-gauge railway to transport the heaviest shells, runs along the northern perimeter while to the south lies the underground standard-gauge railway station with its locomotive shed and refuge siding. The depot's power station is situated just to the north of the station.

Above: The Main Surface Loading Platform (MSLP) at Tunnel Quarry. Smoke in the background is issuing from the chimney of the surface boiler house.

Below: No.5 slope shaft, with conveyor and incline for rope-hauled trucks, photographed shortly after the installation of the conveyor in 1943.

Below: The bottom of No.5 slope shaft at the junction with the conveyor leading to the main underground loading platform and Districts 5 to 9.

Left: The virtually disused MSLP, photographed in 2005.

Originally a winch situated on a balcony floor of the MSLP drew wagons carrying heavy shells up on to the upper level via a slight extension to the slope shaft. Here the wagons could be unloaded without causing an obstruction and their cargo then lowered to the main floor by means of a short elevator, the location of which is shown on the plan overleaf.

Below: The bottom of No.5 incline today. Compare this with the 1943 view opposite. The conveyor and one handrail have been removed and a new wagon haulage system, incorporating run-away safety stops, has been installed.

Below: In this contemporary photograph of the top of No.5 shaft one can see the diagonal mark on the wall parallel with the haulage cable which marks the position of the extension to the incline that once accessed the upper floor.

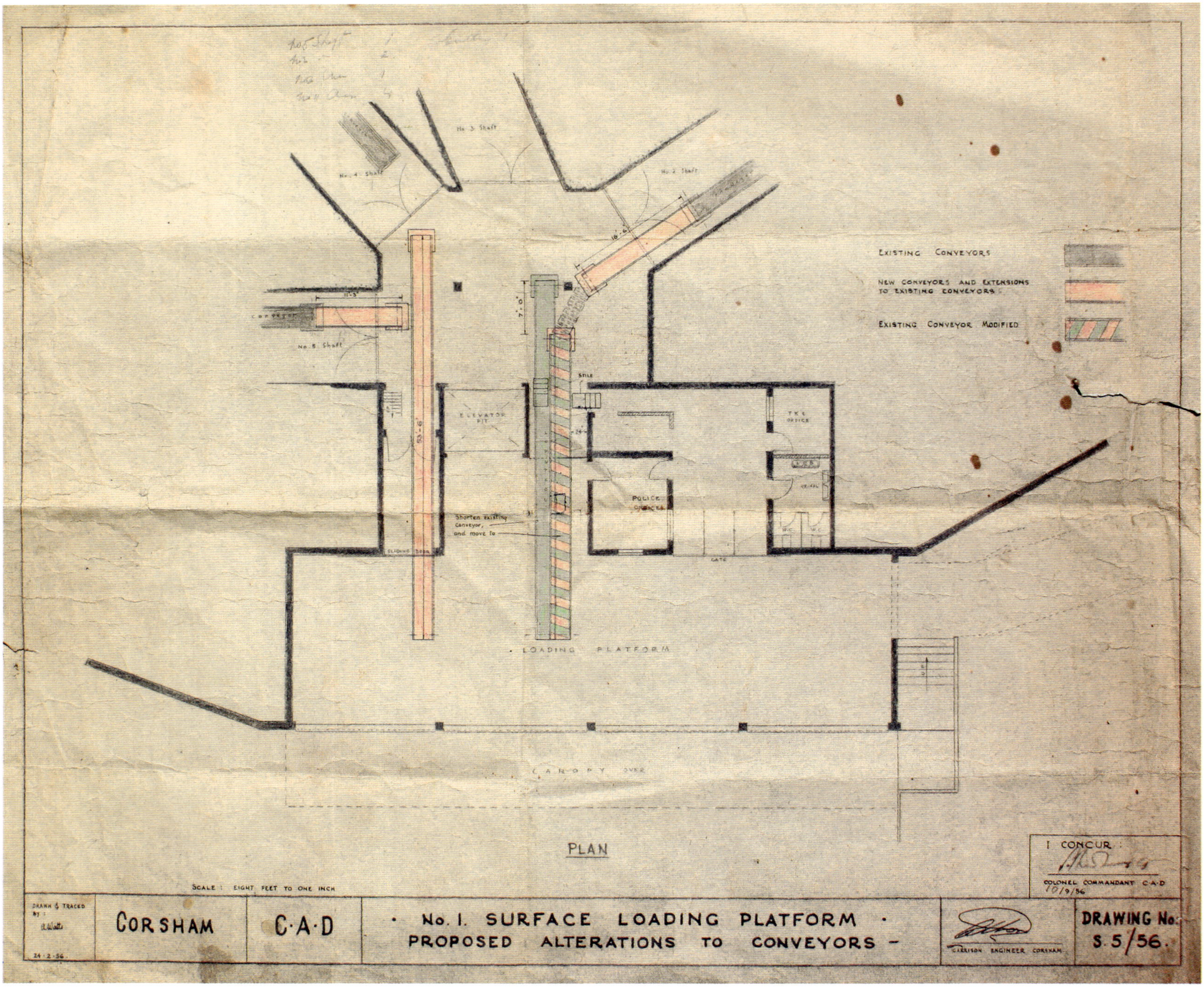

Above: This drawing, prepared to show post-war alterations to the configuration of the conveyors, illustrates the way the four slope shafts radiate from the rear of the building.

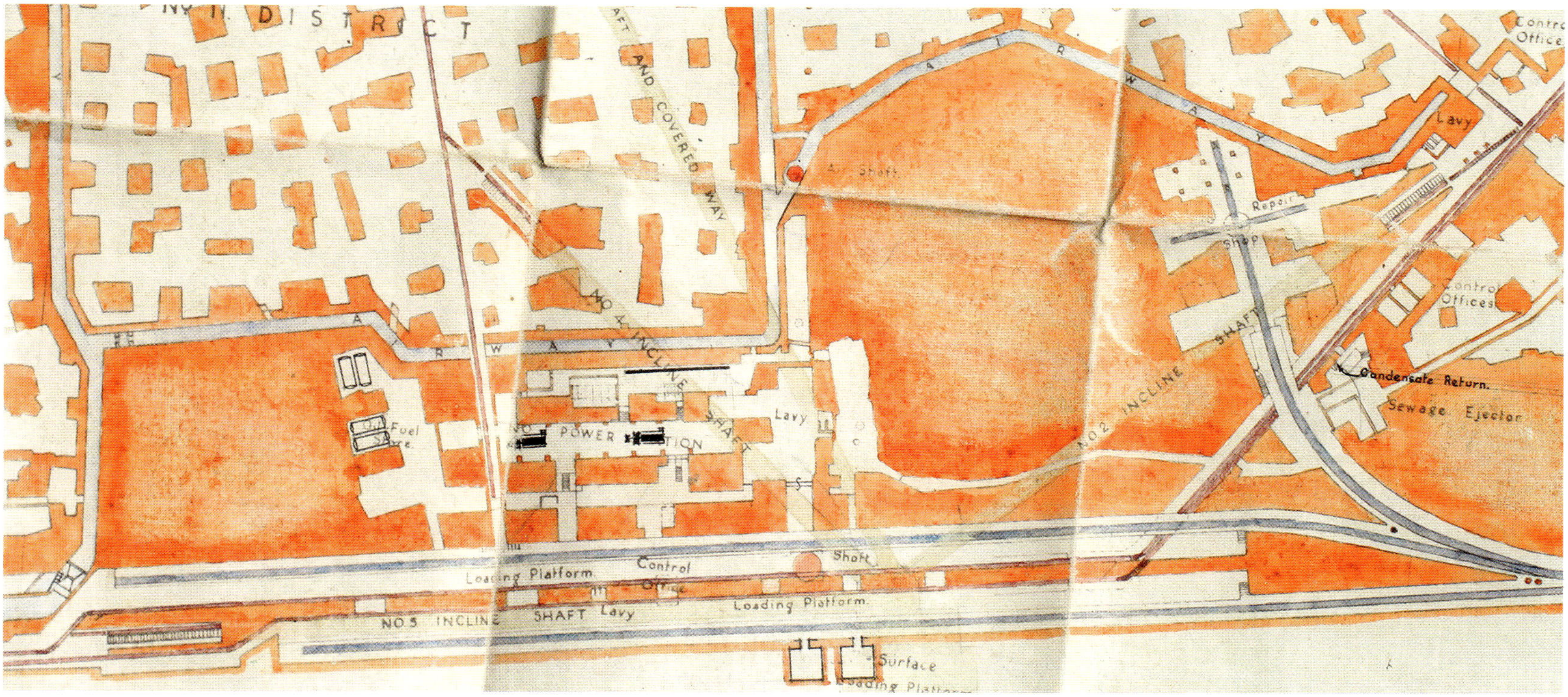

Above: A detail from the Tunnel Quarry survey showing the railway station, engine shed and power house.

Below: The eastern portal of Box Tunnel in 2005 with the overgrown entrance to the ammunition depot to the right of the stairway.

Below: A view along the approach heading from the underground station towards the tunnel portal.

Above: The refuge siding, running north from the east end of the platforms in the underground station.

Above: Seen from the main railway heading, the line branches at this point to the north and south platforms, with a further branch, just visible in the background, to the locomotive shed and maintenance area.

Left: The inner-most end of the southern railway platform. Notice the very extensive steel-work supporting the roof in this area. Originally the far end of the platform opened out onto the Main West haulageway giving direct communication by conveyor with Districts 2-4, but this opening was blocked-off with a concrete block wall in the late 1980s in order to control the airflow through the depot in connection with the adaptation of adjacent quarry workings as a military communications centre.

Ammunition unloaded on the south platform could be transferred onto the conveyor on the north platform for transportation to Districts 5-11 via roller-beds erected through archways in the wall on the right-hand side of this view.

Right: A view along the full length of the north platform from the point at which the conveyor turns beneath a skew arch to run parallel with a similar conveyor from the south platform to run the length of the Main West haulageway.

In the middle-distance can be seen a moveable bridge, suspended from the ceiling by a chain hoist which carries a short length of narrow-gauge railway and a roller conveyor link. When lowered across the track this enables ammunition to be transported in and out of Nos 11 & 12 Districts, the joint haulageway for which emerge through the wall to the north of the railway at this point. This location can be seen in detail on page 67.

Left: The eastern section of the northern platform. The building at the top of the steel stairway is the depot's conveyor control room which provided central control of all the conveyor belts on both platforms and on the Main East and Main West haulageways. This was built after a number of unfortunate incidents occurred when, due to poor communication, ammunition travelling on a moving belt piled-up at an end-on junction with a stationary belt. Requests and instructions for starting and stopping the belts were transmitted to the control room by bell codes and visual electrical indicators.

Left: A view towards the west end of the northern platform. The passage in the right foreground (with a ladder down into a pit) gives access to the depot's sewage ejectors and associated compressors. A second passageway in the middle distance leads to the underground power station.

Below left: A close-up view of the conveyor control room which is built into the concrete wall that separates the north and south platforms and is cantilevered out on both sides.

Below right: One of the two indicator panels in the conveyor control room. The black instrument on the wall had a bell mounted on it with solenoid-controlled flags which indicated from which conveyor the bell signals were coming. A panel on the desk was fitted with start-stop buttons and illuminated indicators to show which conveyors were running.

Right: A train of box wagons in the underground station being loaded with anti-tank mines. *Below right:* The doors to the underground locomotive shed. *Below left:* One of the depot's Hunslet 0-6-0 diesel shunters under repair in the underground workshop. The War Office employed three Hunslet locomotives (WD Nos. 855, 856 and 857) at Tunnel Quarry. Day-to-day maintenance was carried out in the underground locomotive shed but the engines were transferred to the Royal Engineers' main railway workshops at Bicester for major overhauls.

Although the War Department locomotives were supposed to operate only in the underground area, they were frequently used, unofficially, to transfer trains between the depot and the sidings at Thingley Junction.

Above left: Inside the locomotive shed showing the inspection pit and the turntable giving access to the engine stabling roads.

Above right: Storage tanks in the engine shed for locomotive diesel fuel.

Right: Main West haulageway, with the entrances to Districts 2, 3 and 4 on the right-hand side. Originally there were two parallel belts here but the right-hand one was transferred to Monkton Farleigh in 1985. The hump in the conveyor in the middle distance is to allow a roller conveyor to be erected above the adjacent 'low' belt to connect with the conveyor in No.3 District without impeding the flow of ammunition on the low belt.

Right: A leisurely transfer of 25 pdr cartridges from Main East high belt into a storage district. Note the instructions regarding what to do in event of fire. The most likely reaction would probably be blind panic and a desperate rush to the nearest exit.

Below left: Stacking boxed 25 pdr projectiles in No.6 District. This wartime photograph shows civilian labourers who at that time outnumbered RAOC workers in the underground depots. Presumably these men were too old to be called up.

Below right: National Service lads stacking 25 pdr cartridges in No.6 District in 1948.

Above left: A superb view of No.6 District stacked to the ceiling with 25 pdr cartridges. There would have been approximately 25,000 tons of ammunition stored in this district at that time.

Above right: Unloading a stream of 5-inch field gun shells from the conveyors in No.5 District.

Left: A receipt of 5-inch gun shells from the MSLP via No.2 inclined shaft. The shaft conveyor would normally connect with the twin belts in Main East haulageway but here a short portable conveyor is being used to route the shells directly to No.5 District.

Above left: A view of No.6 District today, corresponding with the wartime photograph shown opposite, with the conveyor still in place but ammunition long gone.
Above right: A contemporary view of No.5 District. The rails embedded in the floor are relics of the earlier overhead ropeway system. The conveyor, which had been mounted on the concrete blocks on the left was removed and transferred to Monkton Farleigh Quarry in 1985.

Left: Near the bottom of No.2 incline today. The partially dismantled foreground conveyor is that from which anti-tank mines are being transferred in the picture on page 66. The incline shaft in the background is that from which shells are being transferred in the illustration opposite.

Left: An issue of anti-tank mines from No.5 District in 1943. This view shows the twin conveyors (high and low belts) in the Main East haulageway, connected via a roller-bed to the district conveyor. This photograph illustrates how a roller-bed could be linked from the district conveyor to the high belt allowing transfers to be made without interrupting the flow from adjacent districts on the low belt.

Below: A typical view of artillery shells stacked in Tunnel Quarry. This is just one corner of one bay in one district and could probably be repeated a thousand-fold to give a true image of the quantity stored in the depot at any moment in time. The totally capacity was approximately 120,000 tons.

Above left: Access from No.11 District was only possible by crossing the main line siding so a lifting bridge, normally raised to ceiling height, was installed. When lowered it interlocked with the conveyor and narrow-gauge rails in No.11 District.

Above right: Because the district sloped towards the station an electric winch was provided to draw wagons up the incline.

Left: Districts 10 and 11 share a common conveyor to the railway platform. This conveyor link is broken at the point where it passes through a ventilation passage separating the districts, normally sealed by double blast doors. When access is required a mobile 'piggy-back' conveyor is used to join the two district conveyors.

Above left: Main East haulageway, crossed in the foreground by a main cable route and in the middle distance by a bridge carrying the lines of the northern railway platform. In the background the conveyor turns to the right and climbs an incline to emerge at platform level.

Above right: This contemporary view of a section of No.3 District shows excellent examples of existing stone support pillars that have been encased in concrete, together with new concrete pillars supporting steel roof girders.

Left: The bottom of No.4 slope shaft in No.11 District. Here a portable conveyor links the shaft and district belts. Conveyor 'Stop' and 'Start' buttons and bells for sending and receiving instructions can be seen attached to the wall beside the incline. The rails on the right-hand side of the shaft are relics of a railway system that predated the conveyors in the depot.

Above: No.4 District haulageway. Because conveyors cannot bend around corners it has been necessary to utilize two belts in the angled haulageway in this district. These conveyors were the first installed in the Corsham depot and were supplied by the Meco Engineering Company. Subsequently, the War Office standardized on Sutcliffe conveyors which were more heavily constructed and required more substantial concrete supports.

Right: Initially all transport in the depot was by means of narrow-gauge railway trucks propelled by continuous overhead ropeways of a type widely used in collieries at that time. However, the systems installed in the first-completed districts at Tunnel and Monkton Farleigh quarries were soon found to be inefficient, noisy and dangerous when used to handle ammunition. At first, it was thought that belt conveyors would not be suitable because up to that time they had been designed to run in only one direction, i.e. out of mineral mines and quarries. At the request of the War Office the conveyor manufacturers Richard Sutcliffe & Co developed a drive system that would track accurately in both directions and by the end of 1942 all the overhead ropeways had been replaced by belt conveyors except for those carrying very heavy shells in the Main East haulage at Monkton Farleigh and, as seen here, in Huddswell Drift at Tunnel Quarry.

Left: The drive mechanism for the Huddswell Drift overhead ropeway shortly after its installation. This is incorporated with the lower landing of the Huddswell vertical lifts, one of the cages for which can be seen beneath the winding drum.

Above left: A view to the west along Huddswell Drift, from the raised platform which supports the winding engine. Wagons loaded with 9.2-inch shells are awaiting their turns to be attached to the rope for transfer to their allocated storage bays.
Above right: This is a posed publicity photograph supposedly showing a wagon being manhandled into position beneath the overhead ropeway, but is noticeable that the wheels have been spragged to guard against it running away while the photograph was being taken.
Left: An early view of No.2 District, before the overhead ropeways were abandoned in favour of electric belt conveyors. The star-wheels which support the wire rope allow the haulage chain which attaches the wagon to the rope to pass through without obstruction.

Left: The Huddswell ropeway engine today. The overhead rope and its supports have been removed and the tops of the lift shafts capped. Behind the group of trucks can be seen the corroding, cantilever gates of the lift cages. The wagons are fitted with castor steering and dual-purpose wheels which enable them to run on either the railway system or on flat surfaces, pulled by the depot's Ransomes Sims & Jeffries electric tractors.

Below left: The east side of the Huddswell lifts, giving access to Districts 8 and 9. There are no rails on this side of the lifts so wagons would be hauled away by electric tractor.

Below right: This example of a Huddswell ammunition trolley is fitted with a steel hoop to secure in position a single 18-inch howitzer shell. Star wheels from the dismantled rope haulage system can be seen stacked against the wall in the background.

Above left: The reserve stock of 9.2-inch projectiles for the Freetown Coastal Defence battery in store at Tunnel Quarry.
Above right: Ammunition for the 18-inch railway gun, manufactured towards the end of the First World War for a new gun then under development. Mainly as a propaganda exercise, the gun was sent down to Bekesbourne on the Dover to Canterbury line in 1940. Publicized as a monster that could bombard German troops on the French coast, it was actually a high-angle howitzer and would, from Bekesbourne, have had trouble bombarding the Kent coast. No rounds were ever fired in anger and very few in practice. Most were stored at Woolwich Arsenal until 1938 when they were transferred to Tunnel Quarry. In 1963 they were taken to Barry Docks and subsequently dumped in the Irish Sea.
Left: Ammunition for the 5.5-inch field-gun. Between D-Day and VE Day, 21st Army Group in north-west Europe fired 2,610,747 rounds from these guns.

The Powerhouse

Under normal circumstances Tunnel Quarry was supplied by electricity from the grid at 11,000V. Two 500 KvA transformers in the power station reduced this to 440V three-phase for power and 240V single-phase for lighting. There were also two 500 KvA alternators powered by a pair of five-cylinder Ruston Hornsby 5VLB diesel engines for use in event of a grid failure.

Left: Front view of No.2 generator showing its 500 KvA alternator and exciter.
Below left: A rear view of the generator set. The upright cylinder on the far left is an electrically heated oil filter.
Below right: The switchroom. To the left are instrument panels monitoring the state of the generators and transformers, with a synchronising column at the far end. The switchgear to the right controls low voltage (440/240V) distribution throughout the depot.

Left: A recent view of No. 2 generator. Although suffering surface corrosion, it is in fairly good condition. Many components from No.1 engine, which is in front of it and just out of shot, were removed in 1985 for use in the restoration of a similar plant at Monkton Farleigh. The five-aspect instrument high on the left-hand wall near the handrail is an illuminated display transmitting instructions to the engine driver to speed-up or slow down, etc., from the switchroom in order to maintain the correct voltage and AC frequency.

Below: The switchroom today with the original low-voltage distribution switchgear on the left and instrument panels on the right. The new transformer in the right foreground is a replacement for the wartime equipment which was found to be filled with a highly toxic polychlorinated biphenyl dielectric oil. Between the transformer and the instrument panels is a group of relatively modern 11Kv switches installed during alterations to the Corsham electricity system in the 1980s.

Above: A corner of the kitchens in the underground barrack block. When the depot was first commissioned it was expected that Britain would suffer continuous and devastating aerial bombardment by the Luftwaffe and that the Germans would probably use mustard gas bombs and other chemical weapons. Thus it was thought that surface barracks would be too vulnerable, so sleeping, dining and welfare facilities were provided for the RAOC contingent of approximately 600 personnel. By 1942 the aerial threat had become negligible and this, coupled with the inconvenience of permanent incarceration underground, led to the abandonment of the underground barracks. These were bricked-up and lay undisturbed for the next sixty years.

Above left: The underground telephone exchange at Tunnel Quarry, probably taken towards the end of the war or during the early post-war years.

Below left: This photograph of the telephone exchange was taken in 1943. The girl in the foreground is Edna Bullen from Doncaster, whose story appeared in the Birmingham Gazette on 18th November 1943. In her account she records how, 'after two years of Army life underground, winter ailments disappear because of the clean air and even temperature'.

Above: The empty shell of the telephone exchange in 2009. The distinctively shaped ventilation louvre and the pattern of the wooden beading on the asbestos-clad rear wall are clearly identifiable in the wartime photographs opposite.

Above right: This photograph of the kitchen in the underground barracks was taken from the same position as the wartime photograph opposite. Little seems to have changed, with most of the equipment still surviving and in its original position. One surprise is that a fluorescent lamp has replaced the original fitting, a change that may indicate that the kitchens were briefly re-commissioned during the 1950s to serve the ROTOR radar centre in nearby Brown's Quarry.

Right: A view from the administration area of the barracks looking towards the cookhouse, the door to which is to the left of the servery window in the background. The passageway to the right leads to the dining room. On the left-hand wall is a key press labelled 'Underground Barracks Keys'.

Above: The CDI (Corsham Depot Induction) fan. This huge fan sucked air from the hundred acres of abandoned quarry workings that surround Tunnel Quarry and distributed it around the depot. It was a hope only partially realised that external air passing through the relatively cold quarry workings would deposit most of its moisture before entering the depot, thus avoiding the requirement for an expensive air-conditioning system.

Huddswell Laboratories

Regular checks of small samples of ammunition were made underground in what were known as 'Permitted Areas'. Larger scale inspections, repairs and modifications were, however, undertaken at the Huddswell laboratories, a secluded surface compound situated a quarter of a mile east of the main depot.

The Huddswell complex consisted of a comprehensive group of buildings dispersed around a hexagonal service road and resembled more a small ordnance factory than a conventional laboratory. Three hundred personnel were employed at the site including ATS storewomen, REME artisans, officers of the Ammunition Inspectorate and Pioneer Corps labourers, all of whom wore thick felt over-boots and loose fitting white felt suits without pockets or turn-ups when working inside the designated 'clean' buildings.

Shortly after the end of the Second World War the Huddswell facilities were expanded to include new workshops in which artillery shells in various dubious conditions, returned from temporary stores and depots on distant battlefields, could be examined and mechanically scraped, repainted, banded, stencilled and re-packaged pending long-term storage. A two-cell proof yard was also provided where various classes of ammunition could be test fired.

Thingley Junction

Above: Thingley Junction – the sidings still quite busy with ammunition movements in 1952.

Below: The covered platform in this recent photograph was erected when the sidings were re-configured for an unspecified Cold War purpose in 1976.

A feature of CAD Corsham was that all its sub-depots should primarily receive and issue stock by rail, so plans were laid at an early stage to provide railheads as close as possible to each sub-depot. Although Tunnel Quarry had its own underground station this was not large enough to handle long, trains of mixed cargos, such as whole, ship-load consignments of imported ammunition from the docks or outward cargos for a supply convoy to a distant battlefield. Inward shipments would be distributed throughout the Corsham sub-depots and, similarly, large outward shipments would be assembled from items stored in the various sub-depots. Eastlays and Monkton Farleigh quarries had their own dedicated rail terminals similar in function to the underground station at Tunnel Quarry; Eastlays at Beanacre sidings a mile away by road, and Monkton Farleigh at Farleigh Down Sidings near Box, connected to the quarry by a spectacular one-and-a-quarter mile long tunnel. All three sub-depots were served by an extensive new reception, assembly and distribution yard constructed in 1938 for the War Office by the GWR at Thingley Junction near Chippenham, where the former Wilts, Somerset & Weymouth line branches off south towards Trowbridge.

Brown's Quarry

Early in 1940 the RAF decided to establish a secure underground operations centre for No.10 Group, Fighter Command in the Corsham quarries. It was understood that construction of the underground facility would not be completed until the early part of 1941 so, as an interim measure, Rudloe Manor near Box was requisitioned as temporary accommodation in June 1940. Staff and administrative functions were housed in the mansion while a makeshift control room and associated facilities were established in huts in the grounds.

The underground operations centre was constructed in Brown's Quarry, a remote heading north of Tunnel Quarry but connected to it by a long, narrow passage. Construction was completed in December 1940 and the site handed over to the RAF on 15 January 1941. Access was by means of a passenger lift from the surface, although there was also an emergency link to Tunnel Quarry via the underground heading. This passage also gave access to South West Control, an RAF telecommunications centre controlling voice and teleprinter links between airfields and other establishments in the south-west of England. South West Control was constructed in what had been earmarked as Tunnel Quarry's No.1 ammunition storage district, but which had been abandoned when the Royal Engineers decided that the roof structure was dangerously unstable. It would appear, however, that different safety criteria were applied by the RAF who went ahead with construction despite War Office misgivings.

Brown's Quarry continued in its role as No.10 Group Operations Centre until 1945 when the Group was disbanded and the site became home to the RAF Control and Reporting School. In 1950 it took on a new lease of life as the Southern Sector Control for the RAF's Rotor radar system. Rotor was an immensely complex and hugely expensive radar network intended to provide a nationwide shield against Russian atomic bombers. Unfortunately the concept of manned bombers and atomic bombs gave way to ballistic missiles and nuclear warheads – against which there could be no active defence – and the whole Rotor project, along with the Corsham operations centre, was abandoned in 1958 before the scheme achieved its final fruition. Military communications facilities under different guises continued to operate underground in the Corsham quarries but by 1980 the wartime operations room was long abandoned and is now just an empty shell.

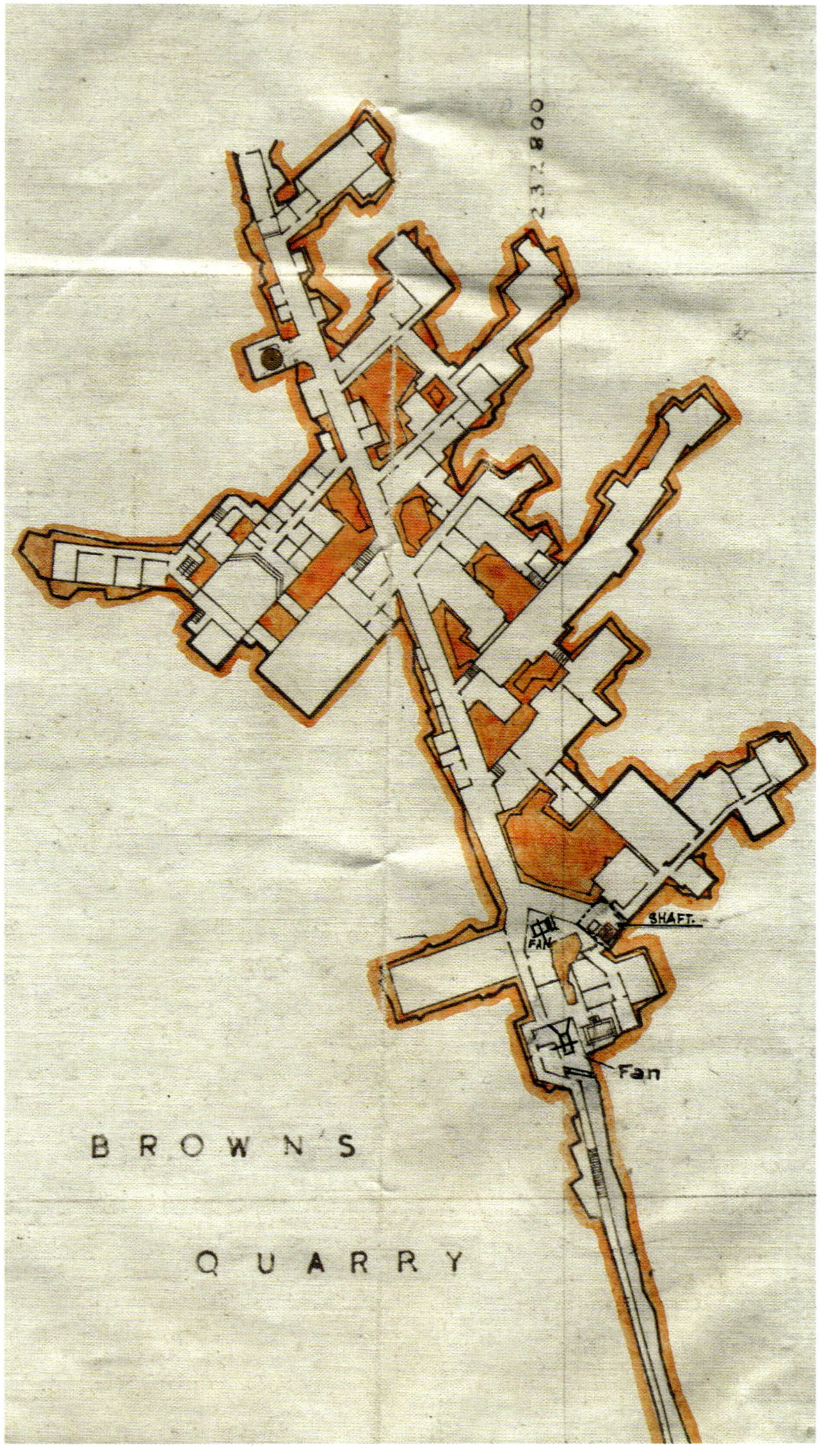

Above: Detail from the 80-inch plan of Tunnel Quarry showing Brown's Quarry and the general arrangement of RAF No.10 Group operations room.

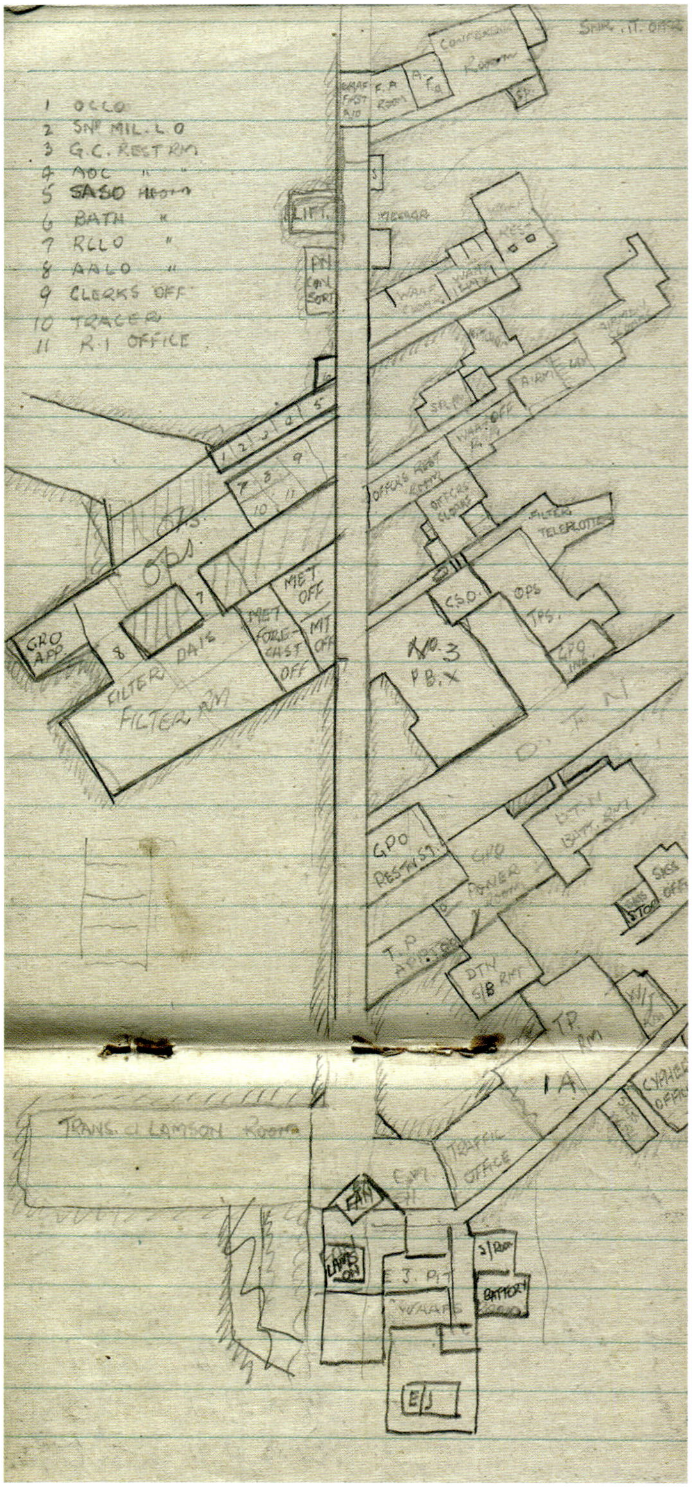

Above: Sketch plan from Fred Allen's notebook showing his proposed layout for No.10 Group operations room and headquarters complex.

Above: A view from the balcony looking down into the plotting room.

Below: The Lamson tube exchange in the No.10 Group headquarters.

Above: The plotting room in 1943 showing WAAF girls moving tallies on the map table to record the positions of British fighters and enemy intruders. The officers on the mezzanine floors control events, issuing commands to and receiving reports from Sector airfields, anti-aircraft gun sites, radar stations and Royal Observer Corps units.

Right: The shell of the plotting room. The rubble-filled trench in the middle of the floor is a cable duct that carried electrical power and communications cables to the plotting table. All of the mezzanine floors, which were of wooden construction, were removed in the early 1980s by which time they were in a serious state of decay.

This large chamber was constructed by first cutting narrow, vertical slots the required height of the side walls and somewhat wider, within which the concrete walls were cast to just below roof level. A horizontal slot was then cut spanning the two side walls at roof level, just deep enough to accommodate the beams. Lengths of greased railway track were then laid on top of the walls and the wide roof-support girders were then slid along them into their required position. When this was completed all the remaining stone between walls, ceiling and floor was cut away.

Left: The area at the far west end of Tunnel Quarry situated between the CDI fan and the barrack area was occupied by the RAF as a communications centre known during the war as South West Control and more recently as No.1 Signals Unit and No.6 Signals unit. Although linked to both Tunnel Quarry and Brown's Quarry, South West Control had its own dedicated entrance in the form of a vertical lift shaft from a small bunker on the surface. This view shows the bottom lift landing and lobby area shortly before closure.

MONKTON FARLEIGH QUARRY

Monkton Farleigh Quarry was acquired in the latter months of 1937 to provide additional storage space for army field ammunition and, more importantly, anti-aircraft ammunition for the air defence of the United Kingdom. As the impending war grew closer the vulnerability of the United Kingdom to aerial attack became increasingly apparent and the role of Anti-Aircraft Command rose higher upon the defence agenda.

With the experience of construction difficulties at the earlier Corsham depots behind them, the War Office developed a more sophisticated scheme for Monkton Farleigh Quarry. Instead of adapting the existing random layout of quarry pillars, these would all be swept away to be replaced by regularly spaced concrete walls and pillars to produce a subterranean complex consisting of six rectangular boxes each 1,420 feet long, 180 feet wide and eleven feet high. Each box, or magazine, would be separated from those adjacent by twin, concrete-walled passageways which would serve as protective blast barriers, ventilation ducts and emergency escape corridors. It was realized that this form of construction would take longer to complete but, at Monkton Farleigh, the War Office had the advantage that the area of quarry earmarked for development was surrounded by some fifty further acres of quarry which had been part of the original purchase but were surplus to the initial requirement. Two five acre sections of these spare workings to the west of the main area, known as 'K' and 'L' areas, (later 19 and 20 Districts respectively), were quickly adapted to a minimal standard to provide temporary storage until the main works were complete. Both were provided with independent incline shafts to the surface for access. 'K' area was commissioned in May 1937 and 'L' area four months later in September. Meanwhile, more than 2,000 men were put to work in No.12 District, the first of the permanent magazines to be completed.

Monkton Farleigh was unusual amongst the Corsham quarries in that, although the workings were 100 feet below the surface, they were burrowed below the top of a high ridge almost 600 feet above sea level. The principal route for issues and receipts of ammunition was via a railway yard at Farleigh Down Sidings in the valley below. Plans had been prepared in December 1938 for the construction of a one-and-a-quarter mile long tunnel to link the sidings with the main depot but, as it was expected that this might take three years to complete, an aerial ropeway was constructed as a temporary

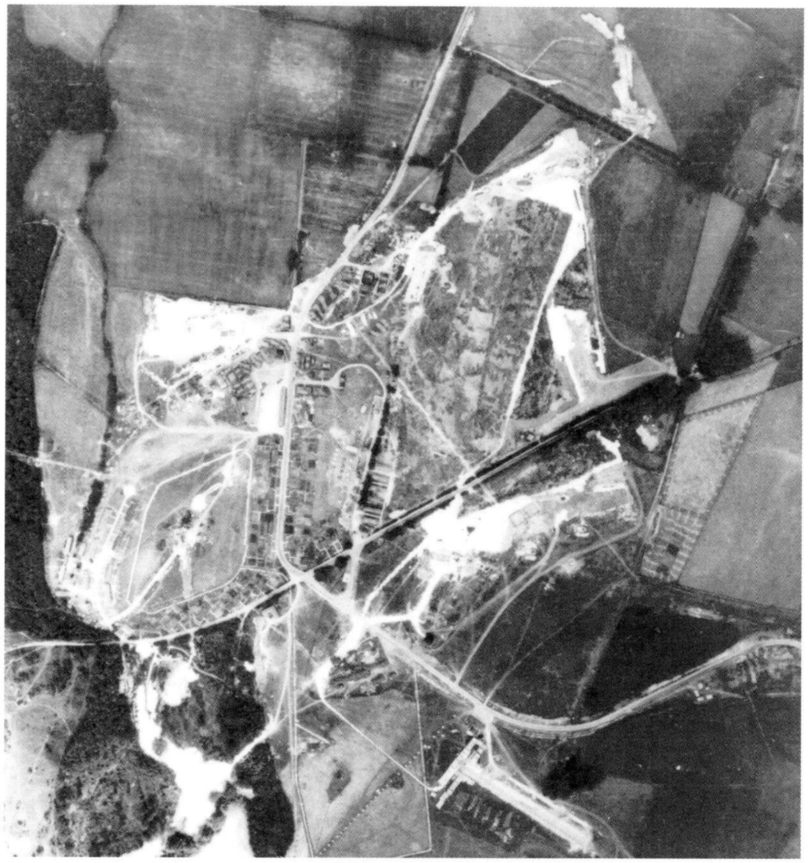

Above: This aerial photograph taken in July 1940 demonstrates how conspicuous the construction work at Monkton Farleigh was from the air. The large expanse of white in the bottom left of the picture is where waste stone from below ground was dumped in long abandoned surface quarries in the woodland near Brown's Folly.

expedient. A terminal building on the hilltop served the surface loading platforms for Districts 19 and 20, while an intermediate station near the unfinished Main West entrance building provided access to No.12 District via a temporary lift erected in the district's ventilation exhaust shaft.

No.12 District was completed and handed over to the Royal Ordnance Corps in March 1940. Buoyed by the success of its quite complex engineering, the Royal Engineers decided upon an even more radical design for No.14 District which involved the complete removal of all the natural stone in the entire area and its replacement by a series of four-foot-thick lateral walls crossing the district and spaced at twenty-two-foot intervals. The walls would be pierced with a series of arches to allow freedom of movement and ventilation, and the middle arches in each wall would form a central access way

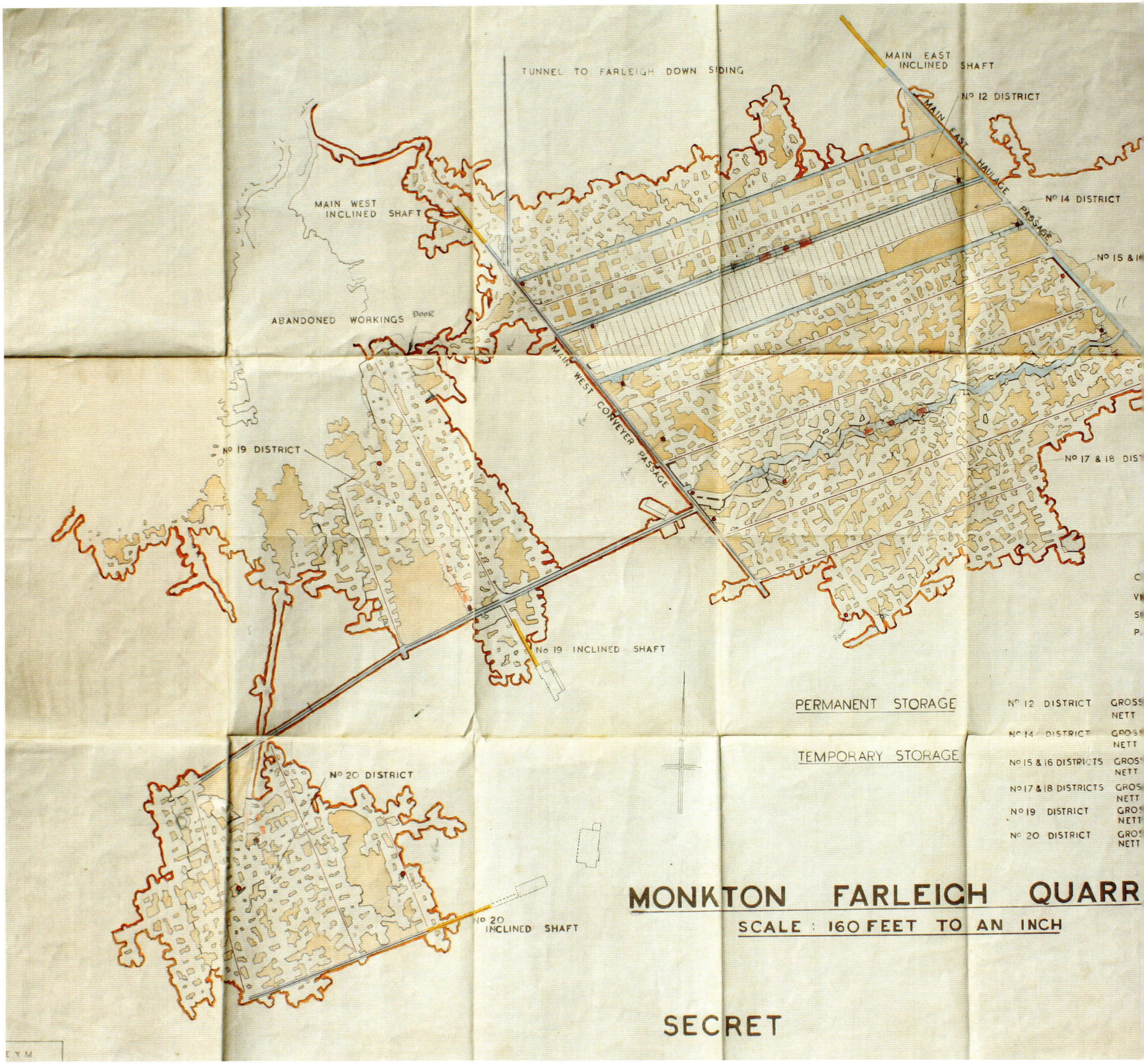

TUNNEL TO FARLEIGH DOWN SIDING
MAIN EAST INCLINED SHAFT
No 12 DISTRICT
MAIN EAST HAULAGE PASSAGE
No 14 DISTRICT
MAIN WEST INCLINED SHAFT
ABANDONED WORKINGS
DOOR
MAIN WEST CONVEYER PASSAGE
No 19 DISTRICT
No 17 & 18 DIST
No 19 INCLINED SHAFT
PERMANENT STORAGE
TEMPORARY STORAGE
No 12 DISTRICT
No 14 DISTRICT
No 15 & 16 DISTRICTS
No 17 & 18 DISTRICTS
No 19 DISTRICT
No 20 DISTRICT
No 20 DISTRICT
No 20 INCLINED SHAFT
MONKTON FARLEIGH QUARR
SCALE : 160 FEET TO AN INCH
SECRET

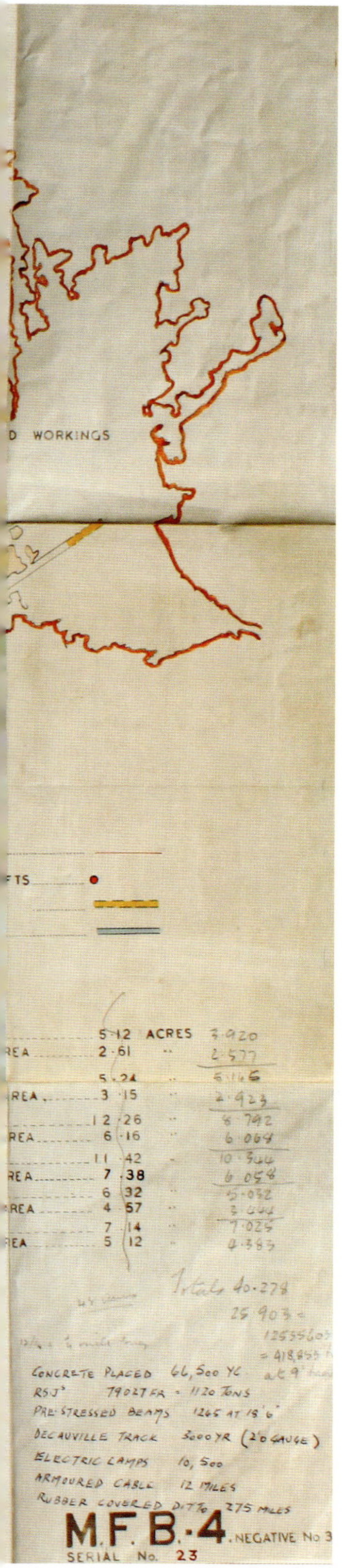

in which would be placed a belt conveyor. Between each pair of walls pre-stressed reinforced concrete beams – experimental in design and the first to be used in the United Kingdom – were attached to steel corbels let into the tops of the walls, spanning the gap in order to support the ceilings in each bay. Development of the district started well but the rush to finish, together with the employment of inexperienced labour, caused the various stages of construction to become unsynchronized resulting in a serious roof collapse. It was then decided to abandon this advanced method of construction and revert to the system of ad hoc pillar strengthening used elsewhere in the depots. By the middle of 1941 the War Office priority had changed with respect to Monkton Farleigh. The idea of utilizing the temporary areas to relieve pressure on the depot while the permanent districts were completed to an exceptionally high standard gave way to a policy of finishing everything as quickly as possible and incorporating the hitherto 'temporary' sections as part of the permanent storage facility. Instead of stripping out the random arrangement of pillars left by the quarrymen in the lower end of the depot the engineers arranged, as far as possible, to take advantage of the existing layout. In this way the work was completed both expeditiously and economically. Towards the end of the war and into the 1950s, when operational pressure upon the depots had eased, a programme of further pillar strengthening and other improvements was begun at Monkton Farleigh.

Amongst the new, post-war works was a plan to fully air-condition the whole of the depot. Throughout the war the underground areas had been heated and ventilated by a system of steam radiators and twelve-foot diameter circulating fans. Induction fans were positioned in underground chambers at the east end of each district with extraction fans at the tops of exhaust air-shafts at the west end. Steam was provided by a surface boiler house containing four large Lancashire boilers. While this made working conditions underground tolerable it did little to reduce the overall level of humidity, which was a more insidious evil. Although obsolete ammunition tended to accumulate in the underground reserve depots to some extent, during the war years there was generally a constant turnover of stock so very little ammunition was kept below ground long enough for it to be detrimentally effected by the environmental conditions. Post-war, however, when the depots were reclassified as long-term storage, dealing with the humidity became more of a problem and it was for this reason that full air-conditioning was installed at great expense at Monkton Farleigh. This installation was intended to be an experiment, the results of which would determine the new plants that would subsequently be installed at Eastlays and Tunnel Quarry. However, soon after the system was started up in 1955 problems developed with the structure of the quarry. Whilst the dry, warm air from the conditioning plant produced perfect storage conditions for ammunition, it also dried out both the natural rock and the clay layers bonding the various stone strata in the quarry, resulting in roof falls and fractured pillars. The cost of rectifying these problems, by a massive programme of pillar strengthening, proved prohibitive and hastened the demise of the depots in the 1960s.

In 1974 Monkton Farleigh and Eastlays were sold into the private sector and were earmarked by their new owners for development as underground mushroom farms. These plans did not come to fruition and Monkton Farleigh, being somewhat out on a limb, was quietly abandoned to the depredations of vandals and scrap metal thieves. Although the quarry has found renewed life as a secure storage facility in recent years many of the original features have been lost.

Fred Allen's original, water-coloured linen layout plan of Monkton Farleigh Quarry. This drawing has been annotated with a number of statistics regarding the quantities of materials used in construction. Notice the diagonal connecting tunnel between No.20 District and the abandoned workings to the west of No.19 District. During construction this was the only route into No.20 District for the transport of building materials. The underground drift connecting Districts 19 and 20 with the main area was not completed until June 1940.

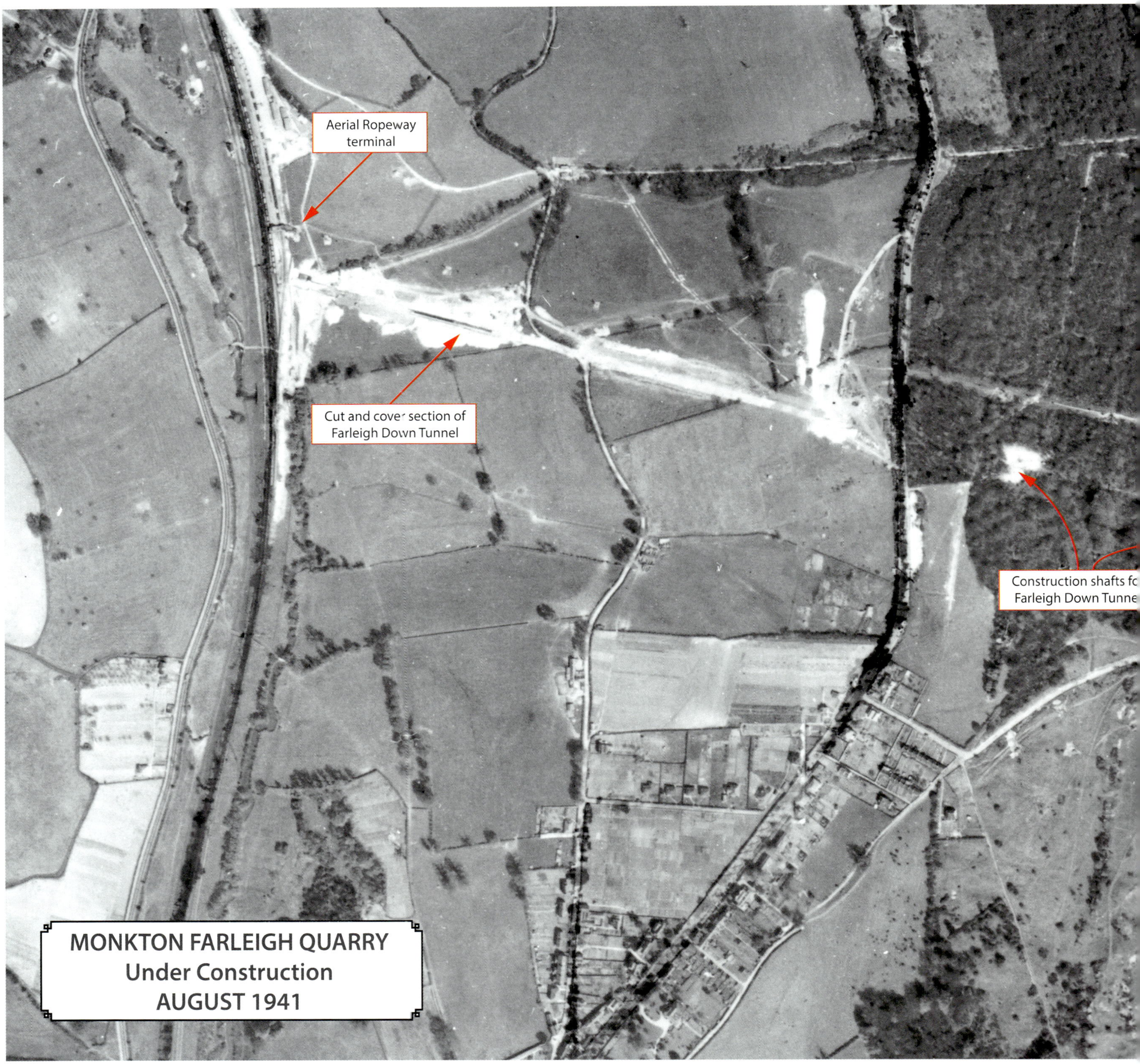
Aerial Ropeway terminal
Cut and cover section of Farleigh Down Tunnel
Construction shafts fo
Farleigh Down Tunne
MONKTON FARLEIGH QUARRY
Under Construction
AUGUST 1941

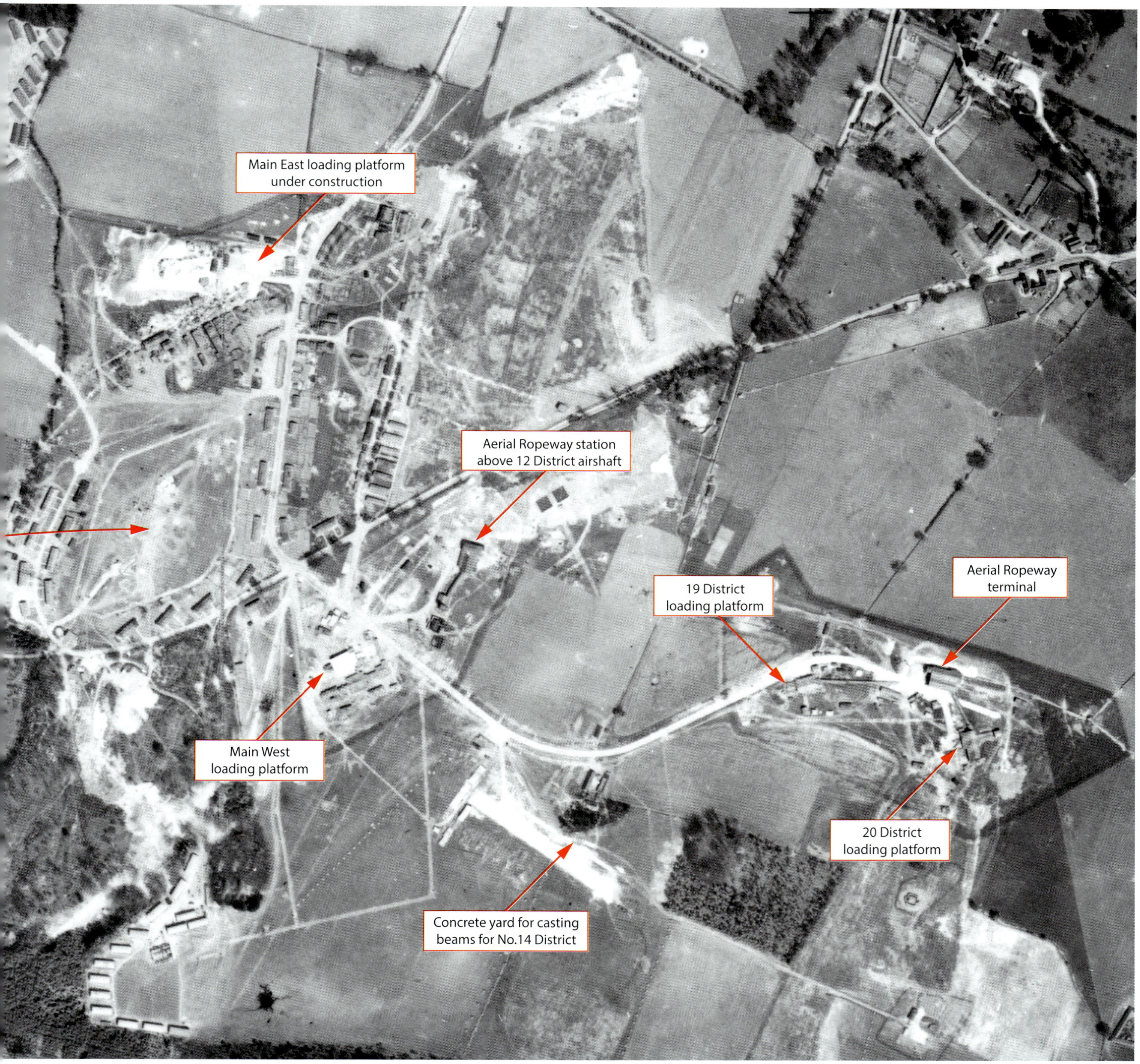
Main East loading platform under construction
Aerial Ropeway station above 12 District airshaft
19 District loading platform
Aerial Ropeway terminal
Main West loading platform
20 District loading platform
Concrete yard for casting beams for No.14 District

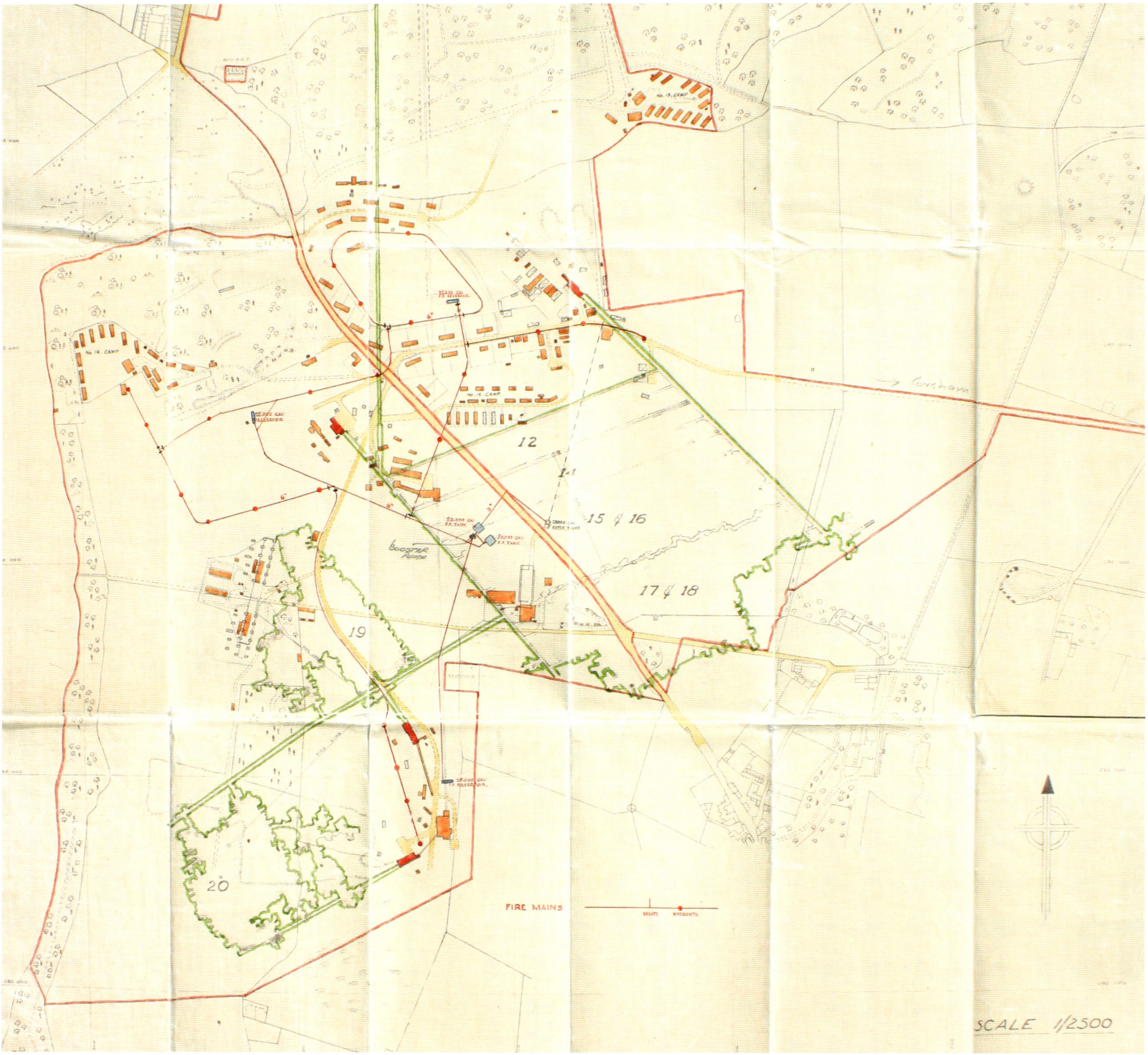

Above: From the same series of Fred Allen's drawings, this plan shows the underground areas at Monkton Farleigh superimposed upon a plan of the surface features.

Above: Aerial view of Main West building in 1991. The concrete patch in the area of grass in front of the building is a pillbox that was mounded over post-war and used to mount a captured German anti-tank gun. Large concrete RAOC and Royal Engineers crests once adorned its sloping sides.

Below: The final number '1' in the date on the Royal Ordnance Corps crest is a separate piece of stone, inserted after the crest was completed due to construction running behind schedule. *(See inset in the image above.)*

Below: Main West Building. The contraband for which one was instructed to search oneself included smoking material, metal objects (that might cause a spark) and food, which if discarded might encourage rats.

Left: The interior of Main West building early in 1942 showing the arrival of one of the first shipments of ammunition to be carried underground by conveyor.

Below left: The last box of ammunition leaving Main West building before the closure of the depot in September 1963. The conveyor belt passes through an aperture, closed by a heavy, hinged rubber flap, in the wall at the top of Main West inclined shaft. There is a pedestrian entrance to the shaft in the alcove near the group of men in the background of this photograph.

Below right: Aerial view of the Main West compound in 1973. Main West entrance lies in the bottom left corner and the concrete bases of the laboratory buildings to the centre right. Note the boiler house, air-conditioning plant and associated pipelines to the left of the picture.

Above: Main West haulageway near the junction with 19/20 drift. The room on the left was originally the office of the Commanding Ordnance Officer but later became the Maintenance Office where records of plant and structural servicing were kept. The next door on the left gives access to the switchroom and powerhouse.

Below: A view north along Main West haulageway from No.16 District in 1985 after removal of the conveyors.

Below: The east end of 19/20 drift showing the heavy concrete-work required to support the badly fissured rock in this location. To the right are toilets and a suite of blast-protected rooms which comprised the Main Permitted Area, where samples of ammunition were dismantled and examined. These rooms were later used as an underground canteen after dedicated 'Permitted Areas', or small, blast-protected examination bays, were established in each of the storage districts.

Above: Main East entrance building. This houses the winch for an overhead rope haulage system in Main East passage. Note the roof of the incline shaft at the right-hand end of the building.

Below left: The overhead rope haulage engine in Main East building.
Below right: The bottom of Main East inclined shaft showing the continuous rope haulage and star-wheel supports.

Above: A truck descending Main East shaft on the overhead rope system. All trucks descend on the left-hand rail and ascend on the right.

Above: The horizontal return roller and tensioning device for the overhead rope at the inbye end of Main East. Heavy cast-iron weights attached to the truck body via a hawser passing over a vertical pulley maintain the tension.

Left: Ammunition trucks lined up in Main East corridor opposite the eastern exit from No.12 District. Most of the wagons used at Monkton Farleigh were steel-framed and wooden bodied manufactured by Hudsons of Leeds, with fixed axles and roller-bearings incorporated in the wheel hubs. These wagons were originally fitted with drop-side doors but it appears that these were soon discarded for operational convenience.

Wagons for use on Main West incline were generally fitted with a 'U'-shaped guide on the end board to prevent the haulage rope cutting in to the wooden end of the wagon. An example of this type can be seen in the photograph above left. Many of the wagons were also fitted with asbestos-clad skids beneath the axles which engaged with the raised steel plates between the rails, also visible above left, in order to retard descending trucks.

Above: Branches from the railway in Main East haulageway radiated into the east ends of Districts 12, 15 and 16. These carried shells too heavy for the conveyor belts. The entrance to District 15 is shown above.
Below: A section of railway in the east end of No.16 District.

Above: The junction of No.16 District and Main East. Within the storage areas trucks were propelled by hand.
Below: The conveyor and narrow-gauge railway line run parallel in the east end of No.12 District.

Above: No.19 District entrance building. The inclined shaft is at the right-hand end of the building. The left-hand extension housed the winding engine for a rope haulage system in the shaft (subsequently replaced by a conveyor in 1942) and the drive unit of a conveyor that linked the loading platform to the nearby aerial ropeway terminal. This conveyor passed through a short tunnel beneath the access road in the foreground.

Left: Looking up No.19 District slope shaft towards the surface. The concrete blocks on the right once carried the belt conveyor. The blocks gradually increase in height towards the base of the shaft to ease the transition between the incline and the horizontal floor of the quarry.

The rails in the centre of the picture are a relic of the early operational days of No.19 District which was briefly worked using narrow-gauge trucks and an overhead rope system until this was superseded by belt conveyors.

Left: This view is looking from the bottom of No.19 slope shaft into the district across the main haulageway that links Main West passage to Districts 19 and 20. The blast doors securing the storage area can be seen in the background with the district name, on a yellow background, inscribed above the lintel.

The steps in the foreground allowed staff to safely cross the now dismantled conveyor. The broken wall to the right of the centre of this photograph is all that remains of the conveyor control room, destroyed by vandals, like much else in the depot, in the early 1990s.

Right: A different view from the same location. The slope shaft is just out of view to the right of this photograph, with the district office adjacent to the red-painted door which gave pedestrian access to the stairway on the shaft. The passageway to the left is the eastern end of 19/20 drift heading off into the darkness towards Main West haulageway and the main area of the depot.

Above: The main haulageway through No.19 District in 1985 after the conveyors were removed. The octagonal pillars are the result of a large-scale improvement scheme begun in 1945 when it was decided that Monkton Farleigh should become a permanent establishment. Previous to this most of the roof supports in Districts 19 and 20 were simple wooden props. Notice the rails embedded in the floor; these are relics of the rope haulage system that predated the conveyors. The steel stanchions with cross girders at the top once carried the star-wheels that supported the overhead rope.

Right: No.19 District conveyor control office in 1985. The panel just visible against the back wall of the office allowed remote control of the two conveyors within the district and also of the three conveyors in 19/20 drift. The flameproof switch-boxes on the right-hand wall operated the lights in the eastern half of the storage area.

Above: Renovation work under way in 1985 at No.20 District loading platform, which was seriously damaged by fire some years earlier.
Below: The bottom of No.20 District slope shaft with the district conveyor control room on the left and sewage ejector pit to the right.

Below: A wider view towards 20 District slope shaft showing the wooden-framed Meco conveyor and the rolled steel mining arches that are unique to this district in the depot.

The photographs on this page were taken in No.20 District during an illicit visit to Monkton Farleigh Quarry in 1973, when, except for the removal of the rubber belting from most of the conveyors, the depot was still in remarkably good condition.

Above: A quick but perilous way to descend the inclined shaft.

Above right: The main haulageway in No.20 District showing the steel-arch roof supports.

Right: Near the bottom of No.20 District slope shaft. The building on the right is the district office and contains control equipment and signalling apparatus for all the district conveyors. The wooden-framed conveyor in the foreground continues up the incline and is a very early example, first used as a trough-belt for evacuating waste stone during construction and then modified to run as a flat belt for ammunition transport.

Above: The central, or No.2 conveyor route in 20 District, damage to the floors is a consequence of the widespread theft of cables buried in underfloor ducts during the early 1980s.

Above: A view west along No.20 drift towards the furthest extremity of the depot.

Below left: The western or No.3 conveyor passage. Both Districts 19 and 20 were substantially reconstructed in the immediate post-war years; the concrete roof supports seen here replaced earlier temporary wooden props.

Below: The incline, driven through a slip-fault, connecting No.20 District with the main area of the depot.

Nos. 12 and 14 - the Permanent Districts

Following the completion of No.12 District in December, 1939, two thousand men were set to work on the underpinning of No.14 District. Four concrete pumps were strategically placed along the southern edge of the district and a large number of Hardiax cutters held in readiness. The task was divided into four stages: first the line of each wall was cleared by cutting away stone pillars which obstructed the route; secondly the foundations were excavated to solid stone and filled with concrete to floor level; next the walls were built up to ceiling height, archways formed and steel corbels inserted to hold the roof beams; finally all the stone remaining between the walls was cut away, roof beams inserted and floors graded. Every third wall – nos 1, 4, 7, etc, – was to be completed from west to east before starting from the west again with walls 2, 5, 8, etc. In this way congestion of labour was largely avoided, and it was hoped that the risk of leaving large areas of roof temporarily unsupported would be obviated.

Construction proceeded favourably with the first series of walls, but late in April, 1940, as excavation was under way for the second and subsequent series, disaster struck. A serious roof fall occurred in the area of walls 12-15, followed by further collapses nearer the east end of the district. Many of the completed walls were badly crushed and the roof was seen to have dropped several inches. All further work was immediately suspended and an inquiry instituted. On 7 May an inspection was conducted by Mr Whitehouse of the Fortifications and Works Directorate and a report prepared for the War Office. It appears that, whilst the first series of walls was constructed satisfactorily, excavation and pillar removal for the intervening walls was pushed on too rapidly, the work getting so far ahead of the building that a much larger roof area than ever contemplated was left unsupported and its weight consequently thrown upon the completed walls. In a number of cases these were unable to take the stress and were badly crushed and pushed out of alignment. It was estimated that, whereas the original plan allowed for 15% of the roof to be taken up with concrete walls, the total roof support in the collapsed area, including the crushed walls, fell to only 5%.

Instructions were given that no further pillar extraction should be undertaken until those walls already started were completed and that all the arched openings except those adjacent to the external wall and the central ones on the haulage should be blocked up. Mr Whitehouse criticized an earlier decision to reduce the thickness of the walls from five feet to four feet and recommended that supplementary walls should be erected where necessary to give lateral support. In compliance with this advice buttresses were built along the line of the central haulageway. In view of what had happened, it was decided that the scheme should be modified and that some sacrifice of storage space should be made in the interests of safety. Where sound pillars were encountered they were to be left intact. In several instances this procedure did not seriously affect the storage space available since the areas cleared for the building of walls were used for storage and the existing pillars left to afford the necessary support.

Above: The entrance to No.12 District as it was in 1985.
Below: A typical area within No.12 District showing the substantial engineering work undertaken there.

Above: The main haulageway through No.14 District viewed from the Main West end.

The collapse of No.14 District

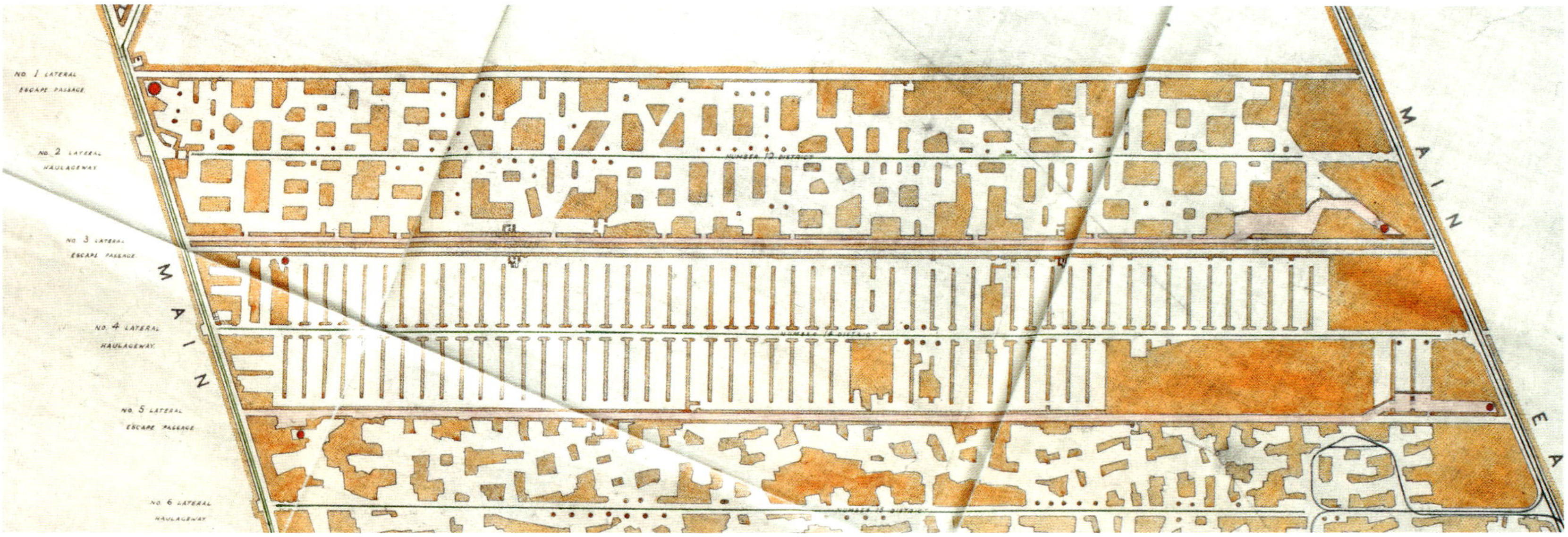

Above: This enlargement from the 40-inch survey of Monkton Farleigh illustrates the extent of the abandoned area at the east end of No.14 District following the collapse of April 1940.

Below: In 1989 access was gained to the collapsed area, within which substantial remains of uncompleted walls were discovered. Slots were cut in the virgin stone to provide space for the erection of walls. The photographs left and right show how little clearance was left for the erection of shuttering and other tasks.

Above: Originally it was intended that all the division walls would be pierced by seven arches, but following the collapse, confidence in the design was lost and all except the middle one and those near the perimeter walls were infilled. This photograph shows a series of these archways and also the ends of two of the pre-stressed reinforced concrete beams inserted to support the roof.

Above right: Taken from inside the collapsed area, this photograph shows an infilled arch, above which can be seen several pairs of rolled-steel girders set into the wall. Corbels supporting the pre-stressed reinforced roof beams would have been suspended from these girders.

Right: Hundreds of pre-stressed beams were cast but a large number became redundant after the 14 District form of construction was abandoned. Many discarded beams are now piled in the undergrowth behind Main East building, slowly breaking up in the frost.

Right: South East entrance. Used only for the passage of maintenance materials, this inclined shaft joins the depot at the inward end of Main East haulageway.

Below left: The tin hut was a military police guard house. An electric winch, used to lower building and maintenance materials into the quarry and to evacuate waste, once resided in a shed at the far end of a raised loading platform at South East entrance.

Below right: The winch was removed for scrap some time before this photograph was taken, but the notice detailing the bell signals for its operation was still extant in 1968.

Above: The Ruston Hornsby 5VLB engine after restoration in 1986.

The Powerhouse

Just as the powerhouse at Tunnel Quarry was designed for three alternator sets but only had two installed, Monkton Farleigh's was designed for two but had only one installed. The cut-backs were due partly to the unavailability of plant during the war and partly to financial constraints. When the depot was reclassified as permanent in the post-war years, consideration was again given to installing a second generator but nothing came of this. Foundations and all necessary pipework for the proposed second plant were put in place when the powerhouse was built in 1940.

Above and below right: Two views of the switchroom in 1986. Control panels were installed for the second generator but were never used. The small transformer in the lower picture supplied power to Farleigh Down Sidings. The brick cubicle in the background of the top photograph contains the 11Kv switchgear.

Below: A large air receiver in the passage behind the powerhouse, the doors to which are visible in the background. The door on the right leads into a chamber containing two 20,000 gallon fuel tanks for the generator.

Air-Conditioning

Plans were laid in 1943 to improve the previous ventilation system by the installation of steam radiators at the bottom of each induction shaft. Implementation of this plan was delayed due to difficulties in acquiring the necessary boilers for the surface boiler house and was not finally completed until 1945. In 1952 a contract was let for the expansion of this heating system to full air-conditioning, a scheme that was finally completed in 1955. The old system was altered from steam to hot water and two of the boilers taken out of use.

Left: Front view of the boiler house in 1968. The gantry is a 5 ton Priestman electric coal grab which lifted coal from the yard beneath, travelled along its rails to a position above the boiler house and deposited its load into a hopper from where it would be fed into the boilers by automatic stokers. Fully operational, the plant consumed 500 tons of coal per week.
Below left: The boiler house in 1968. Although disused for many years the plant remained largely intact. The steam pipes in the original system descended No.17 District air-shaft and were distributed underground. In the 1950s system the pipes were distributed across the surface and descended new air-shafts to the heating plants underground.
Below right: The boiler house in the 1980s, devoid of its pipework and converted for light industrial use.

Right: One of three York four-cylinder ammonia compressors in the refrigeration plant room. By means of three diesel driven ammonia compressors and three sets of condensers, evaporators and circulating pumps, the surface refrigeration plant produced chilled water for delivery to the underground dehumidifiers. The chilled water was delivered via large diameter cork-lagged pipes that ran parallel to the hot water lines.

Right: The three National Diesel R4AU6 six-cylinder diesel engines that drove the ammonia compressors, photographed in 1974. The original plan proposed that the air-conditioning compressors, evaporators and condensers should be housed in an extension to the existing boiler house but it was subsequently discovered that the new foundations would encroach upon the ventilation and engine exhaust shaft for the underground powerhouse.

Above: Monkton Farleigh's air-conditioning plant, on the horizon, in 1972. From right to left: The boiler house with chimney; the large asbestos-clad shed housing the refrigeration plant; a wooden water-cooling tower; pipes crossing the field on concrete stanchions; No.19 District loading platform with, in the background, a bridge carrying the pipes across an internal depot road. The large concrete block in the right mid-ground is all that remains of the No.20 District ropeway terminal station.

Left: Steam and chilled water pipes at the top of No.20 District inlet shaft.

Below left: A view of the pipelines descending the eighty-foot shaft.

Below right: The water-cooling tower (which swayed alarmingly in the wind) shortly before it was destroyed by fire in an arson attack.

Left: One of a pair of twelve-foot axial flow fans that circulated conditioned air through Districts 15 to 18. A new vertical induction shaft was sunk to provide air for these two fans and the two dehumidifiers and heaters associated with them. The new fans replaced a single, much larger fan (identical to the CDI fan at Tunnel Quarry) which previously supplied ventilation air from a group of three vertical shafts, connected by underfloor ducts, at the east end of No.17 District.

Below left: Front view of one of the 15/18 District dehumidifiers. The chilled water spray nozzles can be clearly seen behind the louvres. A certain amount of air could bypass the dehumidifiers depending upon its moisture content. Humidity meters positioned in the airflow automatically adjusted the louvres and thus automatically controlled the degree of bypass.

Below right: A rear view of the spray chamber. The green, asbestos lagged pipes carry hot water to a bank of radiators that raise the temperature of the air exiting the dehumidifier.

Above: The air-conditioning plant building in 1978, at the time when the surface pipelines were being dismantled for scrap. The plastic bags in the foreground contain asbestos lagging from the hot-water line. The missing fan from the cooling tower in the background was given on loan to the University of Bath Department of Engineering.
Below: The gutted interior of the refrigeration building. Only the fuel header tanks for the diesel engines remain in-situ.
Below right: The concrete block in the centre of the picture is all that remained of the bridge carrying the pipelines over the 20 District service road.

Right: The surface land immediately above No.20 District. The concrete and steel structure in the right foreground is the top of the district inlet shaft which contained an eight-foot diameter induction fan. The concrete structure in the middle of the picture contains the switchgear for the fan. The red brick building in the right background housed a substation providing power for the air-conditioning plant in No.20 District. The low concrete structure in the middle background is the top of the district exhaust shaft.

Below left: Inside the chamber at the top of the exhaust shaft. Known as 'turnover tops', these staggered constructions were designed to avoid the risk of a direct hit by an enemy bomb on the surface ventilation grille from descending the shaft and exploding underground. The circular opening at the end is the top of an eighty-foot vertical drop.

Below right: The stub-end of a partially dismantled pipeline near No.20 District in 1978.

Farleigh Down Tunnel

Farleigh Down Sidings, the main ammunition transfer railhead for Monkton Farleigh Quarry, is approximately one and a quarter miles away as the crow flies, and some four hundred feet lower, in the valley below. A spectacular conveyor tunnel links the two sites but until this was completed in April 1942 transfers between railhead and depot were made by means of an aerial ropeway.

Right: The upper deck of the Farleigh Down ropeway transfer station. At the end of their journey containers carried on the wire rope were guided onto the curved rail seen in this photograph, where they were loaded or unloaded. Ammunition containers were transferred from rail level to ropeway by a pair of electric lifts, the counterweights for which can be seen below the raised platform.

Left: A view out of the ropeway transfer station near No.20 District, with 19 District loading platform just visible in the left background taken, probably, in 1940. Just visible also, are two of the short lattice pylons that supported the aerial rope. All that remains of this building today is a very large concrete block that once supported the drive motor and horizontal drum.

Right: An early view along the railway platform at Farleigh Down Sidings. The lifts to the ropeway are visible in the centre background. Ammunition arriving on main line trains was unloaded onto narrow-gauge trucks for transfer to the lifts. When the tunnel was completed the trucks would instead be taken underground via a tram-creeper into an underground marshalling yard before their contents were transferred to the tunnel belt. This photo shows the motor-room and foundations for the tram-creeper under construction.

Left: Unloading American-made 155mm propellant charges in the autumn of 1943. The tram creeper, giving access to the underground marshalling yard, is beneath the corrugated steel shed in the background. Wagon No.18, seen in this photograph, is now preserved in private hands.

Right: The approach to the top of Farleigh Down tunnel near its junction with Main West haulageway. A doorway in the left-hand wall gives access to the tunnel belt control room.

Below left: The top of Farleigh Down tunnel which descends at an incline of 1:8 to the main line sidings at Shockerwick near Box. The notice on the wall strictly forbids men from riding on the belt, which must have been a serious temptation to those working almost a mile and a quarter away at the bottom of the tunnel.
Below right: The derelict remains of the tunnel belt control console, photographed in 1979.

Above & below left: The tunnel belt conveyor control room in 1969. As well as controlling the tunnel belt this console also provided remote control over the six conveyors in Main West corridor that distributed ammunition throughout the depot. Because of the length of the tunnel it required two belts joining end-on in the middle. The instruction to 'Start top conveyor first when on receipt, Start bottom conveyor first when on issue' was to ensure that the pile-ups did not occur if the distant belt was inadvertently left stationary as goods in transit tried to join it.

Below: The control console fully restored in 1986.

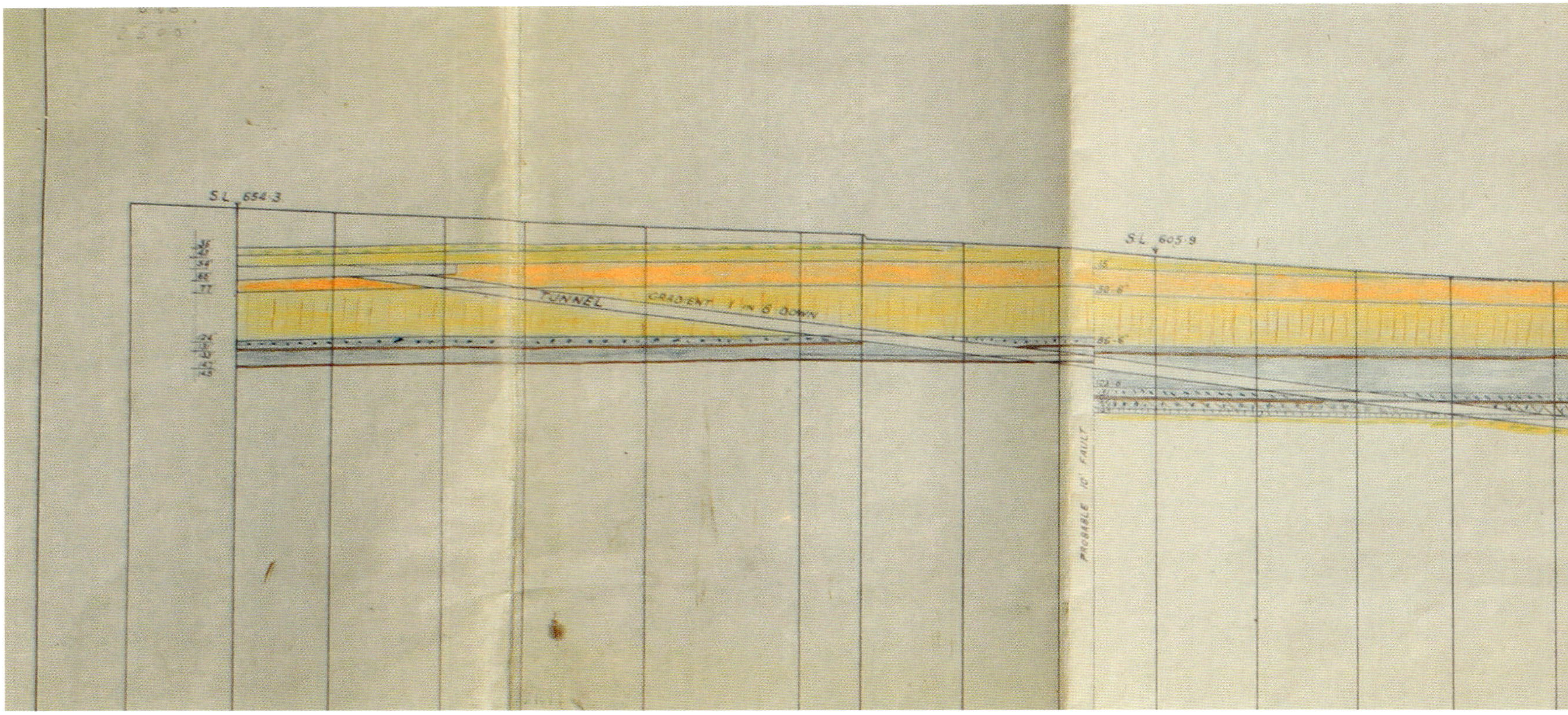
S.L. 654·3
TUNNEL GRADIENT 1 IN 8 DOWN
S.L. 605·9
PROBABLE 10' FAULT

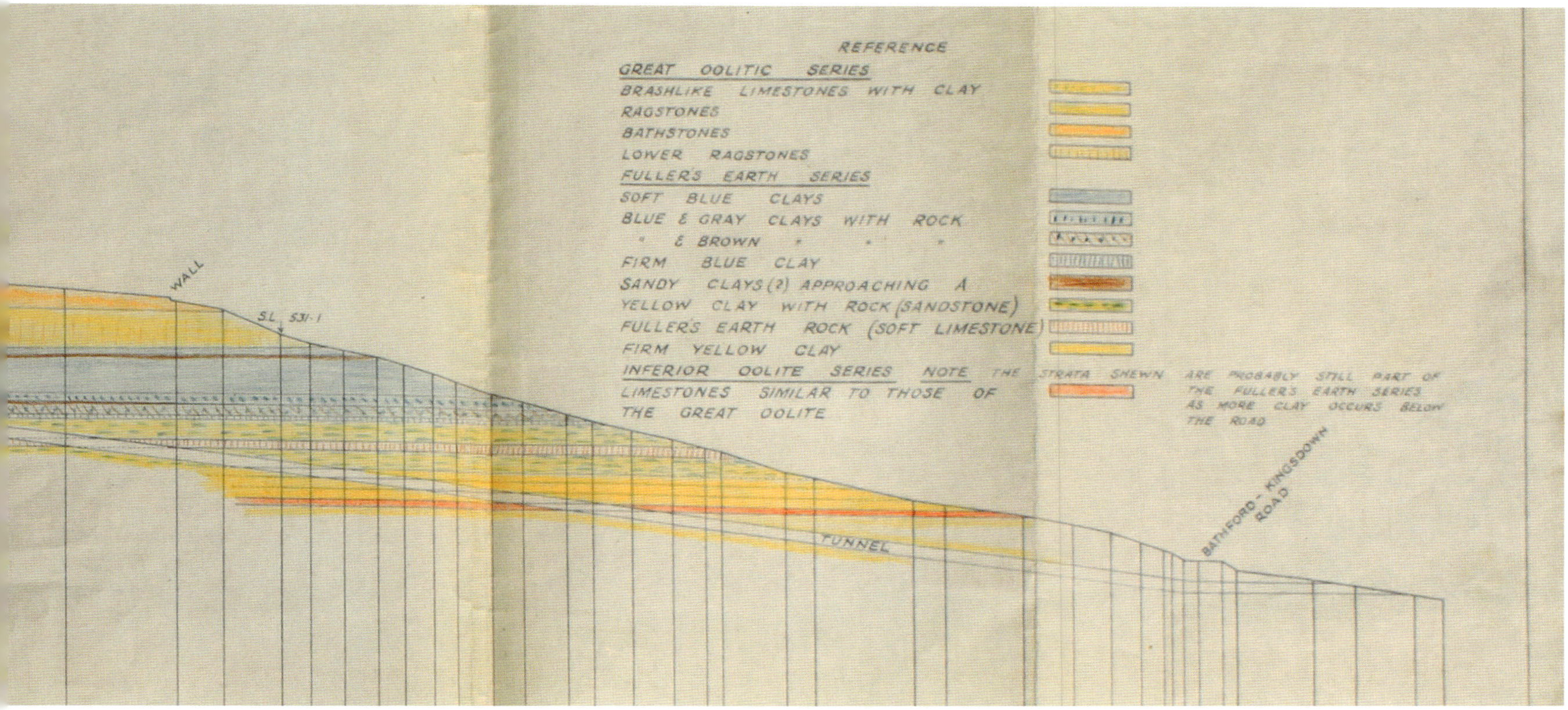

Above: Cross-section drawing of the upper section of Farleigh Down tunnel, above the Kingsdown Road. All this section is a true, ovoid-section brick-lined tunnel. Below the Kingsdown Road the tunnel is much shallower and was built as a cut-and-cover box-section.

Far left: Dave Wright and Harry – two intrepid explorers – in the tunnel during an illicit visit in 1974. At this point the tunnel is approximately 180 feet below ground.

Left: The lower, box-section of the tunnel where it is a cut-and-cover formation. The tunnel fell into disuse in 1950 when the War Office decided that all ammunition movements would be carried out by road, and the rubber belting was subsequently removed. A new, direct road to the Monkton Farleigh depot through Ashley Woods was proposed but the scheme was never implemented.

Right: The drive-head for the lower conveyor; its electric motor protruded into an alcove in the side of the tunnel.

Right: The underground marshalling yard at the bottom of Farleigh Down tunnel in 1974. The tunnel enters the yard in the rear left-hand corner. At the time there were forty narrow-gauge wagons in the yard, all in excellent condition. Unlike those used within the storage areas, these were of all-steel construction and built to a somewhat heavier specification.

Left: The same location in 1984. By this time scrap metal thieves had broken into the site and had begun stripping out the heavy copper power cables from the ducts below the tunnel floor. The cage in the centre of the picture is at the point that the rubber belt ended and its load transferred to a long run of roller conveyors alongside the narrow-gauge tracks. The cage was a safety measure to prevent the operatives becoming horribly entangled with the moving belt.

Opposite: A wider view of the marshalling yard showing the arrangement of tracks in relation to the tunnel conveyor. To the right is a range of administrative offices and a gas decontamination centre. The steel door to the left, adjacent to the nearest wagon, marks the entrance to a substation and switchroom distributing power to the tunnel conveyor, the overhead ropeway, the tram-creeper and all the surface facilities at Farleigh Down.

Left: Farleigh Down Sidings, very busy in November 1943. The tunnel and tram-creeper are now fully operational but the lifts do not seem to be in use. Once the tunnel became functional the aerial ropeway fell into disuse until the weeks preceding D-Day, when both the tunnel and ropeway were working to capacity issuing in excess of 2,000 tons of ammunition per day.

Below left: By 1950 the sidings had fallen into disuse and shortly afterwards much of the steelwork of the tram-creeper fell prey to scrap metal predators. This photograph shows one of the 'dogs' from the up-side chain which managed to avoid the depredations of the scrap men. Spaced at approximately twenty-foot intervals, the dogs would have engaged with the axles of the wagons to propel them up the incline.

Below right: A short length of 'up' chain still in-situ at the bottom of the creeper.

Above: In recent years the underground marshalling yard and tunnel has become something of a notorious venue for raves and parties, and also a magnet for those wishing to breach the security barrier built at the top of the tunnel to seal it off from the main area of the quarry, which is now used by a high-security document storage company. The massive blast doors at the entrance to the marshalling yard have been repeatedly broken through and welded back in place, as can be seen in this image.

Left: The remains of the tram creeper in 2014. Although the rails are still in place all trace of the chains have disappeared and the whole site has been heavily vandalised.

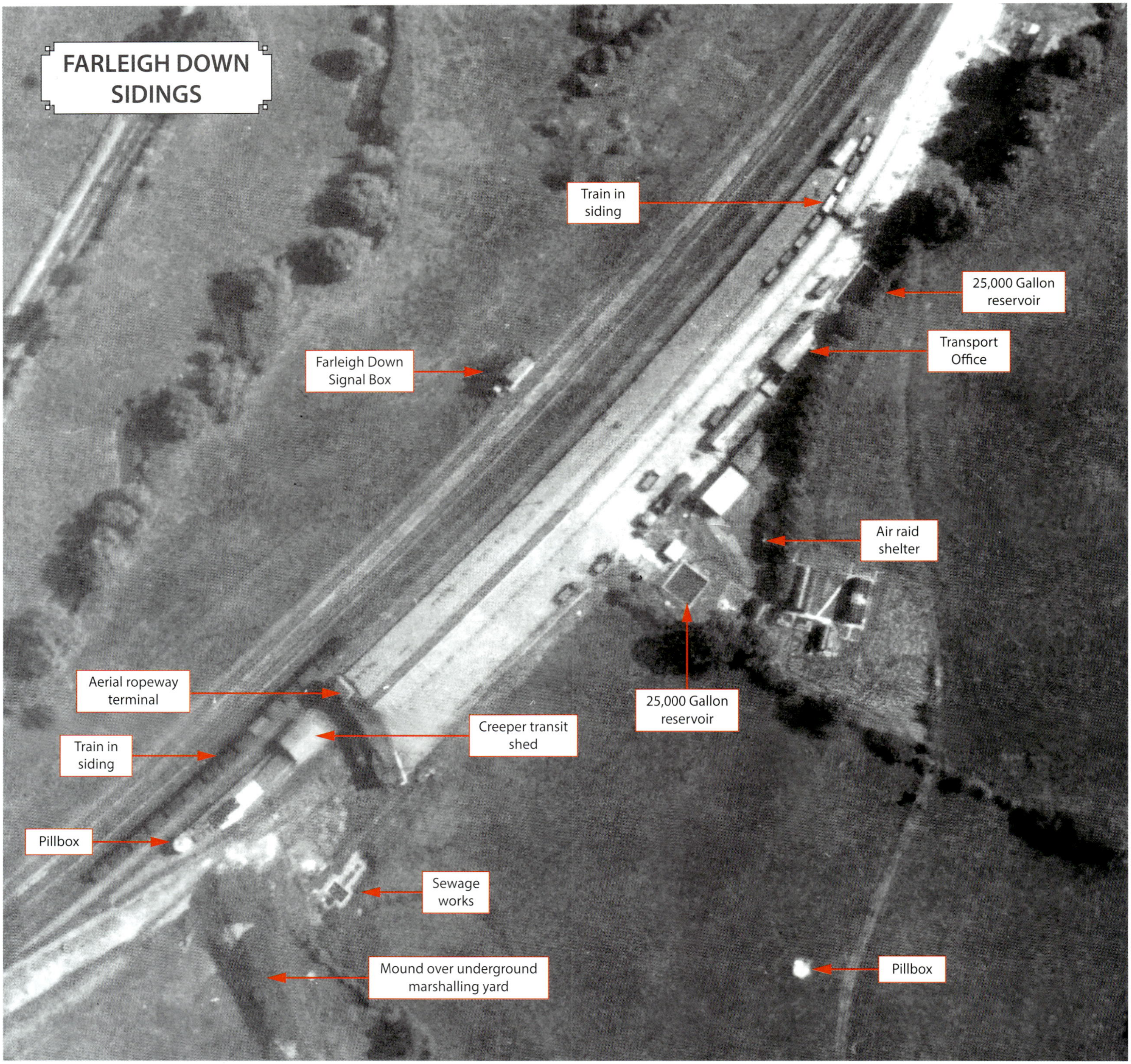

Above: A busy day at Farleigh Down Sidings in the summer of 1945.

Above: An evocative view of Farleigh Down Sidings in 1970. The rail sidings, and the signalbox that controlled them, were taken out of use in October 1950. Many of the ancillary buildings were demolished shortly afterwards and the timber decking that covered the quarter-mile-long platform removed and burnt.

Left: As part of a restoration project at the Monkton Farleigh depot, work began in 1985 in clearing the trees and undergrowth that were threatening to engulf the buildings and platform stanchions at Farleigh Down. At the same time one of the wagons was transferred from the yard for display in Main West building.

Left: The west end of the platforms at Farleigh Down terminate at this unique, round-ended pillbox. A steel ladder on the side furthest from the camera once gave access to an anti-aircraft emplacement on the roof.

Right: The heavily vandalised remains of the Head Wrightson tram-creeper drive gear. The chains were driven by hexagonal sprockets just visible behind the vertical girders. Drive to the large pinions was via a gearbox and worm drive powered by an electric motor, all of which are now missing.

Above: The rather sad remains of the transit shed in February 2014. At the time of writing the threatened blockage of the tunnel has not come to fruition. The drive motor, seen in the photograph opposite, lies in a chamber immediately below the complex railway crossings on the platform.

Monkton Farleigh Mine Heritage project 1984-1990

Left: The depot was sold into the private sector in 1976 and was purchased by a consortium with the intention of developing it as an underground mushroom farm, a scheme which ultimately fell foul of the West Wilts planning authority. The site then lay derelict and prey to widespread theft and vandalism until 1984 when it was acquired by a company intent upon restoring the site as a heritage project. This photograph shows the severity of the damage in the powerhouse before the restoration process started.

Left: All the main power cables for lighting and for the conveyors and ventilation plant were buried beneath the floors of the main haulageways and these, because of their very considerable copper content, proved highly lucrative to metal thieves. In all some twelve miles of steel-wire armoured cable were dug from the underfloor ducts and stripped of its copper content. The mess left by this process was immense, and in this photograph a mini-digger is being used to clear the debris. An open cable trench can be seen against the right-hand wall.

Above left: During restoration of the Ruston Hornsby diesel engine it was found that the governor had seized. In the foreground we see the governor chest cover removed and, in the background, the top section of the valve timing chain.

Above right: Making adjustments to the injector pumps and tappet clearances.

Left: The large 'Wilson' compressor in the centre of the picture supplied air to a ring main encompassing the whole depot and was used to power tools for general maintenance work. The small blue compressor was moved from one of the 1950s air-conditioning plants to its present location to operate the Main East sewage ejector. The ejector was originally supplied with air by two large 8HP compressors located in the generator room, but these were too large for the requirements of the restoration project.

Above: Main West loading platform in 1986, used as the reception building while the depot was open to the public.
Below: Preparing the restoration project's AEC Matador and one of its two Bofor's anti-aircraft guns for a run in 1987.

Above: The interior of Main West in 1987.

Below: Corrosion of the runners made operating th
of a problem. Here they are being closed with the h

Above: This is the second of the project's two Bofor's guns on display in Main West building.

oors of Main East something
Matador and a stout chain.

Below: By the mid-1990s the depot had found a new use as a high-security storage facility. Main West building has now largely disappeared behind a new steel-clad extension built along its frontage.

Chapter 3

UNDERGROUND FACTORIES

SPRING QUARRY

As we have seen in the introduction to this book, the Fall of France and the consequent advantage to the Luftwaffe in its ability to broaden its range of targets across the United Kingdom precipitated Beaverbrook and the Ministry of Aircraft Production into a panic programme of underground factory construction. This programme was once again focussed, initially at least, upon the Corsham area where vast tracts of readily adaptable underground capacity already existed.

Spring Quarry, together with a number of smaller quarries within a ten-mile radius, was requisitioned by the Ministry of Aircraft Production on 7 December 1940. The 3,300,000 square foot quarry was to be transformed into the largest underground factory in the world, housing the entire engine production line of the Bristol Aeroplane Company, currently located in highly vulnerable surface accommodation at Filton near Bristol. The Filton factory produced the Bristol Hercules radial engine which was the standard power plant for the RAF's bomber force during the early years of the war.

It was confidently expected that the conversion could be completed in six months at a cost of no more than £100,000. The scheme was a disaster in almost every respect. With no prior experience of so complex an engineering project, the government handed control to a prominent firm of civil engineers on a 'costs-plus-profit' basis. In retrospect the costs-plus-profit contract, which was widely used for thousands of wartime government projects, has since been recognized as a licence to print money and an open door for corruption and profiteering. There was probably no worse an example than the Spring Quarry factory where an initial six-month, £100,000 scheme burgeoned into a £13,000,000 fiasco, with construction still unfinished at the end of the war. The factory, which was scheduled to begin production in June 1941 turning out Bristol Hercules engines at the rate of 260 each month, had produced only 523 engines by the time of its closure, most of which were development-stage Centaurus engines that contributed little to the war effort.

By mid-1941, despite a haemorrhage of cash, very little progress had been made at the factory site and BAC, which had at first been very keen to go underground, was exhibiting worrying signs of cold feet. The German bomber threat had dwindled to insignificance and the prospect of operating in a claustrophobic subterranean environment seemed increasingly unappealing. Despite its misgivings, the firm was eventually cajoled into taking up half the space that had been originally allotted to them. Dowty of Gloucester expressed an interest in the partially developed north-west quarter of the quarry but later pulled out, as did the Parnall company of Yate who toyed briefly with the idea of establishing a gun-turret assembly plant in the south-central section of the quarry. Eventually, in early 1943, the south-west area, which had already been partially fitted out for BAC, was occupied by the Birmingham Small Arms Company as a barrel mill making barrels for the Hispano cannon.

By the end of 1943 factory development had reached its peak; three-quarters of the quarry was fully occupied and operational and the decision had been taken that no further work would be undertaken in the north-west or 'Dowty' area. The whole concept of the BAC factory had, however, changed. The main Hercules production line was to stay at Filton and, instead, the Spring Quarry site would be used as a development unit for Bristol's new, eighteen-cylinder Centaurus engine.

Despite the fact that the factory was never completed to its full specification the Spring Quarry complex is still an awesome achievement. Personnel access for the 25,000 employees who worked underground was via four high capacity passenger lifts and two Otis escalators, the latter, because new escalators were unobtainable during the war, requisitioned from the London Transport tube stations at Holborn and St. Paul's. Raw materials and finished products were transported by means of four twenty-ton goods lifts and two dedicated machinery lifts – essentially twenty-ton chain hoists suspended above a 100-foot vertical shaft. A separate lift was

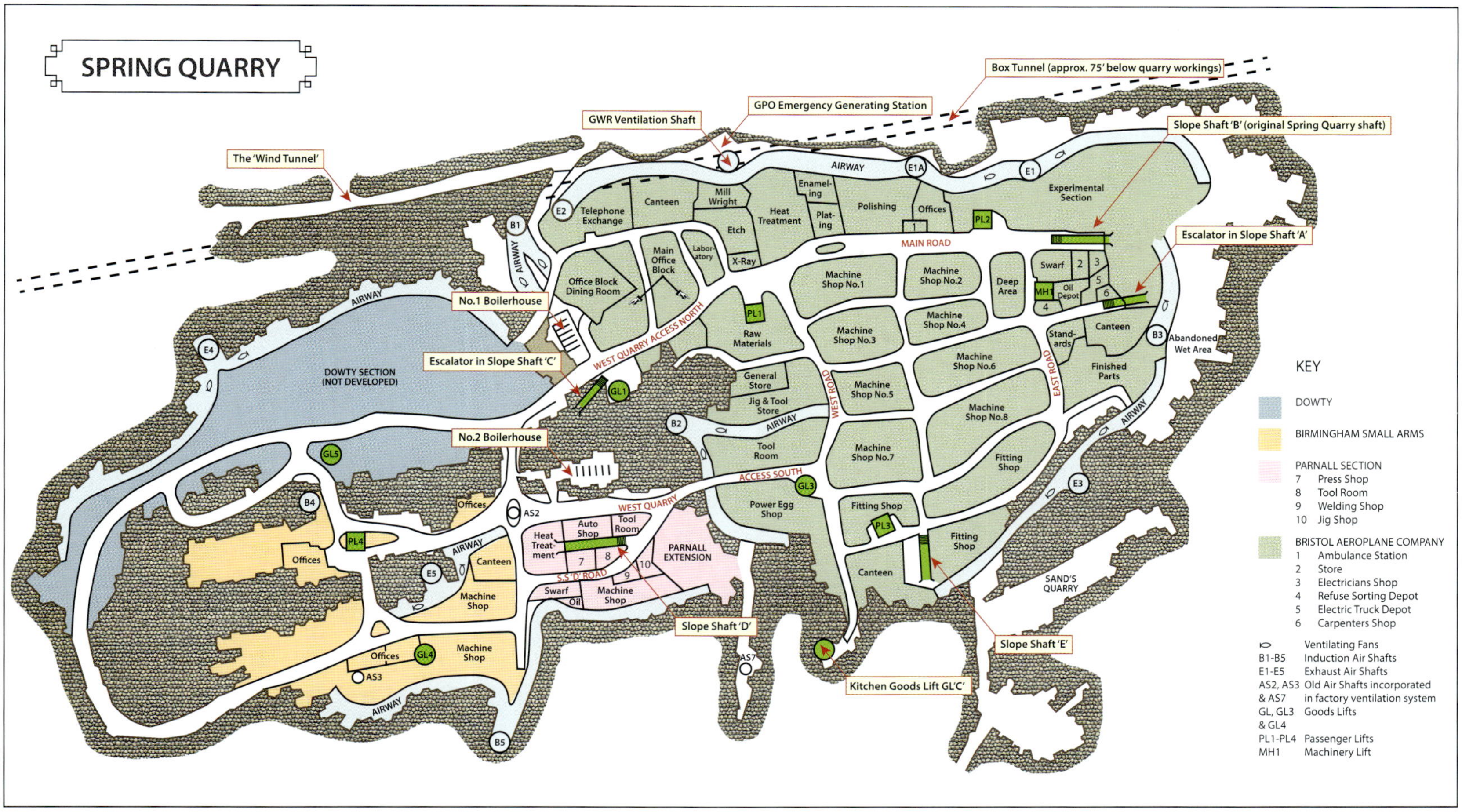

provided to deliver provisions to the underground kitchens while two others were used solely to remove ash from the underground boiler houses. The ventilation system was prodigious; twenty-one air shafts and fifteen axial flow fans, the largest some fifteen feet in diameter, extracted contaminated air and circulated fresh air, heated by a dozen coal-fired Lancashire boilers housed in two underground boiler houses, via underfloor ducts.

The factory closed shortly after the at the end of the war, although the Bristol Aeroplane Company remaining briefly in possession of the site to carry out initial development work on its Theseus gas turbine engine. The massively constructed engine test buildings on the surface were redeveloped at this time as part of the gas turbine project. By November 1945, however, this work was transferred to Filton and BAC's involvement with Corsham came to an end.

The infrastructure was retained by the government and within months the south and west of the quarry were handed over to the Admiralty for the storage of naval optical and electronic equipment, a function which continued, under the umbrella of RNSD Copenacre, until September 1995. By the late-1950s, however, the north-east section was veiled in sinister secrecy. Work had started there on converting the quarry into the Central Government Emergency War Headquarters, (described in detail in *Burlington* by Nick Catford, also published by Folly Books), the site to which the War Cabinet, the Chiefs of Staff and several thousand civil servants would evacuate in the event of a nuclear war with the Soviet Union. 'Burlington', as the Central Government bunker has become commonly known, was declassified in 2004 having fallen out of use some years earlier. Because the government's emergency planning budget had been so restricted during the most critical phase of the development of the bunker, many of the factory services, including the ventilation system, lifts, escalators and sanitary arrangements, were retained and, for that reason survive in good order today.

Above: Four police guard posts controlled access to the factory but only the one securing Goods Lift Access East Road survives unthreatened. This example, on Westwells Road, guarding the entrance to ML1 Road, was demolished in 2012 to make way for the new Corsham MoD centre.
Below: The guardhouse for Goods Lift Access West, on the Bradford Road, was demolished for no apparent reason in 2001.

Above: The guardhouse for Goods Lift 'C' Road and the engine test plant is under threat at the time of writing as part of the Spring Park development.

Below: Slope shaft 'D', originally intended as a pedestrian access to the proposed Parnall turret factory; it was only ever used for maintenance purposes.

Above & below: Interior and exterior views of slope shaft 'E' which allowed pedestrian access to and from the underground main operatives canteen. The top of this shaft was in-filled as a security measure in the mid-1980s.

Above: The heavily reinforced bomb-proof shaft-head building for goods lift GL3.
Below: The bottom landing of goods lift GL3 at quarry floor level. There are two lifts in this shaft, a goods lift to the right and a smaller passenger lift to the left.

Above: This red-brick building contains goods lift GL4 together with a large rectangular shaft, originally designated machinery lift No. 2, above which is mounted a twenty-ton travelling crane. The principal role of ML2, and a similar shaft at the east end of the factory designated ML1, was to lift heavy machine tools in to or out of the factory.
Above right: The 20-ton machinery hoist in GL4.

Below left: The smaller GL4 goods lift.
Below right: A wartime view of machinery lift ML1 in action.

Above: The celebrated shaft-top building of passenger lift PL2 by the side of Westwells Road. The earth mounding is a Cold War addition, designed to increase the structure's blast protection and to cover the side passages, air-locks and blast doors, added to give more shielding to the upper lift landing. Work had begun in 1956 on converting the northern half of the Spring Quarry factory into the Emergency Government War Headquarters where key elements of Britain's Central Government, the Prime Minister and War Cabinet, together with a support staff of some 4,000 civil servants, would have gone if London became untenable in the event of a nuclear war with the Soviet Union. This shaft, together with a nearby escalator shaft and passenger lift PL1 and a similar escalator shaft the east side of Westwells Road, were the designated entry points to the government bunker which, for decades, was amongst the most secret places in Britain.

Left: The lower landing of PL2 retains its wartime appearance despite the Cold War alterations on the surface.

Above left: A view out of the open doors of passenger lift PL1 and through the air-lock and double blast doors of the upper landing of the shaft-head building.

Above right: The ornate bronze control handle in the lift cage.

Left: The lower landing of passenger lift PL1. Notice that there are two independent lifts working in this shaft. PL1 has survived in remarkably good condition due to its continued Cold War use.

The principal employee access to the underground factory was via escalators at the west and east ends of the works. Both escalators were requisitioned from London Transport tube stations at St. Paul's and Holborn in 1941.

Above: Both escalators are now fixed in position and used as emergency stairways in event of lift failures. This is a view up Escalator 'A' at the east end of the site.

Above right: The bottom of Escalator 'A'.

Right: This lubrication reference plate on the drive-motor of Escalator 'A' identifies it as having once been No.4 escalator at London Transport's Holborn underground station.

Opposite: Neither of the escalators requisitioned from London Transport were long enough to reach from quarry floor to the surface. When first installed both escalator shafts terminated some distance below ground level, the last section of the journey being accomplished via a spiral staircase in a short vertical shaft. During the Cold War modifications, the west-end shaft was extended, a sub-surface circulating area constructed, and a second, shorter escalator installed for the final access to the surface. This view is looking from the sub-surface landing up the short escalator to the surface.
Above: A view looking down the lower shaft from the intermediate landing. The inclined concrete structure to the left supports a winch-operated goods haulage system.

CAUTION
SLIPPERY
FLOOR

Above: A panoramic view of the engineering maintenance area at the east end of the factory behind machinery lift ML1.
Opposite below: A scene on the North West Ring Road.
Below: Looking west along East Main Road from passenger lift PL2.

Above: East Main Road at the junction of South Second Avenue, with the approach to Slope Shaft 'B' on the left and a view west along East Main Road on the right.
Opposite below: The vehicle battery charging area behind ML1.
Below: East Main Road looking east from its junction with South First Avenue.

Right: Within the quarry a series of main roads divide the factory into a number of large machine shops and within some of those areas smaller roads create divisions between individual workshops, stores and other discreet, functional areas. Many of these were separated by lightweight mesh screens which were removed long ago.

Left: Abandoned offices in the 'Standards' section. This area gives the impression of a ghost-town with just the shells of buildings remaining. All the fixtures and fittings have been removed along with the doors and the glazing from the windows although, for some reason, the wooden frames have been left in place.

Right: Concrete bases in machine shop No.6 upon which heavy machine tools were once mounted.

Left: In this area of the quarry rather more of the wartime infrastructure has remained undisturbed. On the left can be seen an example of the light mesh screen used to subdivide the workshop areas, while on the right can be seen a series of issuing hatches from one of the factory stores.

Left: One of several staff smoking areas in the Spring Quarry factory. In the background is a street of offices which, unlike those in the Standards area, have survived intact.
Below left: Hundreds of toilets and hand-washing facilities were needed to meet the needs of the several thousand men and women working in the underground factory. Here we see a few of the distinctive hand-washing sluices widely used in MAP factories. These are often mis-described as overall-washing tubs.
Below right: The factory had its own, extensive GPO telephone exchange housed in a suite of rooms underground. Post-war, this was briefly something of a local wonder and a tourist attraction to which school children made frequent organized visits. These trips stopped suddenly and without explanation in the mid-1950s when the site was redeveloped as a nuclear bunker. It is now just a gutted shell and in very poor condition.

Above: The factory ventilation system was extraordinarily complex and built on a prodigious scale. A series of axial flow fans drew outside air down vertical induction shafts and distributed it around the factory via a network of enormous underfloor airways which fed into smaller ducts and thence through ventilation grilles and risers located throughout the factory. Exhaust fans drew stale air from the factory via overhead trunking and perforated, floor-to-ceiling brick-built air ducts that ran around the perimeter of the site.

Left: Large, remotely controlled, centre-pivoted butterfly valves were placed close to each induction fan. These were operated from a central Air Raids Precaution control room in the factory so that they could be quickly closed, sealing-off the ventilation system from outside air in the event of a German poison gas attack.

Above: A typical external view of a fan motor. The vertical red cylinders are lubricators and between them are two dial thermometers measuring the main bearing temperatures.

The ventilation systems in the east and west quarries were isolated from one another, and each had its own underground boiler house to provide steam for heating and process purposes. Because the west quarry was never fully developed the boiler house there was never worked to its full potential. Both contained six Lancashire boilers, originally fitted with mechanical stokers which were soon removed due to their inefficiency, and both boiler houses were provided with vertical coaling shafts and electric lifts to dispose of ash.

Left: Two boilers survive in the east or No.1 boiler house although they are disused and blanked-off. The positions previously occupied by the other four are now home to four diesel generators associated with the Cold War bunker.

Below left & right: The surviving boilers in the bricked-up and abandoned No.2 boiler house. These are now sealed off due to asbestos contamination. Both boiler houses were converted to oil firing and continued in operation under Admiralty occupancy until replaced by a modern, surface plant, with its distinctive quatrefoil chimney stack, off Westwells Road in the 1970s.

Above: The compressor house illustrated here has survived intact from the wartime factory and continued to serve throughout the nuclear-bunker phase of the quarry's history.

Left: One of the three rotary compressors has been taken out of use and now resides in the maintenance workshop but the other two are still fully functional. The switchgear and control instruments are all original.

Below: The brass identification plate denotes the air receiver's origin with the Ministry of Aircraft Production.

Below: Smaller cast-iron identification plates attached to the wall-mounted electrical control equipment seen in the photograph above indicate that it too is of MAP origin.

Left: A second compressor room, housing a pair of conventional vertical piston compressors, also of wartime vintage, survives in the south-east corner of the quarry. This plant provided compressed air for a nearby underground sewage treatment and ejector plant. While both the compressors and the sewage plant survive largely intact it would appear that they have not been used since the war.

Olga Lehmann's Murals

Distressed by the dull colour schemes suggested by the Ministry of Works for the underground canteens at Spring Quarry, Sir Reginald Verdon Smith, Chairman of the Bristol Aeroplane Company, invited Olga Lehmann, a talented young film set designer, to decorate the canteens with brightly coloured floor-to-ceiling murals. The hope was that a more cheerful environment would raise the morale and brighten the spirits of the workforce. Many years later, Olga Lehmann explained the background to her work:

> *"The architect David Aberdeen who studied at the Bartlett while I was at the Slade, approached me to paint murals in the various canteens in the underground B.A.C factory. I was, at the time, a mural painter working in the film industry. Each canteen took about a week to a fortnight to complete and management provided the materials – oil paint and solvents. The first impression of the factory made quite an impact, reminding me of the film 'Metropolis'. It was lit by what appeared to be bright daylight, which was in fact neon strip lighting the likes of which I had never seen before."*

Below and right: These photographs were taken for *Architectural Design* in 1943 shortly after the murals were completed.

M26

M26

M27

Each canteen was decorated to a distinctive theme. The prehistoric theme, seen here, was featured in the operatives' canteen at the east end of the factory. There also, was a stage where ENSA performances were put on and, amongst others, Dame Myra Hess played the piano. Many of the murals in the Admiralty controlled sections of the quarry have been lost – either painted over or destroyed. Those illustrated on the following pages are in the north-west operatives' canteen.

NO TICKETS
CAN BE PURCHASED
UNTIL 12.25 Pm.

Today's Menu
SOUP
MAIN MEAL
SWEET
BEVERAGES Etc

LIMPLEY STOKE QUARRY

Quarries near the junction of Midford Lane and the current A36 trunk road near Limpley Stoke were requisitioned by the Ministry of Aircraft Production in 1940 for use as an underground warehouse for the surplus of Bristol Hercules engines it was confidently expected that the Spring Quarry factory would produce. A survey indicated that only the innermost section of one of these workings – Hayes Wood Quarry – was suitable for conversion, the others being very unstable and very wet. An existing horizontal adit was adapted for use as a primary access while an inclined shaft within the boundary of Hayes Wood functioned as an emergency exit. Below ground, floors were levelled and a large number of brick support pillars were erected. The two access points were linked by a circuitous narrow-gauge railway system that passed through a four-bay surface loading platform in a yard adjacent to Midford Lane on the surface.

Due to the relative failure of the Spring Quarry factory the storage facility at Limpley Stoke was never required. In May 1943 the site was transferred to the Ministry of Supply for use as a warehouse for four thousand tons of TNT destined for eventual consumption in the shell filling factories at Bridgend, Glascoed and Hereford. Most of the surviving surface buildings relate to this later role as an explosives store.

Below: The main entrance to Limpley Stoke Quarry. This is a horizontal adit that passes through several hundred yards of old, disused stone workings before reaching the perimeter of the storage depot.

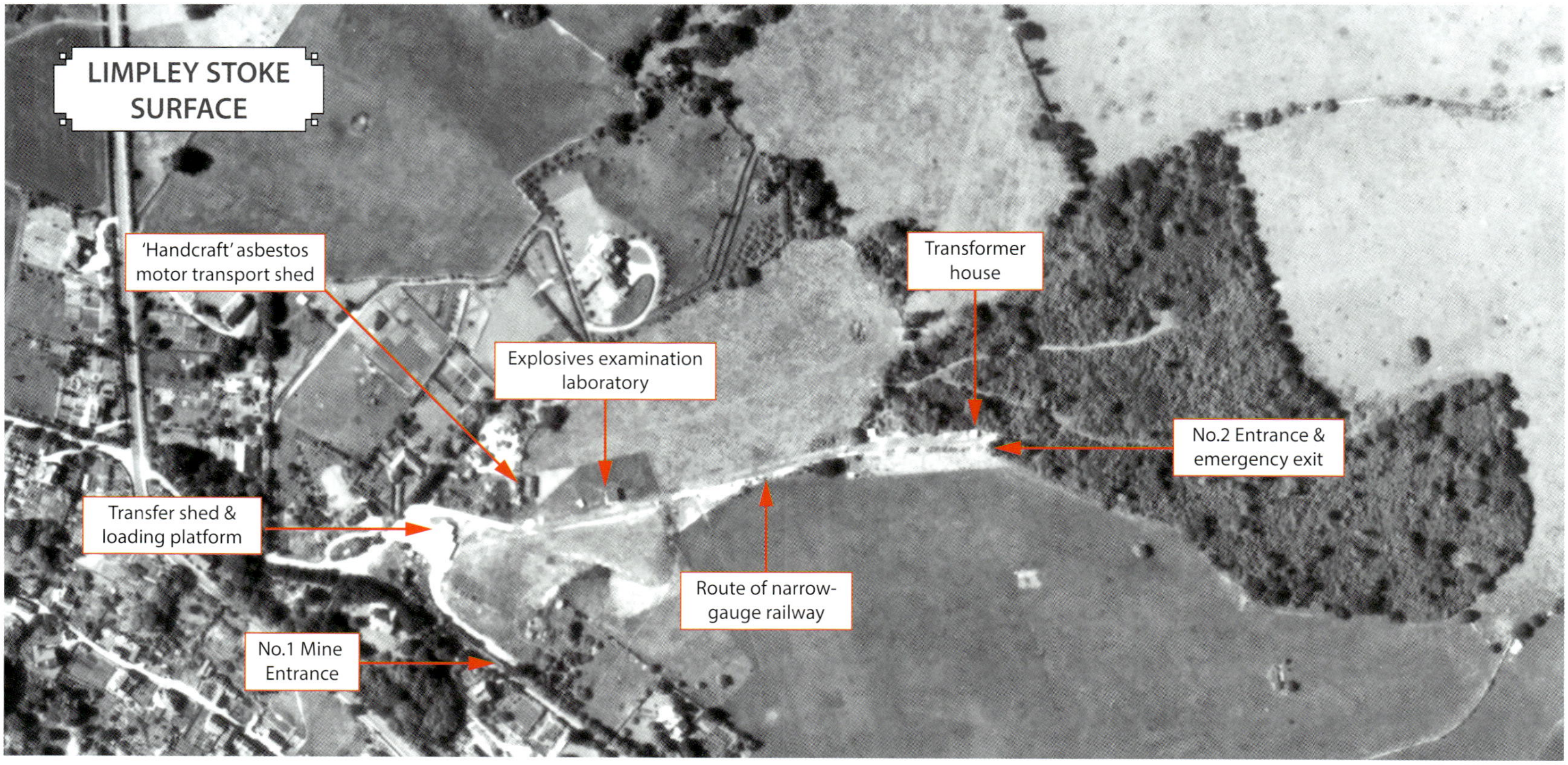

Above: Aerial view of Limpley Stoke Quarry in 1945.

Left: The rear of the surface loading platform. Rails from the main quarry entrance branched into two loops before entering the far ends of the two rear extensions visible in this photograph. In the foreground the rails joined to travel a half mile across fields to the emergency exit.

Above: The approach tunnel to the explosives storage area. This photograph was taken in 1985 when quarrying resumed at Limpley Stoke.

Above: Security gates in the perimeter wall of the storage area.
Below: A typical view showing the profusion of brick support pillars.

Above left: The explosives inspection laboratory. A narrow-gauge railway once ran past the platform at the front of the building, along the route of what is now the farm track seen on the left-hand side of this photograph. Although almost completely eroded away, it is evident that the loading platform was once covered with a layer of spark-proof bitumen. The roof of the transit shed is visible in the background.

Above right: The quarry sub-station and switchroom, now partially hidden in undergrowth near the emergency exit on the edge of Hayes Wood.

Left: The interior of the principal room in the explosives inspection laboratory. This photograph was taken in 2010.

WESTWOOD QUARRY

Westwood Quarry near Bradford-on-Avon was requisitioned along with Spring and Limpley Stoke in December 1940 as part of the Ministry of Aircraft Production's panic response to the threat of a widespread Luftwaffe bombing campaign. No stone had been extracted from Westwood Quarry since 1906 although for a decade or so in the inter-war years it had been used extensively for growing mushrooms. Two events brought this venture to a close: in 1936 a minor earth tremor had caused widespread roof collapses in the mushroom area rendering much of it too dangerous to work and, a couple of years later, the mushroom crop was wiped out by an infection that was impossible to eradicate. Although the government took control of the whole quarry in 1940, large tracts to the east and west extremities were considered unusable and only the 250,000 square feet of the central section was considered suitable for conversion.

The quarry was offered to the Royal Enfield company, but initially their response was luke-warm. Eventually, however, the company agreed to occupy 30,000 square feet of the proposed factory where they would build No.3 anti-aircraft predictors at the rate of twenty units per month. Prior to the Second World War the company was principally a manufacturer of rather out-dated motorcycles and – rather less famously – of lightweight portable diesel engines. During the war, however, like many other established engineering firms, they were encouraged by lucrative government contracts to diversify into other fields which often bore little relationship to their staple peacetime production. Royal Enfield's field of diversification centred upon predictors, gun-sights and other precision gun control instruments. Within a few months of commencing manufacture of No.3 predictors the company agreed to expand production at Westwood. To facilitate this a second, slightly smaller area of quarry was developed as a factory for the assembly of a range of instrumentation including fuse setters, gun stabilizers, gyroscopic sights and anti-vibration mounts for Oerlikon guns, vane-oil motors and self-synchronizing, lag compensating and self-sectoring equipment for a range of anti-aircraft guns.

As the war neared its end, Royal Enfield's output from the Westwood factory became increasingly sophisticated as the original No.3 predictors, which were entirely mechanical in their means of computation and relied upon several thousand precision parts moving in unison, were superseded by radar and electronic gun control systems. Amongst the equipment at least partially developed

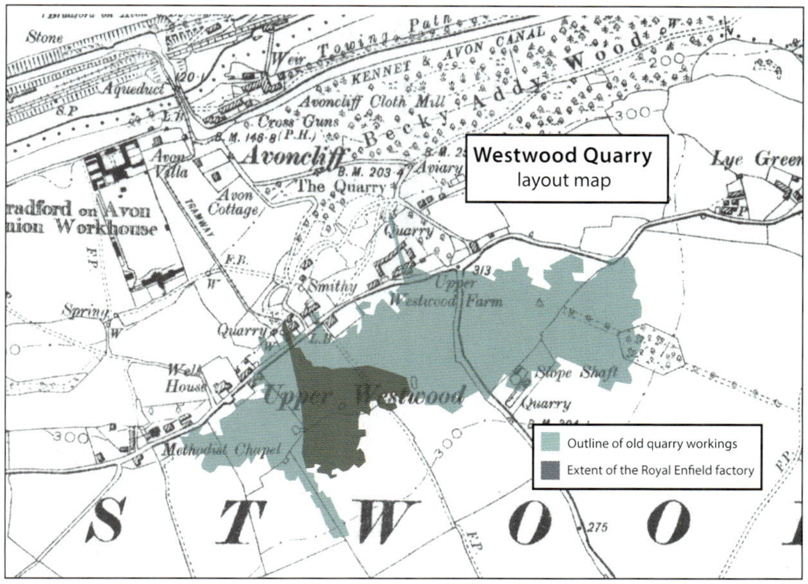

Above: This overlay plan shows the extent of the old quarry workings at Westwood, together with that of the section adapted as an underground factory, in relation to the surface features.

at Westwood during the 1950s was a light anti-aircraft radar system, code-named 'Red Indian' that could automatically direct a battery of eight Bofors anti-aircraft guns. As the government precision engineering contracts diminished, Royal Enfield reverted to its core business of motorcycle manufacture at Westwood. The end of the war saw the return to Britain of many thousands of ex-War Office Royal Enfield 'Flying Flea' motorcycles which were surplus to requirement and which the company agreed to re-purchase. Some of these were unused and had been stored in grease at Army depots throughout the period of conflict while others had suffered long and tortured lives in the deserts of North Africa. Initially at the Westwood factory, but later at other works in Bradford-on-Avon and Trowbridge, all were subsequently refurbished, re-sprayed and sold as new. Motorcycle manufacture continued with the production of twin-cylinder 'Interceptor' and 'Constellation' machines until 1968 when the factory finally closed.

A small section of the works was subsequently taken over by a group of ex-employees of the company and run as a general engineering workshop for a further twenty-five years. The factory is now in a sorry state – Hanson Minerals resumed quarrying at Westwood some years ago and have used large areas of the factory as dumping grounds for waste stone while elsewhere, particularly in the northern sections of the factory, seepage water is causing rapid deterioration of the surviving infrastructure.

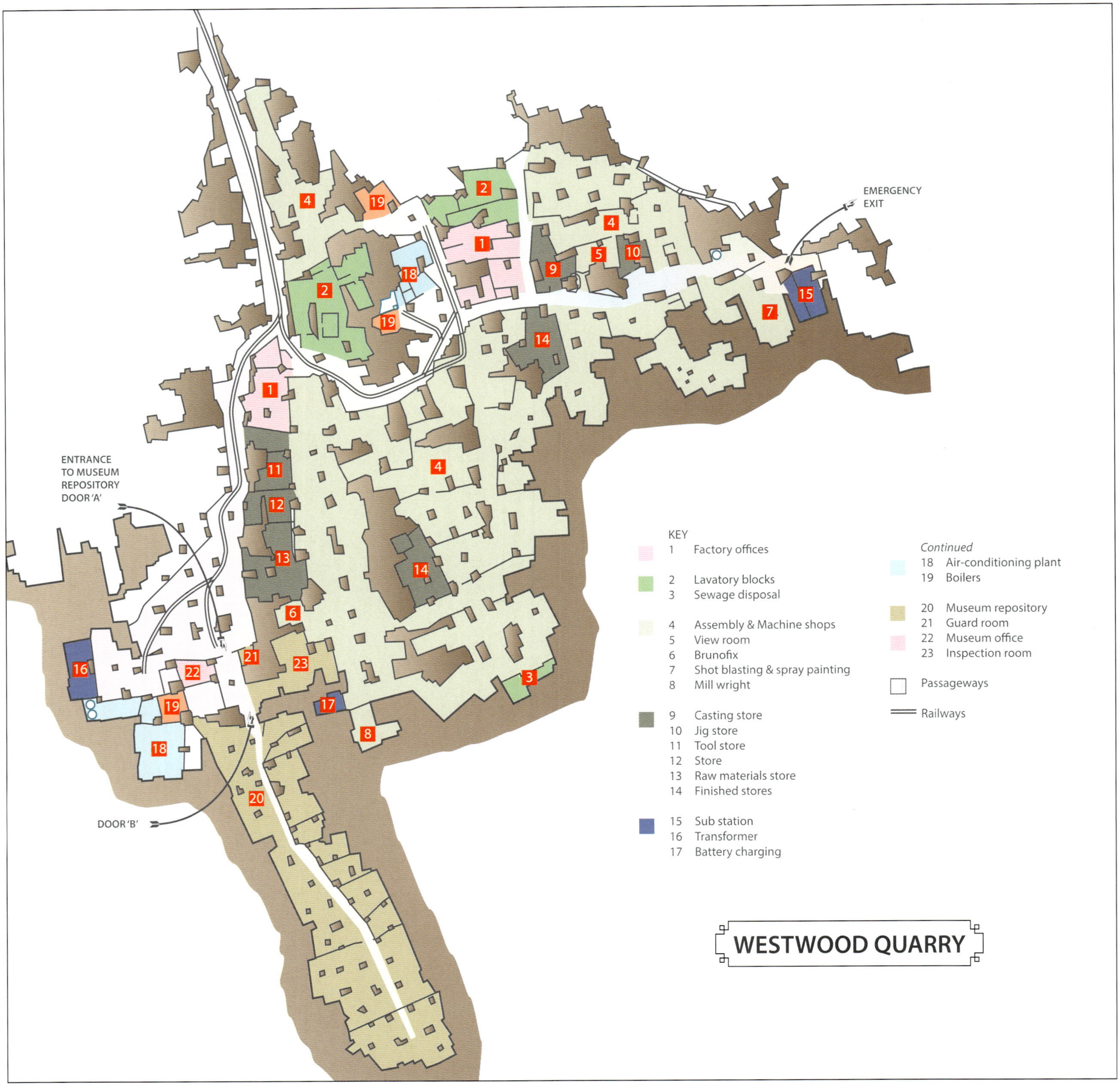
EMERGENCY EXIT
ENTRANCE TO MUSEUM REPOSITORY DOOR 'A'
DOOR 'B'
KEY
1 Factory offices
2 Lavatory blocks
3 Sewage disposal
4 Assembly & Machine shops
5 View room
6 Brunofix
7 Shot blasting & spray painting
8 Mill wright
9 Casting store
10 Jig store
11 Tool store
12 Store
13 Raw materials store
14 Finished stores
15 Sub station
16 Transformer
17 Battery charging
Continued
18 Air-conditioning plant
19 Boilers
20 Museum repository
21 Guard room
22 Museum office
23 Inspection room
Passageways
Railways
WESTWOOD QUARRY

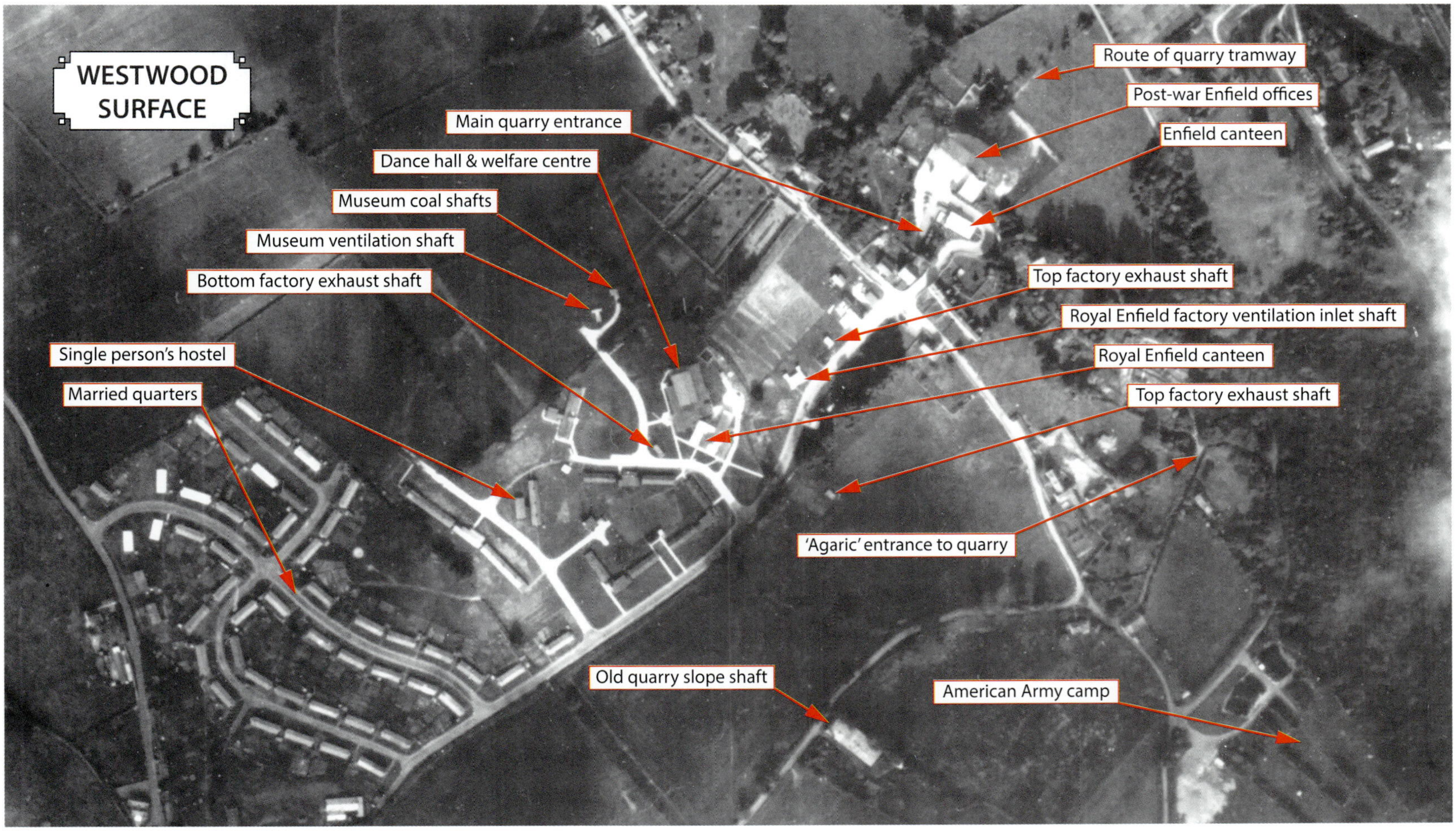

Above: An aerial view of Westwood showing the locations of the most important wartime features. This photograph shows both the surface buildings and shaft-tops associated with the Royal Enfield factory and the British Museum repository at Westwood. The latter is described in more detail on page 275. The American Army camp in the bottom right-hand corner had no association with the underground facilities at Westwood and the reason for its location is unclear. The camp housed the first American negro soldiers to arrive in Britain much, apparently, to the delight of the female population of Bradford-on-Avon.

Left: Clocking-off time at the quarry entrance. Approximately six-hundred people worked in the underground factory, the majority being young local girls with no previous engineering experience. A handful of skilled Royal Enfield engineers were sent down from Redditch to train the girls who quickly proved to be receptive and adept machine operators.

Above: This sequence of three photographs shows the progress of the development of the quarry entrance. To the left is the entrance in 1940 when work began. Loose rock immediately above the entrance has been stabilised and side retaining walls built. The original quarry tramway is still in use evacuating rubble from underground. The centre image was captured a year later. A concrete roadway has been laid and the construction contractor, George Wimpey & Company, are using battery electric narrow-gauge locomotives to transport building materials into the factory. The rails, embedded in the concrete road, were retained for some years solely to transport coal to the three underground boiler houses (two in the factory and one in the museum repository).

The final image shows the entrance in 1944. The retaining wall above the portal is finished, rails have been lifted and all transportation within the factory is now done by means of electric trucks. By this time coal for the boiler houses was delivered via coal chutes in vertical shafts.

Left: The entrance tunnel, looking into the quarry. At the end of the passage the factory entrance is to the left and that to the museum repository on the right.

Above right & left: Two wartime views of the upper machine shop. The notice above the row of lathes in the photograph top right reads, 'First component in each batch must be inspected'.

Right: Compulsory, fortnightly ultra-violet treatment was provided for workers doing long shifts underground who, in the winter, would rarely see daylight.

Below left: The underground tea bar; notice how young some of the girls working in the factory appear to be.

Below right: Experimental 'Red Indian' gun control radar under test in the factory yard circa 1957.

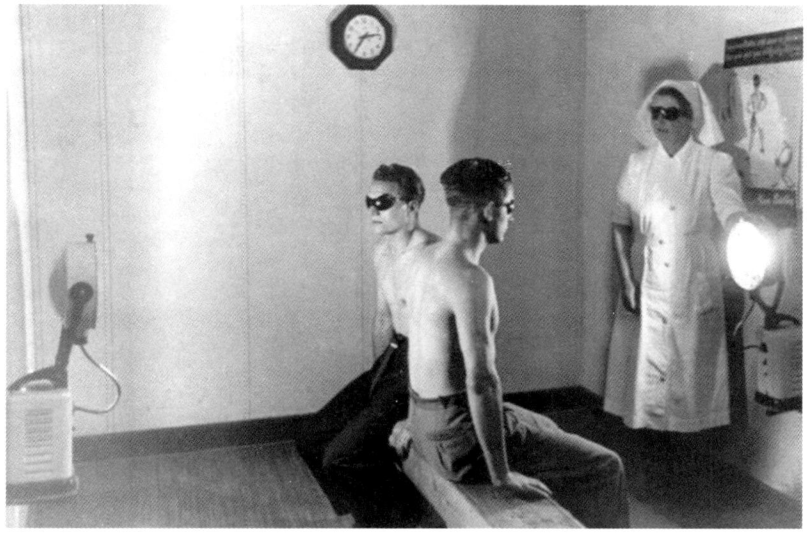

Left: A wartime photograph of the degreasing and plating shop. This is located to the south of the extreme east-end of the main roadway through the factory close to the main electricity sub-station.

Opposite: The degreasing and plating shop in 2012. All the tanks and other plant have been removed, having been disposed of when most of the contents of the factory were auctioned after it closed in 1968. Some of the pipework and electrical fittings visible in this photograph can be identified in the wartime image opposite.

Left: The north-east corner of the top factory main machine shop in 1944. Notice that the grinders on the left-hand side are being operated by women while men appear to be monopolizing the lathes at the far end.

Opposite: The same location in 2012. All the machine tools were disposed of decades before this photograph was taken but the scene is clearly identifiable. The arrangement of very early fluorescent lamps has survived, as has the electrical conduit and switchgear that provided power to the machines. The group of four conduits fanning out on the pillar in the middle of this image can be seen behind the head of the machine operator on the far left of the photograph opposite.

Left: Rather surprisingly, the works drawing office was located underground despite the fact that the invariably high and fluctuating levels of relative humidity was hardly conducive to the safe keeping of paper documents.

Opposite: A recent view of the abandoned drawing office. It is more difficult to relate this to the wartime photograph opposite, but the shape of the ventilation trunking suggests that the earlier image shows the area to the right, behind the pillar in the centre of the room. There is a shadow of a grille on the wall and there is a grille, behind which a light might throw a similar shadow, visible in the background of the wartime photo.

Left: A stoker and his dog in the boilerhouse in the north factory in 1944. At a date unknown, but probably towards the end of the war, the south factory boilerhouse was closed down and the ventilation system adapted so that this plant would serve the whole complex.

Opposite: The boilerhouse today. Three boilers survive, where once there were four. The nearest boiler is one of the originals, seen in the image opposite, but without its insulated cladding which has corroded and fallen away. It has remained coal-fired. The other two, clad in blue asbestos, are post war replacements and were oil-fired. The flue to the surface can be seen behind the old boiler; the bottom has rusted away and debris thrown down the shaft from the small public park above has accumulated beneath it.

Main factory road looking west towards quarry entrance.

Incline to south factory with test and assembly shops to the left.

Main factory road looking east towards the electricity sub-station.

Looking north towards the boilerhouse with offices to the right.

Above: A 360 degree panoramic view of the crossroads in the middle of the works, taken from the junction of the boilerhouse passage and the main road through the factory.

Left: The doorway to the right is the main access to the bottom factory. Large teak double-doors, now missing, once controlled access at this point. The louvres in the wall to the right are outlets from underfloor ventilation ducts.

Right: The central service area. No.2 boiler house is to the left of this picture; the boilers have been removed but the steel flue can be seen in the ceiling. It is probable that the adjacent room formerly housed hot-water circulating pumps but latterly functioned as an electroplating shop. During the early war years a short narrow-gauge railway spur passed through the centre of the area, discharging coal for the boilers in the foreground space.

Left: The shell of No.1 boiler house, bereft of plant. The beam for an overhead travelling crane, a large steel flue on the ceiling connecting to a vertical steel-lined chimney shaft to the surface, and some just discernible brick-footing for three boilers, are the only evidence that any plant was ever installed here. The capped and truncated steel flue for this boiler still survives on the surface, partially concealed within a shrubbery.

Below left: Header pipes and circulating pumps in No.1 boiler house valve chamber. Here three thermostatically controlled electric pumps (two always in service, one as a standby) circulated hot water from the boilers through radiators in the main underfloor air ducts serving the two sections of the factory. *Below right:* Grinding-wheel dust extraction ducting in the upper machine shop.

Above: A collapsing pillar in the north machine shop. Although it would appear that pressure from the quarry ceiling has crushed the pillar, this is not the case. Bricks used in the construction of the pillar, like those in a number of other non-load-bearing brick structures in the factory, have simply burst spontaneously due to faulty firing in their manufacture, probably brought about by the internal build-up of moisture since the factory closed and the heating was turned off.

Above: A panoramic view of the shot-blasting shop. Most of the factory plant was sold by auction following its closure, but, it would seem, no one wanted a second-hand shot-blaster.

Left: This pendulum hardness-testing device is in the inspection department of the south factory and is one of the few pieces of engineering equipment to survive intact. An office door in this department bears the legend 'CIA' which, at first glance, appears highly sinister but, in fact, is the acronym of the Chief Inspector of Armaments and probably dates from the years when Royal Enfield were manufacturing anti-aircraft predictors.

Left: The main assembly shop at the north end of the factory. Notice the extensive use of corrugated sheeting to control seepage water. Given the current state of this area it is difficult to envisage precision opto-mechanical and electronic equipment being assembled here. In later years it was the area where Royal Enfield motorcycle engines were tested before despatch. The pipework attached to the right-hand wall is where the engine exhausts were ducted through to a ventilation shaft.

Below left: Paint spraying booths, with turntables, located at the far east end of the factory close to the exhaust ventilation shaft. The debris visible in the left of this image is waste stone dumped by Hanson Minerals after the company resumed quarrying at Westwood.

Below right: The doors to 'K' store in the bottom factory.

Left: The compressor room which supplied compressed air throughout the factory. It lies directly south of the No.1 boilerhouse valve room and steam pipes from there can be seen crossing the ceiling and heading towards a bank of steam radiators in the ventilation air duct on the far side of the right-hand wall. Concrete bases and electrical connections for the two compressors can be seen in the middle of this view.

Left: No-one appears to remember what this small, triangular room at the east end of the factory was used for. The very heavy rolled-steel girders and narrow benches on each side of the room, together with the proliferation of electrical and compressed-air connections suggests that it contained test equipment that required a vibration-free environment.

Left: The entrance to the lower factory finished parts store, with the assembly area to the right behind the wall with half-height grilled openings. Note the very early fluorescent lighting fittings, each with its separate starter and ballast unit mounted on the ceiling nearby. Elsewhere in the factory these units are mounted in groups on the walls.

Below left: The top factory ladies toilet. The hand washing sluices are similar to those we have seen already in the Spring Quarry factory, although provided on a less lavish scale.

Below right: A corner of the gentlemen's toilet for the lower factory. At least one of the rather attractive revolving soap dispensers has survived intact here.

Above: The rusting remains of the factory's 11Kv sub-station. This station switched two alternative 11,000 volt incoming grid supplies to three transformers which in turn provided current at 415 volts three-phase and 240 volt single-phase for local power and lighting. One transformer, which provided power for the underground factory, can just be seen in the background and is illustrated in detail opposite. The others were located in the adjacent British Museum quarry sub-station and in a surface sub-station that supplied power for the workers' residential site and welfare facilities. A bizarre feature of the quarry's high voltage installations is that they were fitted with water sprinkler fire suppressing systems.

Right: One of two low voltage (415/240 volt) switchboards that supplied current for power and lighting in the factory.

Below left: The transformer and battery room for the factory's low-voltage emergency lighting system.

Below right: The 11Kv transformer in the main factory sub-station. This fed two separate distribution boards for the north and south sections of the factory which were initially designed as independent units. The sprinkler nozzles are clearly visible in this photograph. The switchboard for the north factory is pictured above.

Left: The electrically driven 'Keith' centrifugal fan at the bottom of the ventilation shaft at the east end of the depot. This fan draws contaminated air from a large underfloor duct which in turn connects to smaller ducts with ventilation grilles in the walls of the factory and directly by means of steel trunking to dust and toxic vapour producing equipment such as paint sprayers, shot-blasters, electroplating apparatus and grinders.

Right: The heating plant for the bottom factory. A hot water radiator connected to the induction fan outlet chamber is visible in the left background, with the fan motor on the far right. The concrete slope in the foreground is an air passage connecting the fan to the underfloor ducts. The ceiling mounted ducting provides warm air to various offices and service areas.

Above: The former police post at the entrance to the factory yard.

Right: The main entrance to the quarry. Originally secured by teak double-doors, but for many years left open to the elements and to intruders, the entrance is now secured by a sturdy roller shutter door.

Below: This building, now used as a motor car body shop, was once the factory canteen.

Above: The shaft-head building for the top factory eastern ventilation exhaust shaft.

Above: The top factory west exhaust shaft. From here, in later years, as well as stale ventilation air, exhaust gasses from motor cycle engines under test was evacuated.

Below: The top of the lower factory exhaust shaft. A sub-surface duct from this shaft carried warm air from the factory into the surface canteen and welfare centre to supplement the heating there. A chain-hoist attached to an old forty-gallon drum suspended from a beam above the shaft was used to raise swarf from the machine shop to the surface for disposal.

Above: The top of the inlet plenum shaft. Until recently this building had extensions attached which contained banks of inlet air filters and a filter-washing chamber.
Below: This range of surface offices was built for the Royal Enfield company in the immediate post-war years.

Above: The factory motor transport garage. During the 1950s a barrel-less 4.5" field gun breech and mounting were parked here for testing automatic fuse setters built in the factory.

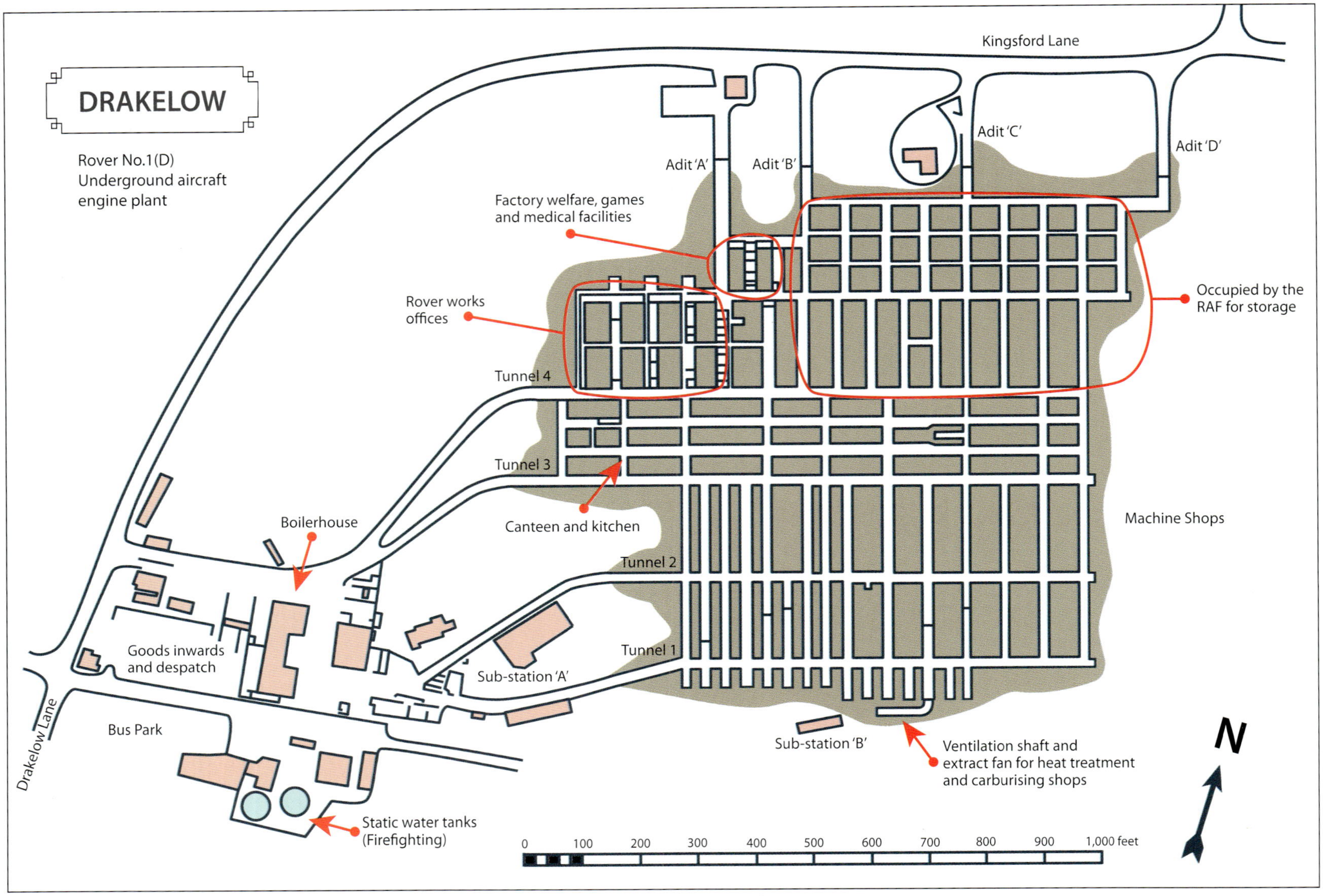

By June 1941 there were 1,200 men working on the construction of the underground factory at Drakelow. With only a vague idea of who might occupy it and what might be made there, the MAP had estimated that construction and fitting out would cost £285,000 and would be completed within six months. By July, 1942 the cost had risen to £983,000 and the selected tenant, the Rover Motor Company, was insisting on a further £184,000 programme of modifications to meet their specific needs. The Rover Company was part of a government sponsored shadow group of motor manufacturers – including Austin Motors, Rootes, Daimler and Singer – formed in 1936, that in the event of war would expand the Bristol Aeroplane Company's aircraft engine manufacturing capacity in a series of dispersed factories.

The original scheme envisaged a series of four parallel, 1,000-foot-long service tunnels, each approximately eighteen feet high and sixteen feet in width, connected by a further series of tunnels at right-angles to the main tunnels, which would form workshops, stores and offices. Once construction was under way it found that the spacing between the lateral passages was too narrow, leading to roof falls and structural instability. Thereafter the spacing was enlarged, as can be seen on the map left, and the number of workshops reduced. This reduction was of little practical consequence as the Rover Company was not particularly enthusiastic about the whole underground scheme and, indeed, they were quite happy to give up a significant portion of the north end of the factory to the RAF for general storage.

Left: The main entrance to the T1 and T2 area, viewed from the weighbridge. The boilerhouse is in the centre of the image with the ventilation tower for Tunnel No.4 prominent above it.

Below left: The ventilation tower for T2 with the roof of the factory sub-station visible in the left foreground. Beyond the tower is a Victorian school building, used during the war as the factory's ARP centre.

Below right: One of the main factory access tunnels photographed after the demolition of its ventilation tower.

Overleaf: A typical tunnel crossing in the factory illustrating the self-supporting nature of the sandstone strata and the ease with which the tunnels were bored.

23

Right: A view of tunnel T4 looking west. In the distance the tunnel curves to the left as it approaches the entrance. At first glance it appears that the tunnel at this location has a flat ceiling but what one sees is in fact the bottom of a very broad steel ventilation duct that spans the width of the corridor, supported by steel girders set into the side walls. The large clock suspended above the office is one amongst many scattered throughout the factory.

Left: Another view of tunnel T4, this one looking east, into the factory, from the inner pair of heavy wooden doors which, it is assumed, formed an air-lock to prevent the ingress of poison gas in the event of a German chemical weapons attack which, was a threat taken very seriously in the early years of the Second World War.

Left: Bay 24 to the north of tunnel T1; this was formerly the factory tool room. This section of the tunnels was one of the first to be completed and was built to the original plan with relatively narrow lateral division walls left between each bay. This proved an unstable design and the factory was completed with much wider supports between the bays. The diagonal steel girders supporting the ceiling beams is evidence of the weakness in this area.

Below left: The wages office in the factory office complex north of tunnel T4.

Below right: Bay 40, north of tunnel T2 which housed the gear section.

Above: A section foreman's office. This steel and mesh form of construction was common in both office and stores areas.

Below: The gutted remains of one of several tea bars to be found in the factory.

Above: The Works Clerk's office with an original Rover Company noticeboard attached to the wall. A sign on the wall to the left, just out of shot, gives directions to the Canteen, Cam Sleeve, Conn Rod and Artic Rod sections.
Below: A typical gentlemen's toilet in the Drakelow factory.

Above: The timekeeper's office near the entrance to tunnel T4.
Below: A corner of the factory's extensive kitchen facilities.

Below: A wartime view of the cylinder head and reduction gear casing section in bay 47 immediately east of the kitchen and canteen between tunnels T3 and T4. The machine tools seen in this view are radial arm drills. Notice the light steel girders just below roof level to which are attached the lights and various service pipes and conduits. These also seem to support corrugated steel sheeting above the machines on the left-hand side, presumably to prevent dust or other debris falling from the roof onto the work in hand.

LONGBRIDGE

Work began in 1936 on a shadow factory on a site adjacent to the existing Austin factory at Longbridge near Birmingham. While the new East Works shadow factory was under construction, plans were prepared for an extensive network of tunnels to be excavated in the soft sandstone beneath the site to provide air raid shelters for the 15,000 strong workforce, and also to provide bomb proof production and storage facilities. Of the six main tunnels, varying in length from 400 feet to 3,500 feet, only one, the twin East Works tunnel, with cross passages totalling 1,700 feet, was built specifically for production purposes; the others were associated with the pre-war West and North works and were essentially personal air raid shelters that could, in emergency, be used for limited manufacturing or storage purposes.

Below: A typical entrance to a semicircular steel-lined tunnel beneath the Longbridge plant. This design is typical of that used for factory air raid shelters.

Above: The overgrown entrance to Tunnel MT-1. This was initially constructed as an employee air raid shelter but periodically utilized for storage.

Left: The entrance to Tunnel MT-8. This is an example of the inverted-U, steel-framed tunnels that were specially constructed for aero-engine assembly.

Right: A typical section of steel-framed factory tunnel showing the U-girders and heavyweight corrugated steel lining.

Below left: An example of a brick-lined shelter tunnel. These were much slower and more expensive to construct than the steel-lined pattern.

Below right: This steel-lined tunnel, which can be sloping away to the right in the background of this shot, appears to be in a precarious condition with wooden props supporting its centre line.

Factory ARP Centre

The factory also had an underground ARP control centre, beneath the Trentham building, consisting of three steel cylinders sunk into the ground; two small entrance and emergency exit cylinders fitted with spiral stairways – one of which is illustrated here – and a larger three-level cylinder accommodating, on the upper floor, domestic and welfare facilities with a telephone exchange, offices and other communications equipment on the middle level and ventilation and other service plant on the bottom level.

Above: A tee-junction in the steel-lined tunnels in the stores area of the factory.

Below: A massive blast door sealing a shelter tunnel.

Above: A tunnel ventilation shaft in the factory yard.

Below: A severely corroded sliding blast door at a junction in the factory tunnels.

RHYDYMWYN

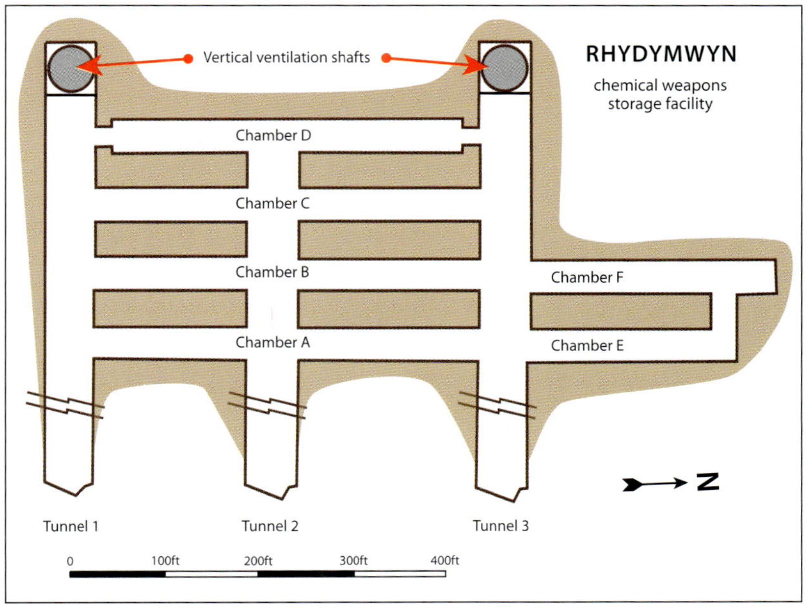

Construction of the tunnelled storage facility to the north of the Valley Works mustard gas factory at Rhydymwyn was completed in November 1940 and on 11 December the first shipment of mustard gas was received from the ICI works at Randle. Initially it was intended that chambers 'C' and 'D' would be used for the storage of mustard gas in bulk, each chamber containing forty-eight, sixty-five-ton lead-lined steel tanks, and that chambers 'A' and 'B' should be used for filled mustard gas bombs and vesicant in drums. Before construction was completed a change in government policy increased the requirement for bulk vesicant and to meet this demand it was decided to install a further twenty-four bulk storage tanks in chamber 'B'. In order to make up for the lost storage capacity for filled bombs, the two front tunnels were extended to form chambers 'E' and 'F'.

To obviate the risk from spillage and other contamination, deep drainage channels were laid in each tunnel and maintained under a slight negative pressure by a vacuum plant exhausting into tall ventilation towers at the heads of vertical shafts at the innermost ends of entrance tunnels 1 and 3. The towers were demolished in the early 1980s.

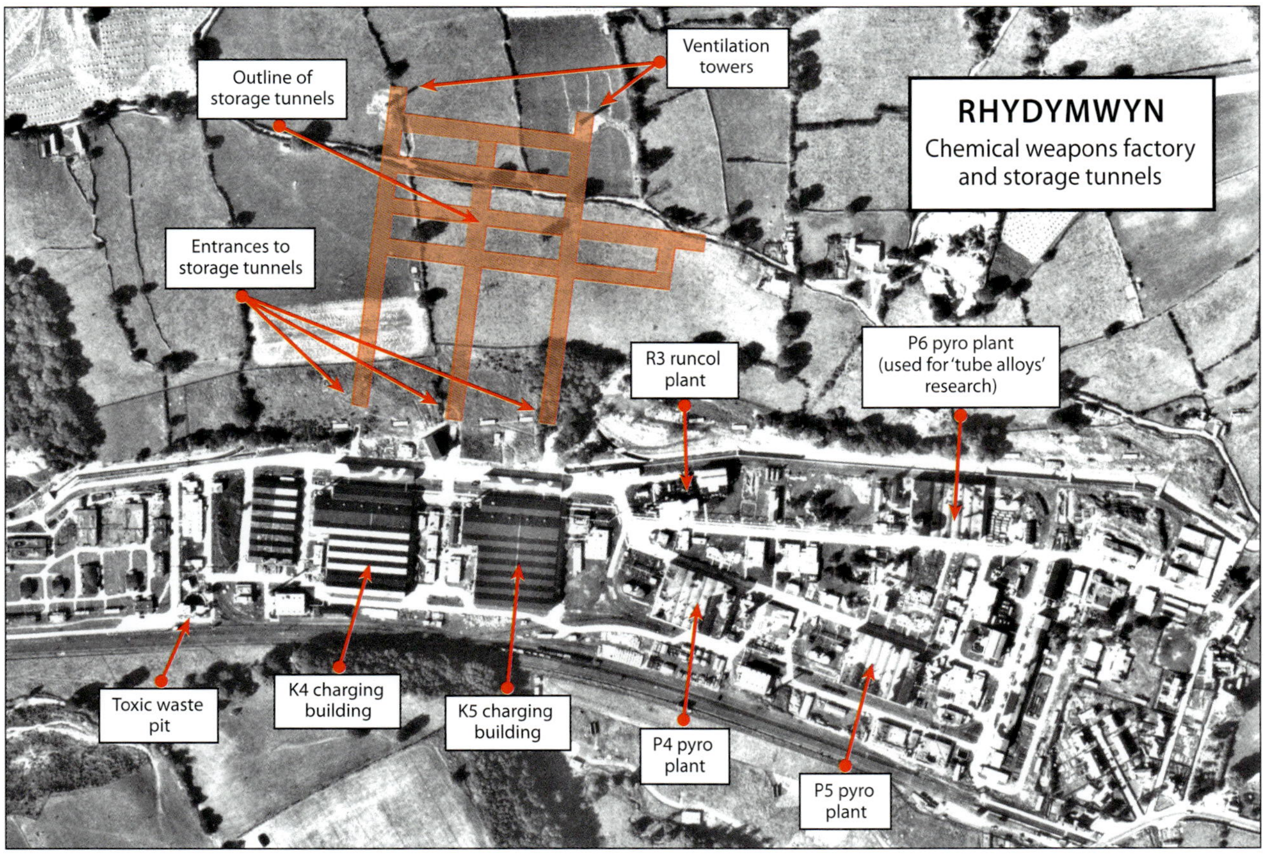

Left: Aerial view of Valley Works with the position of the tunnels superimposed. Major production buildings are annotated. 'Pyro' and 'Runcol' are codenames for mustard gas synthesised by different production processes. Bombs and shells were filled with mustard gas in charging buildings 'K4' and 'K5'. Building 'P6' was designed for mustard gas production but was handed over in 1942 to the Department of Scientific and Industrial Research for use in Britain's 'Tube Alloys' project, the development of the atomic bomb. At Rhydymwyn, professors Simon and Peierls erected a large-scale plant to isolate uranium isotopes by a gaseous diffusion process.

Above: The entrance to tunnel No.2 with the lights on underground in 1988. The structure on the right is Charging Building K5, with Charging Building K4 and its ancillaries on the left.

Below: A more recent view of No.2 Tunnel. Originally there was rail access to the tunnels but many alterations were made in the post-war years.

Below: The entrance to the eastern or No.3 tunnel.

Left: A view down tunnel No.2 from its junction with storage chamber 'A'.

Right: Storage chamber 'A'. Note the grilles in the floor which cover the underfloor spillage, drainage and extraction duct, and the concrete corbels which once supported the rails of an overhead travelling crane.

Above: The outer-most end of entrance tunnel No.2. Unlike the other tunnels, which are of rough rock formation, this section is lined with concrete.

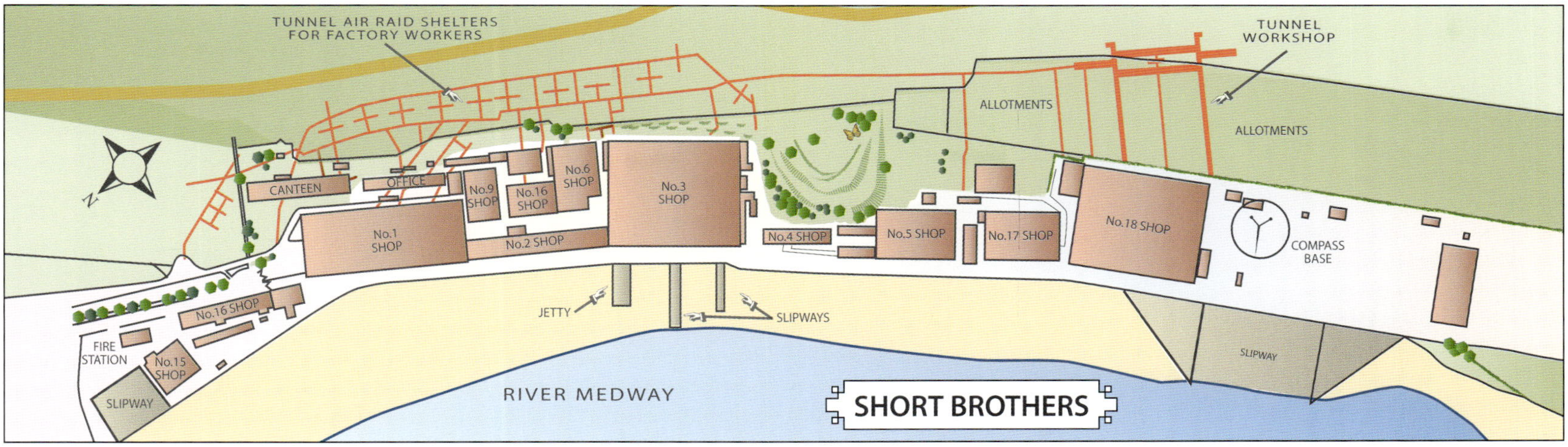

SHORT BROTHERS, ROCHESTER

Short Brothers Ltd had a long-established seaplane works on the south bank of the river Medway at Rochester. In the summer of 1941 the company was faced by two immediate problems. Firstly, German occupation of airfields in northern France meant that the factory was highly vulnerable to enemy bombing and, secondly, capacity in the factory was becoming strained; there was an urgent need to find room for a further seventy-five machine tools to meet the increasing demand of war production but no available factory space to accommodate them. To satisfy both requirements an agreement was reached on 23 September 1941 between the company and the Ministry of Aircraft Production to excavate underground workshop tunnels in the chalk cliff-face immediately behind No.18 machine shop, a recently erected extension to the surface factory, financed by the MAP. The twin, parallel tunnels, each 100 yards in length, provided 12,000 square feet of factory space at a cost of £20,000.

At the same time a series of shelter tunnels was excavated in the hillside behind the older section of the factory at the north end of the site, these and the underground factory being joined by a 400 yard linking tunnel. Four horizontal adits joined the factory tunnel to No.18 machine shop while a series of nine adits gave convenient access to the shelter tunnels from various sections of the old factory.

At the end of the war the underground machine shops gradually fell into disuse although a large part of the complex remained in use for general storage well into the 1980s. In more recent years the whole site has been redeveloped and most of the adits have been sealed either by backfilling or the erection of block-walls, those which remain have been securely gated for reasons of safety.

Above: Layout plan showing position the of the tunnels in relation to the factory buildings.
Below: The western factory tunnel (ie the one closest to the surface factory).

Above: At the end of one of the factory tunnels is this pile of casting sand-boxes and wooden formers for cast-iron components manufactured in the factory.

Above left: One of two ventilation shafts located in ventilation plant rooms at the north-east and south-east extremities of the factory tunnels. These climb vertically for ten feet before inclining at forty-five degrees to the surface.

Above: The north ends of the factory tunnels are linked by a traverse passage from the centre of which this broad passageway continues northwards for a further twenty metres before linking to a long passageway of smaller dimensions to join the shelter complex to the north.

Left: Miscellaneous wartime switchgear adjacent to the doors to the factory's male and female toilets.

Above: These heavy steel blast doors secure one of the factory ventilation plants.

Below: The ventilation trunking is prominent in this view of one end of the factory tunnels. Waterproof fluorescent fittings and emergency lighting indicate relatively recent occupation.

Above & below: Within the shelter section of the tunnels there are three ventilation shafts to the surface and two emergency exits. All are of a similar design consisting of long inclined passages terminating in short vertical shafts to the surface. Originally the airshafts were secured by gates, as seen below but the one for No.3 shaft, seen above, was removed long ago.

Above: At the north end of the shelter tunnels a few bays, as seen here, have been utilised for storage.
Below: The remains of wooden benches still survive in this length of shelter tunnel.

Above: A typical junction in the shelter tunnels, the engineering required to achieve the correct roof geometry at this point is quite complex.
Below: An unlined, rough-hewn passageway through the chalk from the west factory tunnel to the cliff edge near the Medway.

PLESSEY FACTORY

Prior to the Second World War the Plessey Company, based in Ilford in Essex, was already an important player in Britain's electrical and engineering industries. During the 1930s the company had acquired licences from American firms to produce a number of assemblies which would later prove to be of immense importance to the nation's war effort. Most important amongst these was a licence to fabricate integrated, plug-in wiring looms which greatly simplified the wiring of military aircraft, together with rights acquired to manufacture Coffman engine-starter cartridges, and an agreement with the Borg-Warner company to build aircraft fuel pumps designed by one of its subsidiary companies.

Production had expanded during the years immediately leading up to the war with new factories built at Swindon and Cardiff and, as part of the government-sponsored shadow factory programme, several dispersed wartime factories were also established. The main facility, however, remained at Vicarage Lane in Ilford, a site whose vulnerability was highlighted in September 1940 when the machine shop was severely damaged by enemy bombing. Further damage was incurred during further raids in the month that followed. Plessey was one of the companies that became embroiled in Lord Beaverbrook's grandiose scheme to find alternative underground accommodation for Britain's entire aircraft production industry initiated in November 1940, the scheme that led to the construction of the vast and ultimately disastrously inefficient Spring Quarry factory beneath Corsham in Wiltshire. Plans for the temporary acquisition and adaptation of the nearly-completed Central Line extension tube tunnels between Whipps Cross and Gants Hill were proposed by Plessey's managing director, Sir Allen Clark and agreed by the Ministry of Aircraft Production in November 1940. The scheme, including development of the tunnels and the construction of numerous new surface buildings that did not figure in the original London Underground construction programme, was completed in March 1942 at the surprisingly reasonable cost of £25,000.

The tunnels provided 300,000 square feet of manufacturing space and at its peak the factory employed 2,000 workers, the majority of them women. Personnel access was via a pedestrian stairway at Redbridge, where the station was only seventeen feet below ground level, and by escalator at Gants Hill and Wanstead. Additional goods lifts in vertical shafts were provided at Cambridge Park and Danehurst Gardens. A notable feature of the factory was that, due to its linear nature, internal transfer of materials and finished products was made by means of an eighteen-inch gauge railway system using twelve small electric locomotives provided by the Liverpool firm of Wingrove & Rogers.

The factory which, as well as the company's pre-war range of wiring looms, engine-starters and fuel pumps, also manufactured artillery fuzes, engineering components for various armoured vehicles and a range of field telephone systems, ceased production shortly after the war ended in 1945. Clearance of the firm's plant and equipment took five months and a further seven months were required to remove the concrete slabs that had been laid to provide a horizontal floor within the circular tunnel sections. The line through the tunnels finally opened for passenger service in December 1947.

Above: Lady machinists in the drilling section of the Plessey factory.
Below: Another view in the Plessey factory, again with women doing most of the skilled work. Note the narrow gauge-railway on the right.

PARK PLACE, HENLEY ON THAMES

Although only a relatively small company within the British aircraft industry, Sir George Godfrey & Partners of Norbury in south London was important to the war effort as it was the only firm equipped to manufacture hydraulic equipment and other components for the Phillips Master trainer. By the spring of 1941 Norbury was regarded as a dangerous area and under the Beaverbrook plan alternative underground accommodation was sought. The directors of the company identified a small, disused chalk mine at Park Place near Henley on Thames as a suitable location and following an agreement with the Ministry of Aircraft production made on 11th June 1941 the local building firm of Gordon Carrington & Company contracted to complete all the necessary conversion work for a fixed fee of £23,025, later reduced to £18,723.

Shortly after completion of the Park Place factory work began on a second site, also a disused chalk mine, nearby at Warren Row. Both factories consisted, in plan view, of simple, elongated 'U' shaped tunnels with the main entrance at the end of one leg and an emergency exit at the other. All the machine tools and offices were laid out on one side of the tunnel with an open walkway opposite.

After the war Park Place remained in use as a privately owned engineering works until the mid-1980s, leased from the Ministry of Defence. Thereafter, for a brief period, it functioned as a Cold War emergency armed forces communications centre. Warren Row was transferred to the Ministry of Supply in 1945 for use as a store for redundant machine tools and other engineering equipment. In 1958 the site was transferred to the Home Office and redeveloped (and very soon became notorious after its infiltration by Spies for Peace) as RSG-6 one of the government's supposedly secret network of Regional Seats of Government from which the country would be administered in the event of a nuclear war.

Below: The main entrance to Sir George Godfrey & Partners underground factory at Park Place near Henley on Thames.

Below: The emergency exit from the Park Place factory.

Above: A typical view underground in the Park Place factory. In 1985 the disused factory was utilised for a short time as the emergency Armed Forces Headquarters for No.6 Region.

At Park Place the underground facility complemented a substantial surface complex which functioned as a rural, dispersed site for Godfrey's vulnerable works at Norbury.

Several of the buildings, particularly the administrative and service buildings in red brick, were constructed on an apparently lavish scale despite the limited budget that was available. Most of the workshop buildings however, like those shown above right, were built of asbestos and lightweight concrete panels to a more austere design. Surprisingly, the surface buildings survived for a considerable time after the closure of the factory.

WARREN ROW

KEY

1 Camp Commandant
2 Security
3 Works Stores
4 Messengers
5 National Insurance
6 National Insurance
7 Ministry of Labour
8 Ministry of Aviation
9 Home Office
10 GPO
11 Counter Room
12 Voice Comms
13 Teleprinters
14 COI
15 BBC
16 Treasury
17 Ministry of Power
18 Conference room
19 Comms Directing Staff
20 MOWS
21 Ministry of Health
22 Directing Staff
23 Min of Transport
24 Ministry of Housing
25 Scientific Section
26 Civil Defence
27 Combined Ops
28 Conference Room
29 Conference Room
30 Operations Director
31 Assistant Ops Director
32 Regional Commissioner
33 Principal Officer
34 Secretariat
35 Information Centre
36 Police
37 Fire Brigade
38 Min of Agriculture
39 Armed Services Liaison
40 HMSO
41 WRVS
42 Common Services

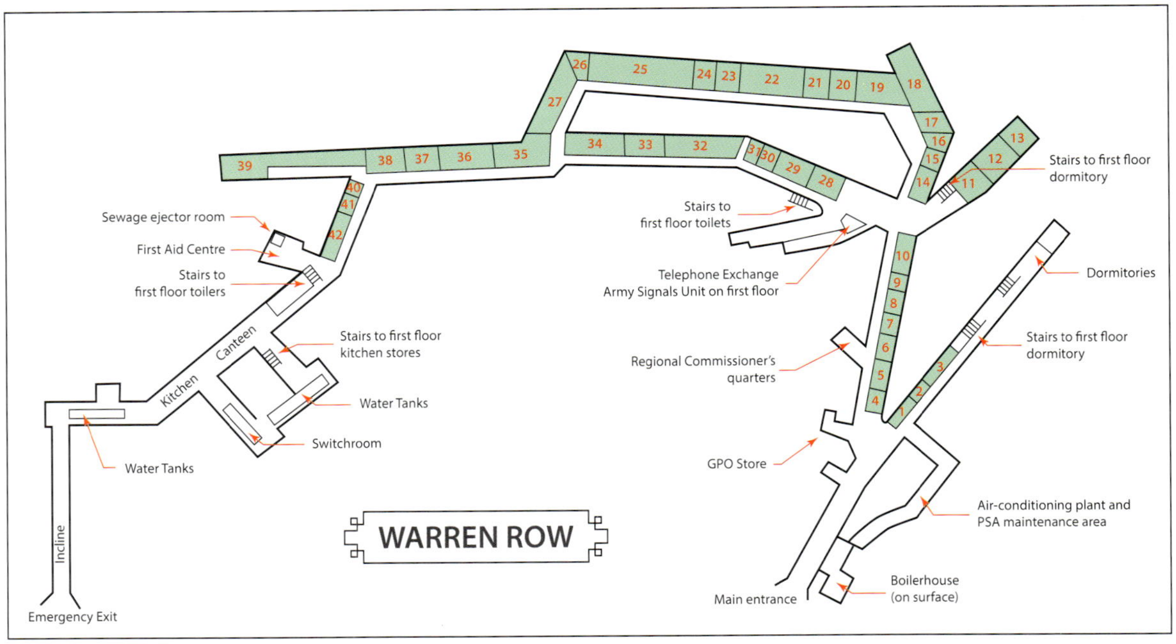

Above: During the Cold War the tunnels at Warren Row became the Regional Government Headquarters for Region 6. This plan shows the layout at that time.

Below left: A wartime view inside the Warren Row factory. The limited amount of engineering work carried out here is very apparent.
Below right: The emergency exit from Warren Row.

Chapter 4

ADMIRALTY STORAGE

BRADFORD-ON-AVON

Although the Admiralty was opposed to the underground storage of ammunition, they did, for a short while at the start of the war, occupy two small quarries in Bradford-on-Avon for the storage of optical equipment and other general stores.

Bethel Quarry

Right: The unassuming entrance to Bethel Quarry in Bradford-on-Avon, one of three small quarries, previously used for Mushroom cultivation, located on the Frome Road that were requisitioned by the Admiralty in October 1939. Bethel, which was used primarily to store RDF and electronic fire-control equipment, was found inadequate for the task and most of the stores were transferred to Copenacre when construction was completed there at the end of 1942.

Below: Layout plan of Bethel Quarry. The road names were allocated by the Agaric Mushroom company who previously occupied the site.

Above: A typical view of Bethel Quarry. At the end of the war the Bradford quarries were quickly de-requisitioned and mushroom cultivation resumed. By the mid-1990s the small-scale cultivation at these locations was not economically viable and the business was run down. This photograph was taken in 2012, some years after mushroom growing ceased.

Left: Land on the opposite side of the Frome Road from the quarry entrance, sandwiched between the road and the Kennet & Avon Canal, was developed as an Admiralty transit depot for material stored in the Bradford quarries. Post-war, many of the buildings there were adapted for mushroom cultivation. These are the last two such buildings to survive on the site shortly before their demolition in 1991.

Paulton Quarry

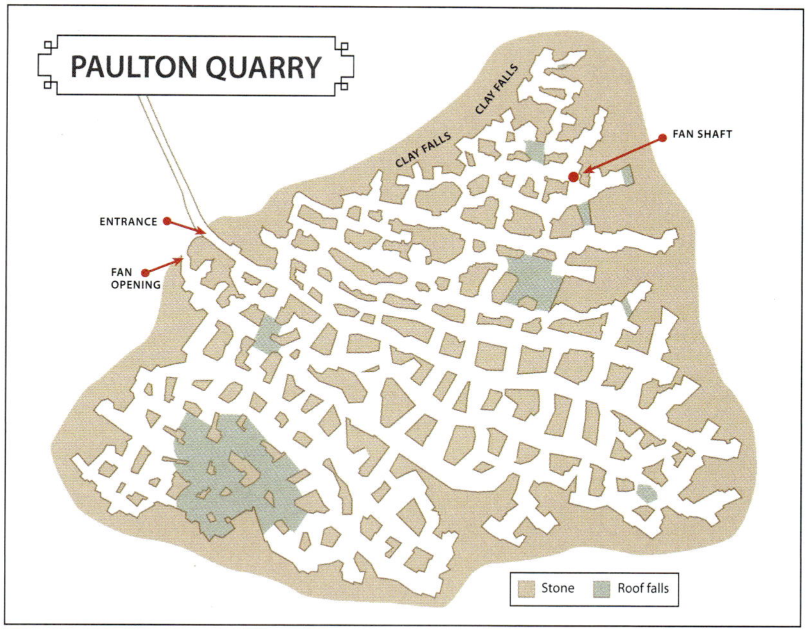

Above: Layout plan of Paulton Quarry.
Left: The entrance to Paulton Quarry which lies to the south of the Kennet & Avon Canal just to the east of the canal bridge on the Frome Road. The entrance is now obscured by a new housing development.
Below: A roadway in Paulton Quarry. Note the steep inclination of the stone strata which rendered the quarry somewhat unstable.

Elm Park

Despite their earlier misgivings, the shortage of suitable storage space (they were reduced to keeping large naval shells in railway trucks lined up in dockside sidings), and their increasing vulnerability to aerial bombardment, the Admiralty found themselves with little option but to adopt some form of underground ammunition storage. Like the two other services, they turned to Corsham but found that very little suitable subterranean real estate remained. Three very small quarries were available: Brockleaze, Pickwick and Elm Park, and the latter was on the point of being taken up by the Air Ministry. After a rather bitter exchange of memos the RAF were defeated and the Admiralty took possession. No major engineering work was undertaken in these quarries.

Above right: A wartime view of Elm Park while under RAF occupation.

Centre & bottom right: Two underground views of the quarry. The steel hooks in the ceiling supported corrugated sheeting used to drain away seepage water.

Below: The quarry entrance in 1990.

Pickwick

Right: The shaft-head structures for Pickwick Quarry stand amongst the newer agricultural buildings in the foreground of the photograph, with the much larger Copenacre complex in the background. The transit shed is prominent in the middle of the site with the long, single-storey range of the picket-post and administrative offices to the left adjacent to the road.

Below: A detailed view of the transit shed. The vertical entrance shaft to the quarry is a simple rectangular opening surrounded by a low brick wall, hidden by the white bales in the background of this photograph.

Left: As well as the vertical shaft there was a slope shaft route to Pickwick quarry which gave a less direct access to the underground storage area. This view shows the winding engine house in the early war years, little changed from the time it was used to haul stone from underground.

Below left: Naval small-arms stored underground at Pickwick.

Below right: This storage bay contains depth-charges and what appear to be Fleet Air Arm 250lb bombs in the background.

Above: The Pickwick slope shaft today. Quarrying resumed at Pickwick in recent years, exploiting highly lucrative reserves of Box Ground stone.

Above right: The main underground roadway in Pickwick Quarry, approaching the vertical lift shaft, with railway track still in-situ. Notice, too, the electric wiring still in place on the wall to the right.

Below right: Typical storage bays in Pickwick Quarry. Compared with the development work done in other Corsham quarries, the engineering undertaken by the Admiralty was not particularly sophisticated.

COPENACRE

Much of the Admiralty's warehouse capacity for non-explosive Fleet Air Arm stores was destroyed during the bombing of Coventry and Woolston on the nights of 27 and 29 October 1940. A frantic search for suitable surface premises proved fruitless so, in January the following year, they approached the Ministry of Works in the hope of commandeering one of the larger Corsham quarries that had, the previous month, been requisitioned by them on behalf of the Ministry of Aircraft Production. Within a few days the Admiralty had accepted the ten-acre Copenacre Quarry and began an immediate and expensive programme of conversion. New shafts were sunk to house vertical passenger lifts and two spectacular inclined cargo transporters; an underground boiler house and heating system was constructed and standby generators installed. Once the first stage of the Copenacre conversion was completed in July 1942 stores displaced from Woolston began to arrive along with large quantities of RDF equipment, fire-control gear and Asdic equipment previously held in the small and highly unsuitable quarries in Bradford-on-Avon. As soon as Copenacre was fully commissioned the Bradford quarries were relinquished and returned to their former owners, the Agaric Mushroom Company.

Below: Aerial view of the Copenacre complex during its last year of operation.

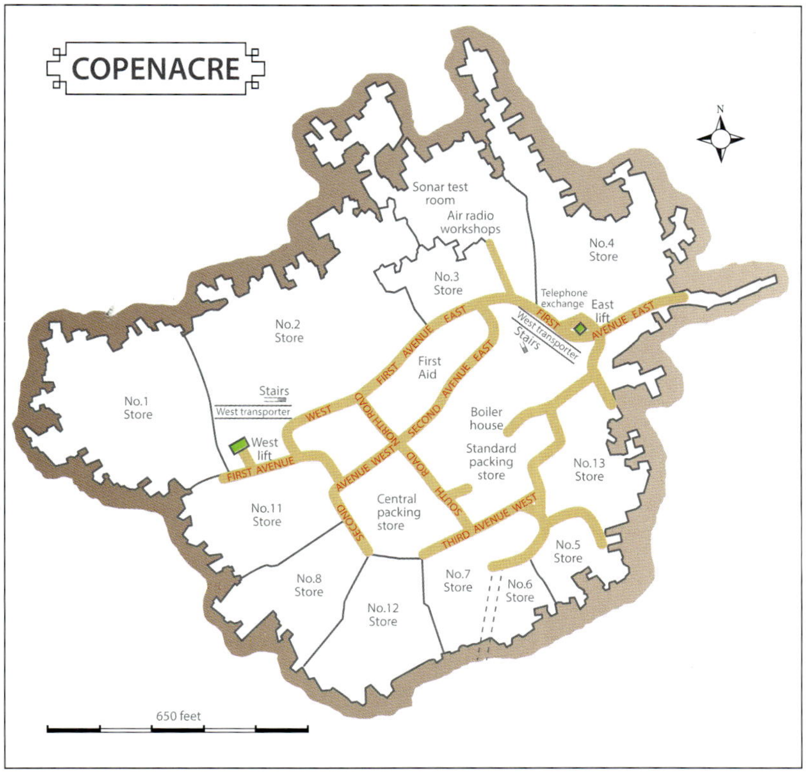

Left: Outline layout plan of Copenacre Quarry showing the positions of the roadways, lifts and transporter shafts.

Below left: The principal goods access to Copenacre Quarry was via two inclined transporter shafts. This rear view of the east transporter shaft-head building shows the massive concrete construction.

Below right: An overhead view of the east transporter surface building, with its security gates located immediately adjacent to the main A4 trunk road. The lorry loading platform is on the right, beneath the corrugated asbestos shedding.

Above: Sunk below ground level, the west transporter shaft-head building is almost invisible from the nearby public road. By the time this photograph was taken the loading platform, beneath the overhanging canopy, had been sealed off by a concrete block wall.

Above: Inside the west transporter building looking down the inclined shaft with the upper loading platform behind the blue steel barriers on the right. There is a pedestrian staircase to the left of the transporter shaft.

Left: The bottom of the east transporter shaft showing the cradle at rest on the lower landing. The undercarriage of the cradle is triangular in shape in order that the travelling platform remains horizontal on the inclined shaft.

Below left: The bottom of the west transporter shaft. A considerable amount of structural steelwork was required at this location to stabilise the rock ceiling above and to the left of the shaft.

Below right: The east transporter winding engine in the shaft-head building.

Above: The rather sinister shaft-head building for the west goods and personnel lift.

Left: The lower lift landing for the west lift in Copenacre Quarry. The door to the left gives access to an emergency staircase in the lift shaft.

Below: The shaft-head building for the east lift. This lift was taken out of use many years ago and all access points on the surface securely sealed by concrete block walls.

Left: First Avenue East, one of the main roads through the Copenacre depot. Although there were some areas in which the ceiling height was somewhat lower, throughout much of Copenacre Quarry the headroom was unusually generous. The standards of engineering here are much higher than at the smaller Admiralty-controlled quarries at Bradford-on-Avon and elsewhere in Corsham.

Right: Heavy doors like those seen in this photograph segregate areas of the quarry. Often referred to as fire-doors, they were intended to control the flow of ventilation air and to contain the emission of smoke in the event of a fire, rather than control the spread of fire itself. This picture also illustrates the varying ceiling heights found within the quarry.

Right: A storage bay adjacent to the very high wooden doors that controlled airflow between North Road and First Avenue.

Below: In the post-war years Copenacre Quarry was used to store an enormous range of naval hardware. Within the quarry the depot was divided into a series of discreet stores each dedicated to particular classes of goods classified according to an obscure, numerically indexed 'Vocabulary of Admiralty Stores'. This is the entrance to No.4 store and appeared to contain, amongst a plethora of other items, gauges and other equipment relating to the Lynx helicopter.

Left: One of the depot's heating and ventilating plants, with a belt-driven circulating fan visible through the mesh screen in the middle of the picture, and a bank of steam-heated radiators behind.

Below: A corner of the power supply room in Copenacre Quarry. Extensive laboratory facilities existed in the quarry for testing electronic components including radar equipment. It is alleged that at one time engineers working there erected their own ad-hoc surveillance radar on the roof of a surface building, by means of which they could monitor traffic movements in the local vicinity. Such equipment required electric power at a wide range of voltages and frequencies which were provided by a number of motor generator sets, two of which are visible in this photograph.

Above left: Three new Cochran boilers for the depot's boiler house being prepared for lowering underground in 1942.
Above: The first of the boilers being lowered into Copenacre's 100-foot deep main ventilation shaft.
Below left: Manually manoeuvring a boiler out from the bottom of the shaft using hand-winches and levers.
Below: The three boilers fully installed in the underground boiler house and fitted with oil-firing apparatus.

Above: At the end of the war Copenacre was retained by the Admiralty as long-term storage and over the following decade Spring and Monks Park quarries were added to the Royal Navy storage facilities at Corsham. The future of these depots looked uncertain in the early 1970s but, once the cloud of closure had lifted, major refurbishments were put in hand. At Copenacre the three wartime Cochran boilers were replaced by the three modern, packaged units seen above. Copenacre was finally shut down in 1997 and the underground area is now used as a dumping ground for nearby quarrying operations which were resumed by Hanson Minerals shortly after the closure.

TRECWN

The principal objection of the Admiralty to underground storage facilities of the type utilized by the War Office at Corsham concerned the logistical difficulty of handling very heavy shells on inclined shafts and in confined spaces in converted quarries. Plans were, however, in hand since 1938 for the construction of two immense, purpose-built depots at Trecwn near Fishguard in West Wales and Dean Hill near Salisbury, at a cost in excess of £6,000,000.

At Trecwn a total of fifty-eight 200-foot long concrete-lined storage tunnels were bored, herringbone-style, into opposite sides of a long narrow valley. Approached by a two-mile long private road and standard-gauge railway branch line, the depot included a range of ammunition maintenance facilities and was served by its own narrow-gauge railway system which branched into each of the storage tunnels. Trecwn was originally designed to store naval mines but was later adapted to handle a wider range of ammunition.

Above: The entrance to storage magazine No.12. Originally, there were railway tracks running up into the magazine, but now the road has been tarmaced across the whole of its width.

Below left: The entrance to storage magazine No.13.
Below right: Interior view of a storage tunnel. Note the spark-proof bronze railway track within the magazine area.

DEAN HILL

The Dean Hill depot, which opened in 1941 and closed in 2003, consisted of twenty-four storage tunnels bored into a chalk hillside south of Salisbury. Eighteen of the tunnels are 100 feet long, six have been extended to 250 feet. The depot included extensive ammunition inspection and maintenance facilities on the surface, all linked, like the tunnels, by a 2' 5" gauge railway system with connections to the depot's main line interchange yard.

Above: Aerial view of the Dean Hill depot. Railway spurs leading into the underground storage tunnels can be seen at the bottom of the photograph. In the centre of the frame are a number of bunded, semi-underground storage bunkers.
Below left & right: Two typical tunnel entrances at Dean Hill.

NO ENGINE
SHUNTING
BEYOND
THIS POINT

Opposite: Interior view of a storage tunnel showing an overhead crane and modern air-conditioning units. This view, looking north towards the entrance to the magazine, shows the curved approach tunnel in the background.

Right: A view looking into a storage magazine with the narrow-gauge railway siding on the left. A 3-ton Fellows Stringer overhead travelling crane, used to load and unload heavy naval weapons, runs on rails supported by concrete corbels set into the tops of the side walls.

Below: Two of the depot's narrow-gauge locomotives; a Baguley Drewry 0-6-0 to the right with a smaller Hunslet loco behind.

Chapter 5

RAF BOMB STORES

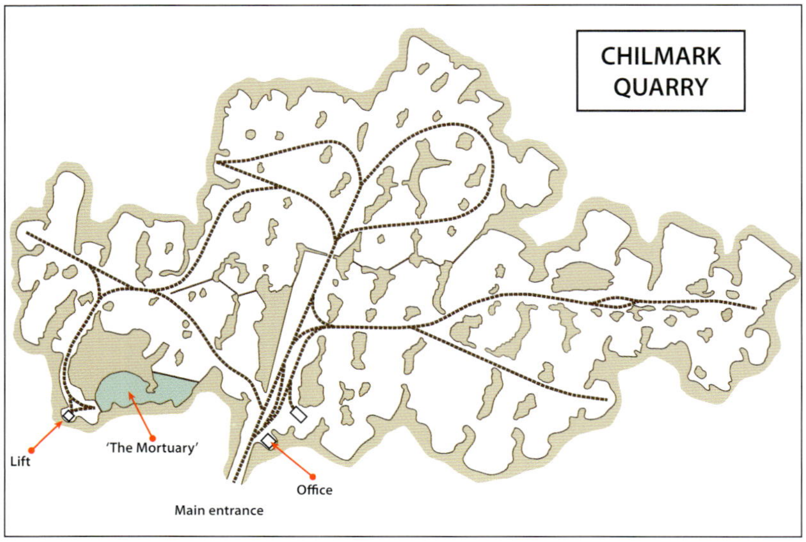

CHILMARK

Two small quarries at Chilmark, in the Nadder Valley west of Salisbury, were acquired by the Air Ministry in June 1936 for conversion into underground bomb stores. The largest of the two, generally referred to as the Main Quarry, is just north of the Ham Cross to Dinton road while the smaller is to the south. Both are connected, along with numerous surface and semi-buried magazines scattered over an area of several hundred acres, to extensive main line interchange sidings at Ham Cross.

The quarry, which provided stone for the construction (and continued maintenance of) Salisbury Cathedral has similar characteristics to the Corsham quarries except that the average ceiling height of ten feet is somewhat lower, and the ceiling stratum seems more stable. The latter characteristic has allowed for very wide unsupported areas underground and, in consequence, only minimal and inexpensive engineering works. Artificial supports, where required, consist of no more than upright steel joists supporting short cross members at roof level.

Above: Gates securing the entrance to the Main Quarry. The pipe in the foreground is a fire-fighting water main.
Below: Inside the main gates showing the open blast doors.

Above: The approach to the lift shaft, which has a rise of no more than fifteen feet and was used as an emergency exit and as a transit route for bombs found to be in suspect condition and stored temporarily in the 'Mortuary'.
Below left: The massive sliding blast door used to seal-off access to the lift shaft and the mortuary.
Below: A detail view of the lift cage showing the narrow-gauge railway turntable, necessary due to the orientation of the rail siding on the surface.

Above: A general view of the storage area towards the west end of the depot showing part of the network of narrow-gauge rails that serve the storage bays. The wide expanse of largely unsupported roof, and the slender steel girders put in place where it was thought extra roof reinforcement was required, are evident both in this photograph and the one below.

Left: The approach tunnel from the main quarry entrance is visible in the centre background of this photograph, just to the right of the quarry foreman's office. Inside the gates a short length of reinforced concrete tunnel was constructed through an area of fractured rock on the hillside edge.

LLANBERIS

Construction of the two-storey, 'artificial' underground depot in the bottom of a seventy-five-foot deep slate quarry near Llanberis was completed by civilian contractors, almost a year behind schedule, in June 1941. Once completed, the structure was overlain with forty feet of loose slate waste as a protective measure. A similar single-storey structure had been completed in a limestone quarry at Harpur Hill near Buxton a year or so earlier. At Llanberis a standard-gauge branch line entered the heart of the depot via a tunnel pierced into the side of the mountain while another smaller tunnel carried a narrow-gauge line from interchange sidings on the south bank of Lake Padarn. Three electric lifts provided communication between the two floors of the bomb store.

All seemed well at Llanberis until the morning of 25 January, 1942 when, without warning and when a train was unloading underground, half of the depot collapsed within seconds, burying over 75,000 high-explosive bombs and other ammunition.

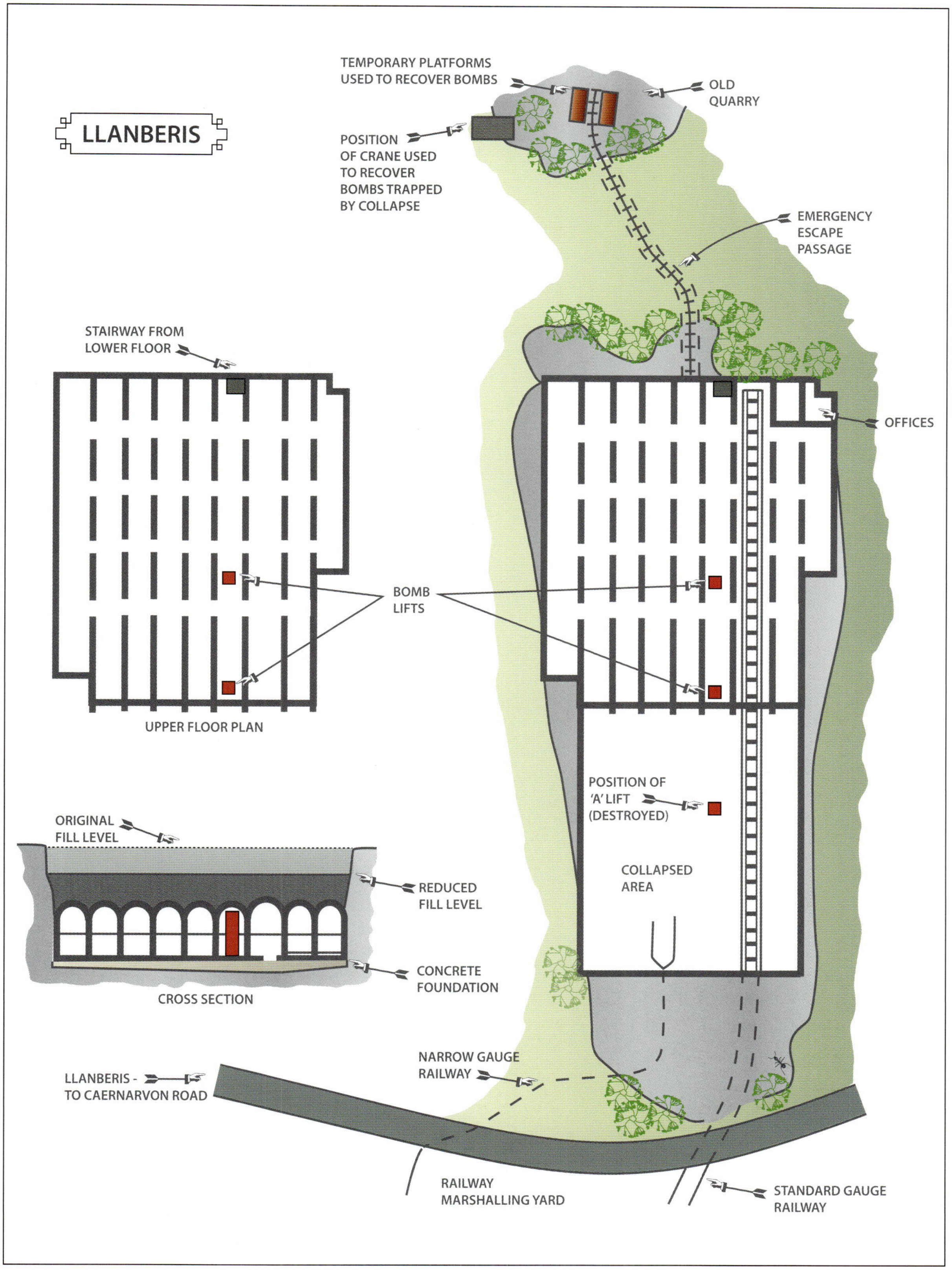

Right: Plan and cross-section of the underground depot at Llanberis following the collapse in January 1942, showing the extent of the damaged area.

Right: Aerial photograph taken after clearance of the wreckage was completed. All the bombs in the damaged area were recovered by 28 April 1942 and the remaining 6,047 tons trapped in the debris by 22 October. Note the small-arms ammunition stacked in the open space left where the tunnels had collapsed.

Below: 500lb high-explosive bombs stacked on the upper floor of the Llanberis depot prior to the collapse.

Above: The truncated tunnels of the Llanberis depot. The lightweight construction, particularly the thin reinforced concrete floor slab to the upper level, is evident in this picture. The shallow arch formation of the roof was designed to transfer the weight of the rubble overburden to the side walls; the problem with this geometrically balanced design was that a failure of any element would inevitably lead to a total, rather than localised, collapse. Shortly before the disaster of January 1942 small cracks were observed in the concrete, but these were considered to be just due to settlement and of no structural significance. The subsequent Court of Enquiry concluded that poor design and the use of concrete with too little cement were the principal contributory factors to the collapse.

The large arch, second from the right, marks the position of the railway platform. The rails were laid in a cutting, with the concrete floor of the lower level at wagon-loading height. The cutting was in-filled with rubble in the late 1990s when it was proposed to use the tunnels as a waste dump.

A small emergency exit tunnel from the rear of the lower floor led into a deep open quarry behind the bomb store and it was via this route that bombs from the undamaged section were evacuated following the collapse.

Above: This view illustrates even more graphically the apparent frailty of the structure. When the depot was rebuilt the end of each chamber was sealed by a brick wall erected approximately ten feet in from the truncated end of the tunnel. The steel ladder in this picture gives access to the exterior of these walls on the upper level, presumably for inspection purposes.

Left: A view from the tunnels looking across the collapsed section towards that standard-gauge railway tunnel entrance. Notice that the end wall of the depot was almost completely destroyed in the collapse but the side wall survived up to the spring line of the arch.

Below left: The standard gauge railway approach to the truncated tunnels. Note the larger dimension of this tunnel to accommodate the width of the platform.

Below right: The innermost end of the underground railway platform. The cutting in which the railway runs is now partially flooded and the rails submerged. It was along the centre line of this tunnel, further to the north, that the first cracks appeared that led to the catastrophic failure of the structure.

By June 1943 the depot had been cleared and stabilized with a view to its re-commissioning. Many of the intermediate archways between adjacent chambers in the surviving section were reinforced with additional brickwork but the Air Ministry had lost faith in this form of construction. For the rest of its life the tunnels at Llanberis were used only for the storage of unfilled bombs and packing cases.

Above right: The ground floor of No.1 tunnel, immediately west of the railway platform, showing the slender reinforced concrete columns supporting the weight of the upper floor.

Below right: Un-reinforced openings between tunnels on the upper level.

Below: This view of the upper levels show the arches reinforced with several rings of brickwork. This treatment has been applied to the majority of the arches on this level. The concentric red circles on the wall mark the position where fire-fighting pipeline was to have been installed had the tunnels continued in use.

Three electric lifts, situated in the tunnel to the east of the railway tunnel, were installed to raise bombs from railway platform level to the storage chambers on the upper floor. No.1 lift was destroyed in the disaster but it is thought probable that the rigidity of No.2 lift, in the centre of the depot, helped stabilize the structure and halted the progress of the collapse.

Above right: No.3 lift cage, more or less intact, still survives on the upper floor of the depot.

Below right: The lower floor landing of No.3 lift, now in very poor condition. The motor, gearbox and control gear have been smashed in order to recover valuable scrap metal.

Below left: The cage of No.2 lift at rest on the top floor. Contrary to popular belief, when lifts fail they do not generally plummet to the bottoms of their shafts but instead drift upwards by virtue of the large counterweights attached to their haulage cables. During rebuilding, No.2 lift was left in place to help strengthen the structure but could not be used because its doors opened directly on to the new end wall of the chamber.

HARPUR HILL

Harpur Hill was built in a similar manner to Llanberis, in the bottom of an open limestone quarry near Buxton. Although initially planned as a single-storey facility, the sloping floor of the quarry allowed the construction of a second, lower level beneath the tunnels east of the railway heading. This lower floor was for a while the RAF's principal chemical weapons store. Following the collapse of Llanberis, an investigation of Harpur Hill revealed disquieting cracks in the structure which led to emergency remedial work and its relegation to a storage facility for empty cases and obsolete weapons only.

Right: The north railway access in 1988, by which time the depot was used as a commercial warehouse served by road transport.

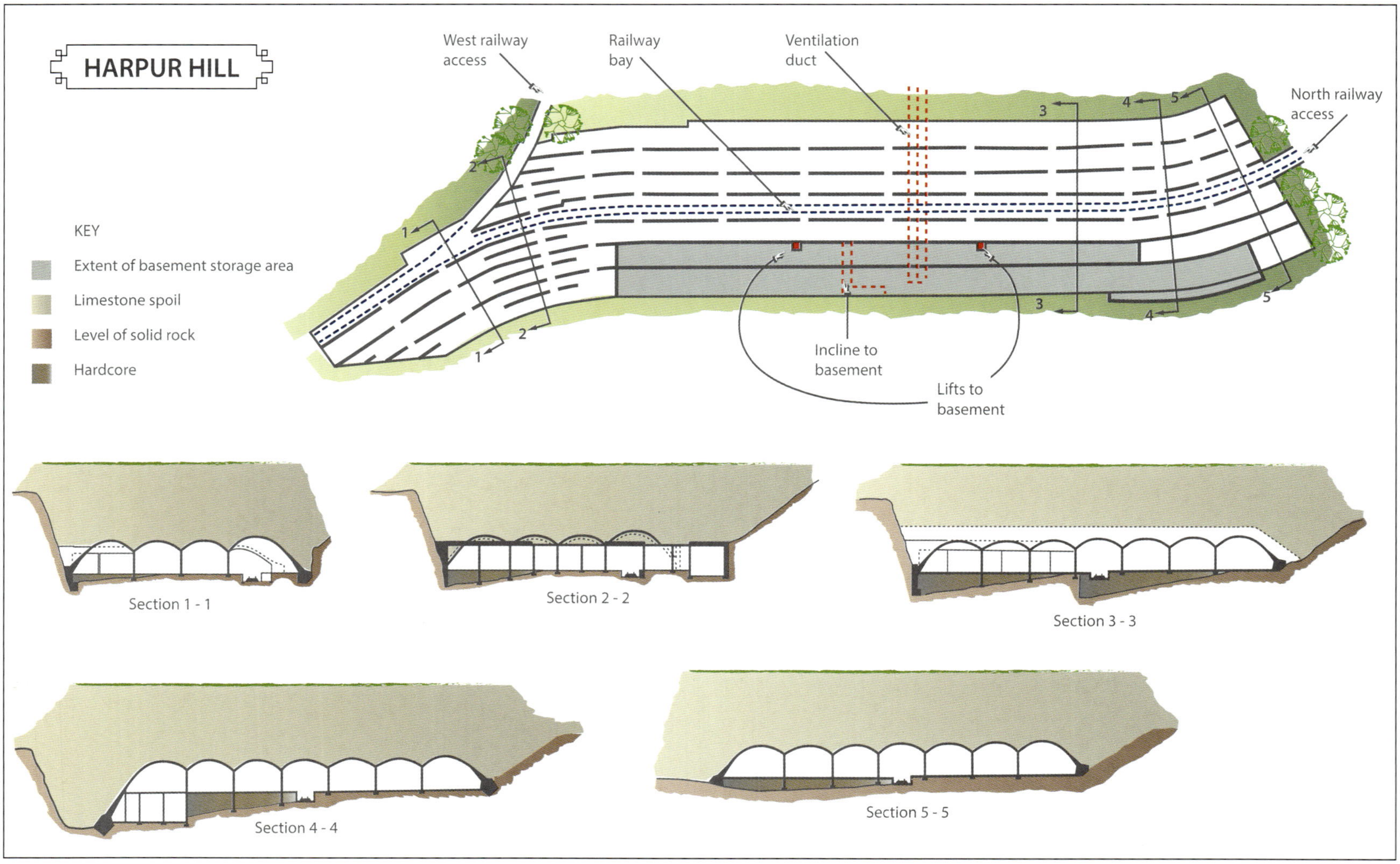

Above: A view of the west railway access taken after the depot was abandoned, showing the derelict remains of the Military Police guard hut.

Below: A detailed view of the portal of the west railway access.

Below: The south end of the underground railway platform at Harpur Hill.

GRANGE CAVERN, HOLYWELL

The deficiencies of Grange Cavern (it small, inconvenient and damp) were acknowledged from the start, but it was requisitioned in September 1939 as a satellite to RAF Fauld until the main depot there was completed. In July 1942 it was transferred to Llanberis to house recovered bombs following the collapse and thereafter saw intermittent use, mainly as a store for obsolete bombs, until 1946 when it was permanently closed.

Right: During the 1980s the quarry housed a small military museum. This photograph shows a few of the military vehicles abandoned there when the museum closed.

Below: The west entrance to the storage facility.

Below: The entrance to the smaller, subsidiary cavern to the east of the site.

FAULD

Fauld was the largest and most important of the RAF's underground bomb stores. Negotiations for the purchase of the worked-out Fauld gypsum mine from Peter Ford's plasterboard company were completed in June 1938. The disused workings consisted of approximately thirty-eight acres to the east and ten acres to the west of a large pillar of unworked gypsum, known as the Castle Hayes Pillar, left to support the weight of Castle Hayes Farm some ninety feet above. Initially the RAF acquired only the area east of the Castle Hayes Pillar, twenty-five acres of which would be used for high-explosive bomb storage with a further seven acres to the north east, separated by a fifty-foot thick barrier of compacted rubble, serving as a store for incendiaries. North of this area a further acre, separated by a 110-foot barrier, was used as a detonator store. Four new entrances were cut into the hillside on the eastern side, two to serve the HE store and one each for the detonator and incendiary stores. Two original entrances at the west end of the depot were retained as emergency exits. Conversion of the HE store was complete in the summer of 1938.

Increasing pressure for storage space led the RAF, in the spring of 1941, to acquire the remaining ten acres west of the Castle Hayes Pillar. It was expected that a gang of skilled workmen could convert the area, known as the 'New Mine', for the storage of 5,000 tons of bombs within six weeks. This proved a little optimistic, the New Mine actually becoming available in October 1942, by which time a relaxation of the RAF explosives regulations had increased its capacity to 10,000 tons.

The New Mine was separated from the original workings by the Castle Hayes Pillar and a 150-foot thick rubble barrier built to the south of it. To the extreme west a further fifty-foot barrier segregated the bomb store from Ford's underground access road. Two tunnels connected the old and new areas, one bored through the Castle Hayes Pillar, the other through the 150-foot barrier.

Left: A train load of 250lb GP bombs emerging from No.2 HE entrance at Fauld in the early years of the Second World War. The train is hauled by one of the depot's Ruston Hornsby diesel locomotives which were later replaced by electric shunters. The wagons are of a double-bogied wooden bodied type peculiar to Fauld.

Notice that several of the workmen are civilians rather than RAF personnel. In fact the majority of the men employed on ammunition movement and transhipment were civilians, the airmen being involved principally on ammunition maintenance work. Towards the end of the war these were supplemented by a large contingent of Italian prisoners of war who became co-operators following their country's withdrawal from the conflict.

Above: A train loaded with 500lb bombs near No.2 entrance to the bomb store. This is probably the same train as that shown emerging from the mine on page 253. In the background can be seen a similar train, consisting of distinctive Fauld-type double bogie wagons, emerging from No.1 entrance. Between the two main lines is a spur in which is parked a train of engineer's skip trucks, used for maintenance purposes.

Above: Stacking bombs in the 'New Mine'. Little engineering work other than the erection of wooden props in the storage bays and steel mining arches to support the roof above the extensive network of narrow-gauge railway lines was undertaken in this area. Similar conditions existed in much of the original area although in some places extensive concrete work, using corrugated steel shuttering, was put in place.

Above: Staff of the Ammunition Inspection Directorate examining 20lb high-explosive bombs in an underground inspection bay. It was a senior member of the Ammunition Inspection Directorate and two RAF airmen seconded to work for the Inspectorate whose actions were the immediate cause of the explosion that destroyed a large part of the depot in 1944.

Right: AID inspectors examining a stack of 500lb bombs in a storage bay. This photograph illustrates the density at which bombs were stored underground at Fauld. Most storage bays were illuminated by a single overhead light fitting and thus, given the manner in which the dark red gypsum absorbs light, conditions would have been fairly gloomy.

The Fauld disaster

At three minutes past eleven on the morning of Saturday, 27 November, 1944 a violent explosion rocked north Staffordshire. From the hillside above the bomb store a black rushing column of smoke, flame and debris – a quarter of a mile in diameter – tore upwards for three thousand feet to form a hideous mushroom cloud in the upper air. From within the mushroom cloud and from the pillar of fire below black objects were seen to spiral out, exploding in the air or falling to the ground before detonating. Minutes later this mass of debris – later estimated at two million tons of earth, rock and boulders and exploding bombs, along with the whole of Castle Hayes Farm – rained down upon the depot and surrounding farms and villages, causing extensive damage and loss of life. On the surface, Castle Hayes Farm and its occupants were vaporized, Hanbury Fields Farm was completely destroyed by falling debris and a large dam holding back millions of gallons of water for use in Peter Ford's plaster works was ruptured by the shock of the explosion. A deluge of mud and water engulfed the factory, killing many of the employees there, before pouring down the shaft into the mine trapping workers underground. Meanwhile, below ground in the gypsum mine the blast had destroyed the barrier between Peter Ford's workings and the bomb store, bringing down the roof and blocking roadways, making escape by that route impossible. Some men were eventually rescued via a vertical ventilation shaft but others died of asphyxiation by the toxic gases from the explosion. Nothing remained of the New Mine except a smoking crater more than a quarter of a mile in diameter and one hundred feet deep.

Everyone working there died instantly in the explosion, the result of the simultaneous detonation of at least 3,800 tons of high-

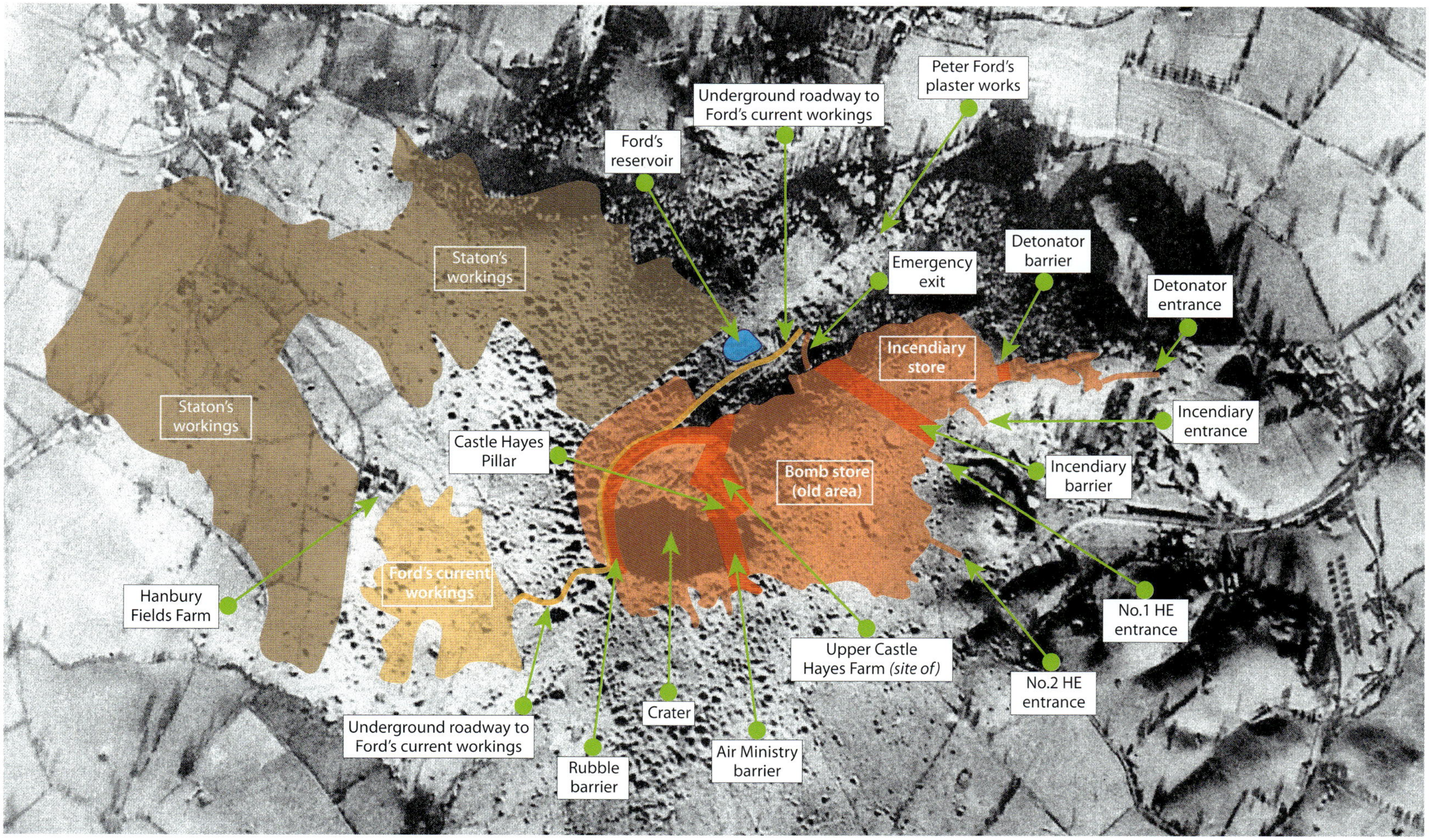

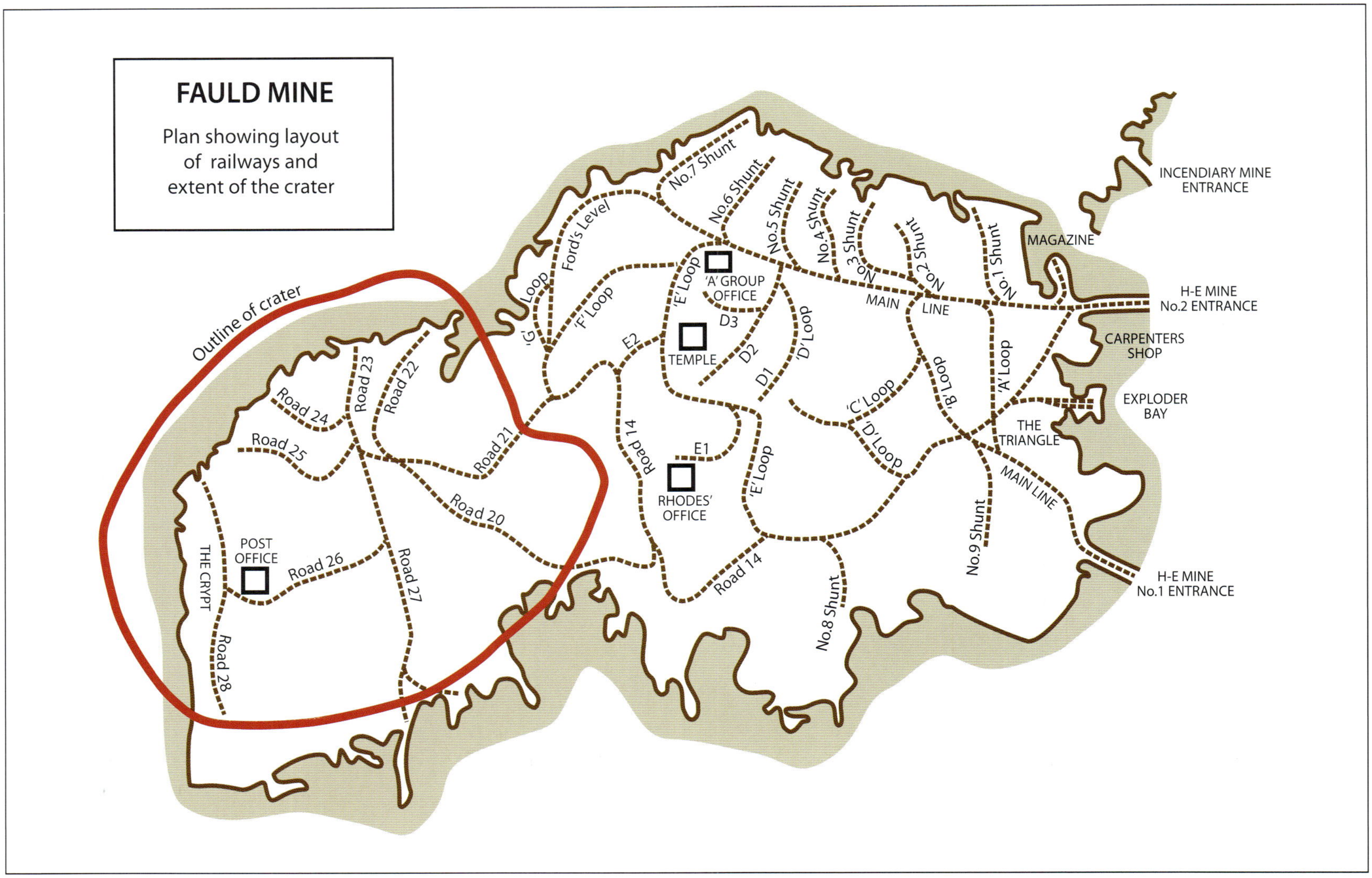

explosive bombs. In all, a total of seventy servicemen and civilians died in the blast.

A number of possible causes were investigated but most were immediately discounted. A Court of Enquiry concluded that the explosion was the result of careless handling of a 1,000lb bomb undergoing repair underground. Repairs were routinely undertaken at Fauld to bombs that had been jettisoned by returning aircraft and subsequently recovered. Strict procedures existed to ensure safety but, after five years of war, staff had become blasé in their handling of high-explosives. It was thought that an airman using a brass hammer and brass chisel to remove an exploder tube from a damaged bomb inadvertently caught a small grain of an explosive compound called 'CE' between the hammer and chisel. It had previously been proved that when CE was compressed between brass surfaces the transfer of energy created a chemical reaction that caused the CE to detonate. The airman concerned had previously been warned about the use of inappropriate tools on several occasions and had something of a reputation for 'cockiness' as regards safety procedures. Ultimately, however, blame fell (somewhat unfairly, in the opinion of many historians) upon the depot's temporary Chief Equipment Officer, Squadron Leader Anness. In his summing-up of the case, Air Marshall Sir Grahame Donald, stated that:

> *"My considered opinion, formed after interviewing Squadron Leader Anness and discussions with the AOC No.22 Group, is that he failed, as Acting Chief Equipment Officer of No.21 MU (Fauld), to exercise the control required by an officer of his seniority in an explosives unit, since he was not sufficiently aware of the work being undertaken in the unit."*

Above: Although bombs in the 'old' mine did not explode, the area was severely damaged by blast. Here we see a train of RAF small-arms ammunition blown out of No.1 entrance into the cutting beyond.

Above: 250lb HE bombs and boxed 10lb HE bombs buried under a collapsed area of the old mine.
Below: 250lb bombs in the innermost end of the old mine engulfed by debris from the crater.

Above and below: Large numbers of 250lb high-exp
lower picture must weigh at least five tons and has

ıbs trapped beneath fallen rock. The large block in the
ıllen fifteen or twenty feet.

Above: A narrow-gauge truck damaged by a roof fall caused by the explosion. In the background can be seen a stack of 250lb bombs and, behind the standing figure, 303 rifle ammunition in boxes.
Below: A scene near the Castle Hayes Pillar showing boxes of small-arms ammunition blown apart and scattered along the railway line by the force of the blast.

Above: A panoramic image of Hanbury Fields Farm, completely destroyed by falling debris from the explosion. The buildings were subsequently demolished and the site cleared and levelled.

Left: The remains of the Cock Inn at Hanbury, since rebuilt. Two wings were completely destroyed and what remained was no more than a crumbling shell.

Opposite: Peter Ford's plaster works the day after the disaster. This was a triple tragedy: first blown apart by the blast, the works were then crushed by falling debris from the crater before, seconds later, it was engulfed by mud and water to a depth of up to thirty feet, released when a dam in the valley above was destroyed by the shock wave of the explosion. Many workers lost their lives here, their bodies could not be recovered for several weeks.

Above: Reconstruction under way near the Ford's Level emergency exit. Blast damage in this area was particularly severe due to its proximity to the open tunnel that pierced the Castle Hayes Pillar. Extensive use of brickwork and heavy rolled steel joists was made in this section of the mine, making it very different in character from the rest of the depot.

Above: Several tons of rock loosened by the explosion are propped precariously by timber beams above two 4,000lb HE bombs. The boxes in the background contain American 23lb M72 fragmentation bombs. Over two million of these bombs were supplied to the RAF under the Lend-Lease agreement and staff at Fauld considered them the most unstable of all aircraft bombs in store there.

Although the New Mine was completely destroyed in the explosion, the base of the Castle Hayes Pillar withstood most of the blast, saving much of the old mine from total destruction. The structure of the entire depot was badly shaken, however, and there were widespread roof falls as well as severe disruption caused by the ferocious blast-wave that burst through the roadways connecting the old and new workings, but there was no sympathetic detonation of bombs.

Once the dead were recovered and the thousands of bombs and other items of ordnance trapped within the old mine had been cleared and made safe, a detailed survey of the surviving structure was made. It was decided that of the 50,000 square yards of the old mine, 15,000 square yards were irreparable and should be abandoned but the rest could be reconstructed and brought back into use. By the end of 1945 most of the repairs were complete and the depot reopened and remained in service with the RAF for a further twenty years.

Opposite: Major roof repairs under way at the bottom end of the depot. Wooden props are being used to support the roof before permanent reinforcements are erected. In the background can be seen shuttering in place for new concrete support walls and arches.

Above: This rather spectacular view shows the junction of the main line and 'B' Loop with branches to 'C' Loop and No.3 Shunt in the distance. The vaulted concrete construction lends a vaguely ecclesiastical air to the scene.

Above: A panoramic view of the 'Triangle'. The left-hand railway track heads towards No.1 Entrance; the centre track is No.14 Road, heading west towards the crater with a branch north to 'D' Loop; the right-hand rail is 'A' Loop, heading north to join the main line from No.2 Entrance. The branch to the right, off of 'A' Loop, is a short spur leading into what was, before the explosion, the Exploder Bay, and after reconstruction, the AID inspection chamber.

Left: Near the junction of 'E' Loop and No.14 Road.

Opposite: The broad expanse of 'E' Loop looking north from No.14 Road.

Above: Although of little use to give protection from an explosion within the depot, this extraordinary, vertical blast door – similar in design to a typical up-and-over garage door but weighing several tons – would be effective against blast from bombs dropped near the entrance to No.2 Tunnel. The door is operated by an electric motor and a vast counterweight in the small room to the right of the door. The blast door was interlocked with a pair of gates normally locked across the entrance tunnel, and could be raised or lowered by means of push buttons on either side.

Above: A superb example of the double bogie, eight-wheeled bomb trucks of the type specially designed for use at Fauld. Most of the wartime examples had wooden superstructures but this one, built by Hudson in 1955, is of all-steel construction.

Left: Most of the railway wagons used at Fauld were unique to the depot. This photograph shows a rather decayed example of the four-wheeled bomb truck. These trucks were supplied by R Hudson Ltd and had extended main frames allowing space for a brakeman to operate the brake wheel.

Above: 'A' Group offices to the left with 'E' Loop disappearing into the darkness and 'F' Loop branching off towards the crater and the emergency exit. Civilian storeman J C Salt was in the office when the explosion occurred. In his evidence to the Court of Enquiry Salt said:

"When the first explosion occurred the lights did not go out, I ran to the door to see which direction the explosion came from, looked down Ford's level then down 6 shunt, then up the main line, and then went back to my office to fetch my torch. I had just entered my office when the second explosion occurred and blew the lights out. It blew me out of my office along with storeman Cresswell and Airman Still."

Above: An example of the reconstruction undertaken in 1945 near the emergency exit in the area of the old workings most severely damaged by blast. The extensive use of red brick, noted above, and the employment of very large cross-section girders as roof supports, is untypical of the rest of the depot.

Above: The junction of No.21 Road, which has emerged from the crater area behind the camera, and No.14 Road where it joins Ford's Level. The roof has collapsed onto the track at this point. Splintered wooden props, blown down by the blast, can be seen in the right foreground.

Left: The blocked entrance to the tunnel through the Castle Hayes Pillar, beneath the rim of the crater. On 27 November 1944 the blast from the explosion roared through this tunnel, wreaking havoc in the old mine. Scorch marks from the fireball can be seen on the walls and ceiling around the tunnel entrance; the unburned surfaces are where slabs of loosened rock have subsequently fallen away.

Right: Near the No.21 Road tunnel through the Castle Hayes Pillar, these rolled steel mining arches have been bent over by the force of the blast. The boulders in the foreground have fallen from the roof.

Above: Pre-disaster concrete reinforcements near the Air Ministry barrier near the base of the crater. Notice how the four-foot-thick concrete wall on the left has been split by the force of the explosion. Through the arch in the centre of the picture mud has oozed in from the crater. Just visible, close to the near-end right-hand wall of the arch, is the tail cap of a 500lb bomb buried in the mud.

Chapter 6

VAULTS & REPOSITORIES

WESTWOOD QUARRY

Following the collapse of the Country House scheme for the safe storage of art treasures, a search was immediately started by Sir Eric Maclagan of the Victoria & Albert Museum and Sir John Fosdyke of the British Museum for suitable underground repositories for the contents of their museums. At first it was thought that all the suitable underground sites had already been allotted to other government departments, but, then it was discovered that space might be available at Westwood Quarry, part of which was being developed as a factory for Royal Enfield. Further accommodation was found in the Manod slate quarries deep below the desolate, mist-enshrouded mountains north of Ffestiniog. Hidden at the end of a four-mile mountain track, Manod was one of the most dramatic government sites in Britain.
On 6 March, 1941, Maclagan and Fosdyke met Mr Bennitt from the Ministry of Works and Buildings, to discuss the difficulties of preparing an area of Westwood Quarry as a museum repository. It was agreed that an isolated 25,000 square foot heading would be sufficient to meet the needs of both museums, and the MoWB was confident that they could satisfactorily air-condition the area. At that time the best tapestries and carpets from the V&A were stored in the long gallery of Montacute House, but conditions there were far from ideal, the roof let in water and the carpets were becoming badly affected with mildew.

The section of quarry available to the museums sloped markedly and it was decided that the eastern half, which was allocated to the V&A, should be terraced to give a series of horizontal stacking areas upon which large items could be stacked. Other than a number of large sculptures, and the Elgin Marbles (which spent the war years below central London in the disused Aldwych tube tunnel), most of the British Museum artefacts were securely boxed and could be easily shelved. There was only one entrance to the repository, and this was sealed by a lobby secured by two strong-room doors transferred from Bloomsbury. Conversion work started in June, 1941, and was completed within six months.

When cleared the area was found to have a very regular pillar formation which required little reinforcement; the main building task being the treatment of the whole exposed stone surface with a special waterproof sealing compound. It was realized from the outset that very careful control over temperature and humidity was required, and a contract to supply air-conditioning plant was awarded to the Norris Warming Company. The installed equipment was very sophisticated and very extensive, requiring a plant room almost as large as the repository. Humidity recorders continually monitored atmospheric conditions in the repository, but adjustment of the plant was performed manually and required great vigilance from the attendants. Men were employed whose sole job was constantly to inspect the walls and floor of the storage chambers checking for damp areas, which were treated with 'Stet', a proprietary damp-proofing compound.

There was a delay in delivery of the air-conditioning machinery, which was not installed until 30 October, three days before the great strong-room doors were finally put in place. By 10 November the plant was up and running but humidity was far from under control, for if the plant was stopped for just a few minutes the humidity in the repository rose immediately to over 90%. It took several months for the quarry fabric to dry out adequately and it was not until 24 February, 1942, that the inward movement of artefacts could begin.

The museum trustees received requests for the safe-keeping of items of outstanding importance from numerous institutions and private individuals, and the quarry soon became a fabulous national treasure-house. Apart from artefacts from Bloomsbury and Kensington, Westwood also held collections from the Bodleian Library, the Imperial War Museum and the Free French Museum of National Antiquities. Among the individual items to spend the war years in Wiltshire were the Rubens Ceiling from the Whitehall banqueting hall, the Charles I statue from Whitehall, the C16th Ardabil Carpet from the V&A and the Wright Brothers' airplane 'Flyer' or 'Kittyhawk', which had been on loan to the Science Museum at the outbreak of war.

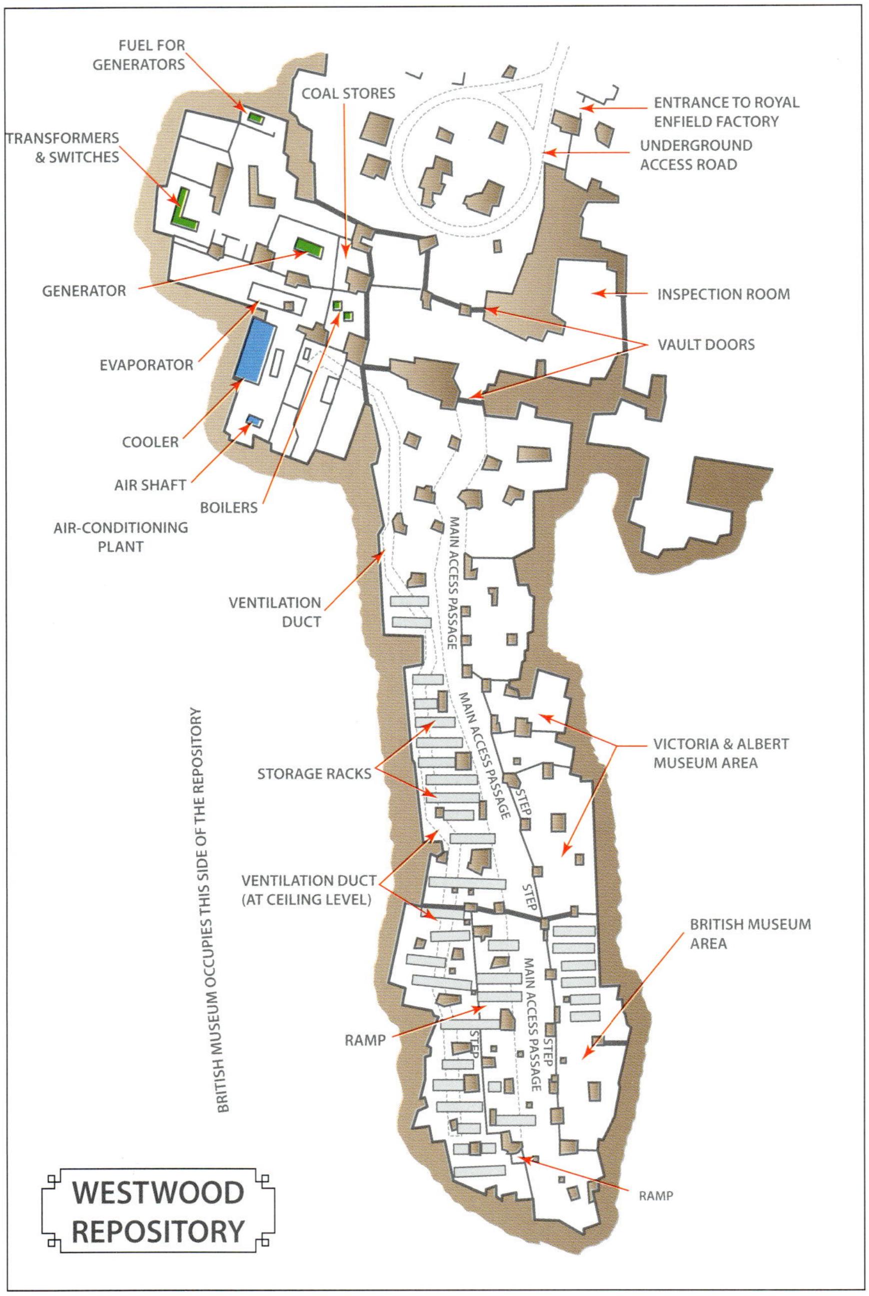

Above right: Part of the V&A's extensive collection of watercolours arriving at Westwood Quarry in March 1942, having been stored under increasingly unsatisfactory conditions at Montacute House since September 1939. The pictures, packed in sealed, waterproof boxes are being transferred onto small electric trucks for transportation into the underground repository.

Below right: The first shipment of V&A artefacts leaving the quarry for return to Kensington in the autumn of 1945.

Above: A view along the central access road in the Westwood Quarry repository shortly after the first artefacts from the British Museum and the V&A had begun to arrive. The gentleman in the foreground is checking the readings on a thermo-hygrograph, an instrument that maintained a continuous record of temperature and humidity variations within the storage areas. The left-hand side of this roadway was allocated to the V&A, and the way in which it has been terraced to accommodate large items of furniture from their collections is clearly visible.

Left: Medieval terracotta panels from the Victoria & Albert Museum stacked against the rough stone walls of the quarry.

Above left: Part of the V&A collection of medieval tapestries and carpets stored in the Westwood repository. Textiles of these types were sewn into tubular canvas bags and laid on mesh or slatted wood pallets raised a few inches from the ground to allow the free circulation of air. Amongst the items stored at Westwood is the mid-sixteenth century Ardabil Carpet – the world's oldest surviving carpet. Measuring approximately thirty-five feet by eighteen feet, it is one of a pair which arrived in London in 1893 in absolutely terrible condition. A public appeal raised sufficient funds to restore one of the carpets using fragments of the second carpet to affect the repairs. The remaining fragments eventually found their way to the Los Angeles County Museum of Art.

Below left: V&A furniture stacked against the wall with little protective packing. In the foreground is a thermo-hygrograph used to monitor atmospheric conditions in the repository.

Above: Miscellaneous items from the British Museum stacked in packing cases underground at Westwood. The boxes to the left of this picture, marked 'G&R' are from the Greek and Roman Department, those on the right marked 'ETH' are from the Ethnographic collection.

Above right: Stacked against a pillar in the left mid-ground are a few of the pictures from the National Portrait Gallery, which, formerly stored at Mentmore House, eventually found their way to Westwood. The crates in the foreground contain large items of statuary from the Greek and Roman department of the British Museum.

Below right: Shortly after the artefacts arrived at Westwood it was discovered that an infestation of moths had made their home amongst the textiles in the ethnographic collection. To counter this, a special chamber was put aside for them to be regularly inspected and given a monthly insecticidal blast of DDT. Health and safety considerations seem to have carried rather less weight in the 1940s.

Above: This view was taken in the main access tunnel at Westwood in August 1945, near the point where the underground roadway diverges to the right into the museum repository and to the left into the Royal Enfield factory. Loaded aboard the small electric truck are boxes of exhibits from the V&A being driven out to a waiting lorry for return to London. On the right-hand side of the corridor are a few of the many thousands of motorcycles that the Royal Enfield Company agreed to buy back from the War Office at the end of hostilities. Some had remained unused, packed in grease, at War Office stores in Britain and abroad while others had spent the war years being constantly ranted around the deserts of North Africa. All were eventually refurbished, resprayed in civilian colours and sold as new.

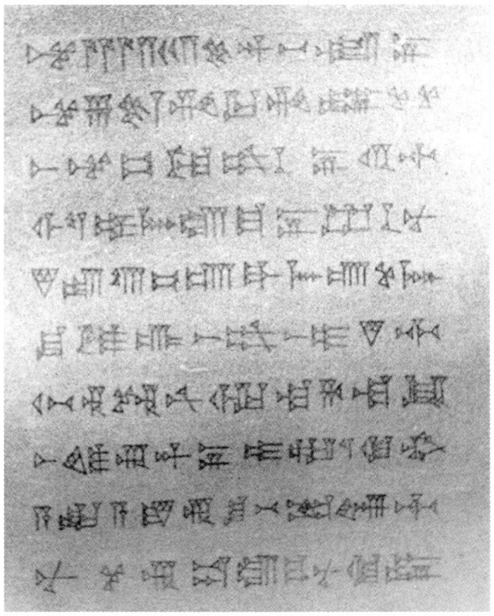

Left: Westwood was under the charge of J C Gadd, the Keeper of Egyptian and Assyrian Antiquities at the British Museum and in a moment of leisure he doodled some graffiti on the wall of his office. Being an expert in Assyrian history, he doodled not in English but in Cuneiform script, a system of writing dating back to the Sumerian civilization of the third century BC. A translation of Gadd's text is shown below.

"In the year of our Lord 1942
The sixth year of George, King of all lands,
In that year everything precious,
The works of all the craftsmen
Which from palaces and temples
Were sent out, in order that by fire
Or attack by an evil enemy they might not be lost,
Into this cave under the earth
A place of security, an abode of peace,
We brought them down and set them."

Above: Because it was imperative that the air-conditioning plant at Westwood should run without interruption, (a stoppage of just twenty minutes, it was said, might allow humidity levels to rise sufficiently to cause irreparable damage to the most delicate artefacts), it was necessary to install a standby generator plant. Unfortunately, in 1942 it was impossible to purchase new equipment so, instead, a very old Lister-Petter set was acquired from the Exe Valley Electricity Company of Dulverton in Devon. When delivered it was found that the diesel engine was completely worn out and that virtually every moving part required renewal. Spares were difficult to find and it was a year before the machine was serviceable. Then, when the engine was first started on test, the cylinder heads ruptured and a large brick exhaust chamber exploded causing widespread damage in the powerhouse.

The blame was attributed to workmen, in a hurry to complete construction, blocking the exhaust chamber with old cement sacks and brick debris. Following the explosion the underground generator was abandoned and emergency power was taken from a mobile searchlight generator, borrowed from Anti-Aircraft Command, parked at the top of a ventilation shaft and connected to the switchboard by trailing leads down the shaft.

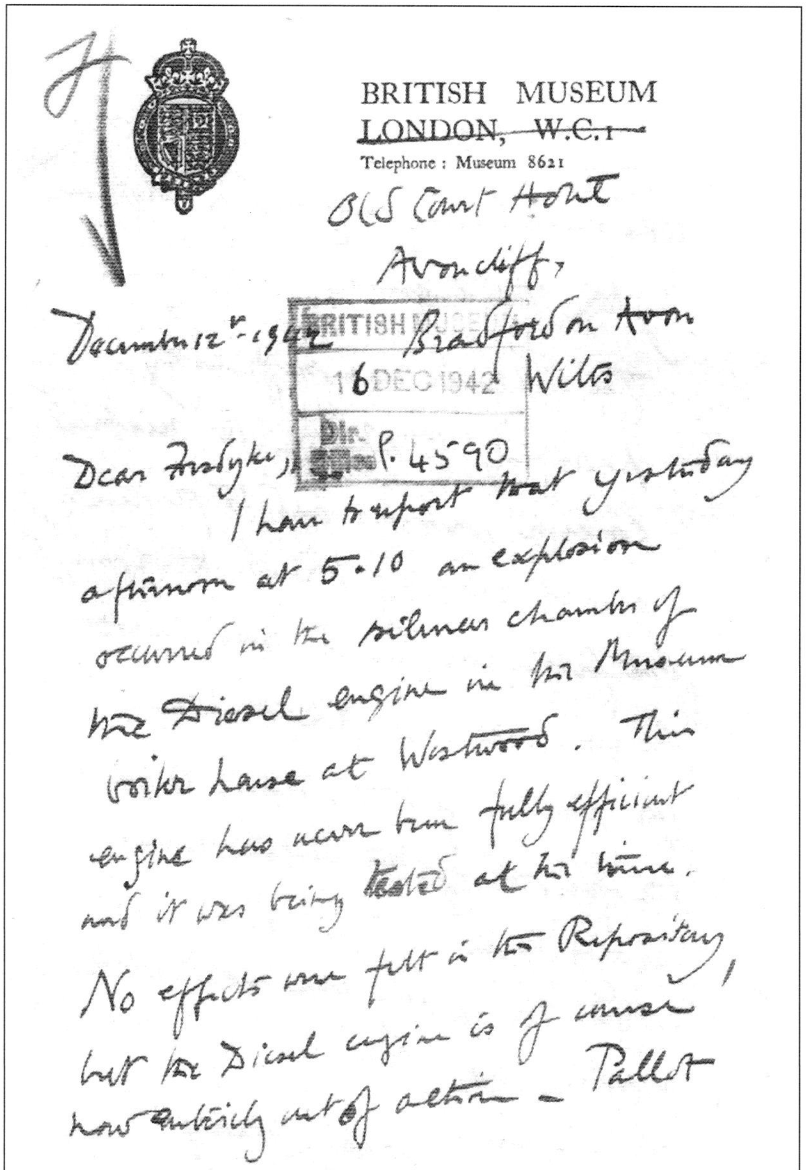

BRITISH MUSEUM
~~LONDON, W.C.1~~
Telephone: Museum 8621

Old Court House
Avoncliff,
Bradford on Avon
Wilts

December 12th 1942

BRITISH MUSEUM
16 DEC 1942
Dir.
P. 4590

Dear Forsdyke,
I have to report that yesterday afternoon at 5.10 an explosion occurred in the silencer chamber of the Diesel engine in the Museum boiler house at Westwood. This engine has never been fully efficient and it was being tested at the time.
No effects were felt in the Repository, but the Diesel engine is of course now entirely out of action – Pallot

December 12th 1942
Dear Forsdyke,
I have to report that yesterday afternoon at 5:10 an explosion occurred in the silencer chamber of the diesel engine in the museum boiler house at Westwood. This engine has never been fully efficient and it was being tested at the time. No effects were felt in the Repository but the diesel engine is of course now entirely out of action. - Pallot

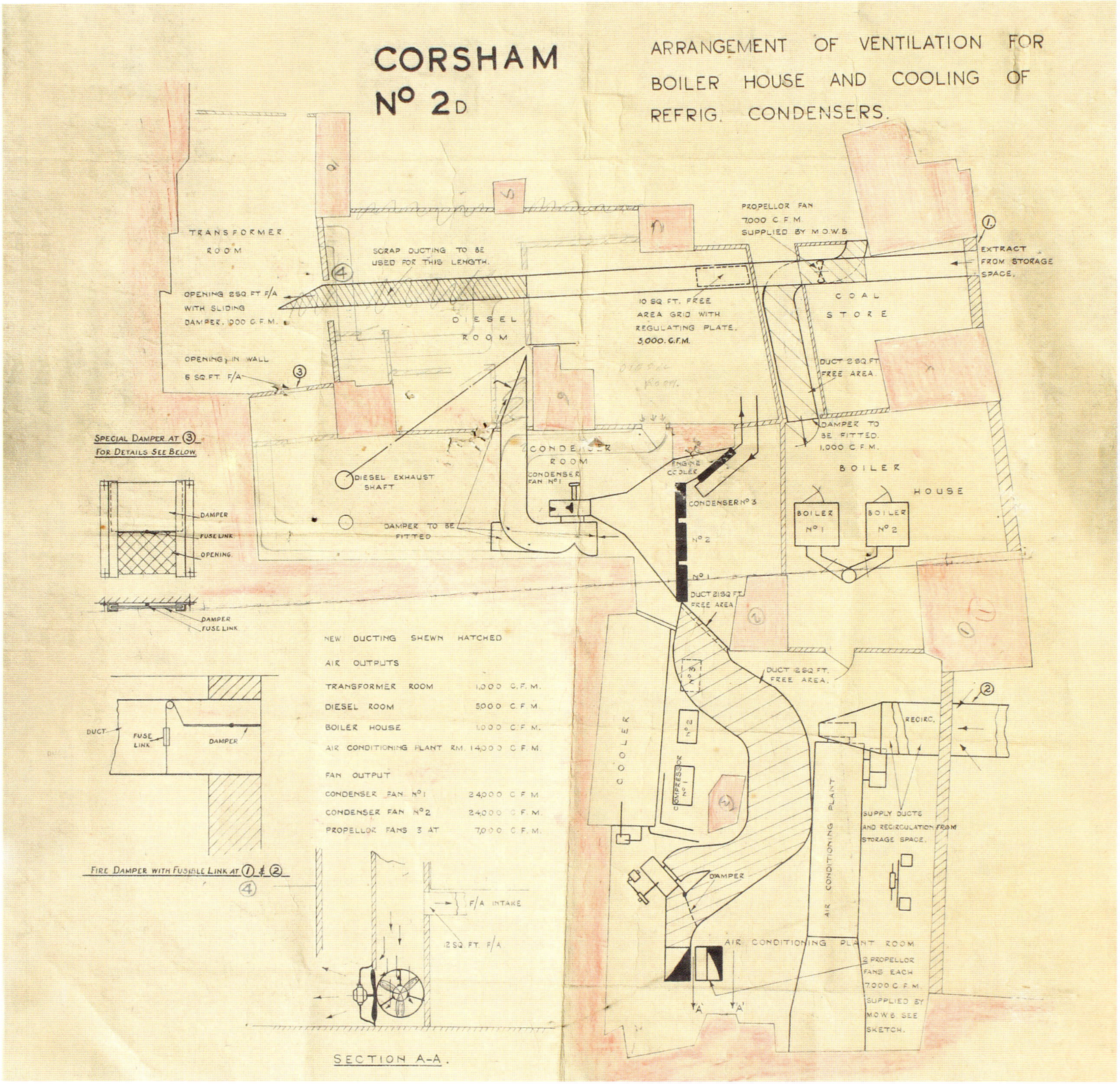
CORSHAM
Nº 2D
ARRANGEMENT OF VENTILATION FOR BOILER HOUSE AND COOLING OF REFRIG. CONDENSERS.
TRANSFORMER ROOM
SCRAP DUCTING TO BE USED FOR THIS LENGTH.
PROPELLOR FAN 7000 C.F.M. SUPPLIED BY M.O.W.B.
EXTRACT FROM STORAGE SPACE.
OPENING 2SQ.FT F/A WITH SLIDING DAMPER. 1000 C.F.M.
DIESEL ROOM
10 SQ. FT. FREE AREA GRID WITH REGULATING PLATE. 5000. C.F.M.
COAL STORE
OPENING IN WALL 6 SQ.FT. F/A
DUCT 2 SQ.FT FREE AREA.
DAMPER TO BE FITTED. 1,000 C.F.M.
SPECIAL DAMPER AT ③ FOR DETAILS SEE BELOW
CONDENSER ROOM
CONDENSER FAN Nº1
ENGINE COOLER
BOILER HOUSE
DIESEL EXHAUST SHAFT
CONDENSER Nº3
Nº2
Nº1
BOILER Nº1
BOILER Nº2
DAMPER
FUSE LINK
OPENING
DAMPER TO BE FITTED
DUCT 2 SQ.FT. FREE AREA
NEW DUCTING SHEWN HATCHED
AIR OUTPUTS
TRANSFORMER ROOM 1,000 C.F.M.
DIESEL ROOM 5000 C.F.M.
BOILER HOUSE 1,000 C.F.M.
AIR CONDITIONING PLANT RM. 14,000 C.F.M.
FAN OUTPUT
CONDENSER FAN Nº1 24,000 C.F.M.
CONDENSER FAN Nº2 24,000 C.F.M.
PROPELLOR FANS 3 AT 7,000 C.F.M.
DUCT 12 SQ.FT. FREE AREA.
DUCT
FUSE LINK
DAMPER
RECIRC.
COOLER
COMPRESSOR Nº1
AIR CONDITIONING PLANT
SUPPLY DUCTS AND RECIRCULATION FROM STORAGE SPACE.
FIRE DAMPER WITH FUSIBLE LINK AT ① & ②
F/A INTAKE
12 SQ. FT. F/A
DAMPER
AIR CONDITIONING PLANT ROOM
2 PROPELLOR FANS EACH 7,000 C.F.M. SUPPLIED BY M.O.W.B. SEE SKETCH.
SECTION A-A.

Above: The bomb-proof top of the British Museum airshaft at Westwood, photographed in 1974.

Above right: In the early 1990s much of the surface land at Westwood was redeveloped for housing. Unfortunately for the developers it was discovered that Hanson Minerals Ltd, the new owner of the underground workings, retained rights over the airshaft, so by way of compromise the top of the shaft was disguised as this 'gazebo' attached to the side of one of the houses.

Left: The fan plenum chamber in the ventilation plant , with the main air-conditioning apparatus in the background. This is contained within the lower right-hand section of the plan opposite.

Opposite: The original engineer's layout plan for the Westwood air-conditioning system.

Above: Although, in 1945, the trustees of the various museums and galleries wanted to return their exhibits to London in order to return to peacetime normality as soon as possible, a certain amount of material remained in store at Westwood until the mid-1950s due, principally, to the fact that some of the British Museum's galleries had been badly damaged by German bombs. During the decade following the end of the Second World War relations with the Soviet Union became increasingly frosty and the possibility of an atomic war was a cause of real fear. In recognition of this risk the government decided that Westwood Quarry should be retained indefinitely and that its facilities should be upgraded. As part of this process a new Crossley diesel generator set was installed in the repository powerhouse in the late 1950s. The quarry was finally released from government control around 1982.

Above right: The reserve fuel tank for the standby generator.

Right: The generator switchgear and control panel.

Above left: The outer vault door of the museum repository. Because a wartime steel allocation could not be obtained for the construction of purpose-built security doors at Westwood, it was necessary to transport two sets of Victorian strong-room doors from the basement of the British Museum in Bloomsbury down to Wiltshire as a makeshift alternative.

Above right: Coal-fired boilers in the museum air-conditioning plant.

Left: Switchgear in the museum sub-station. Included amongst this equipment are interlocked switches that would allow the museum's diesel generator to power the Royal Enfield factory or, conversely, for the factory sub-stations to provide power to the repository should the supply there fail.

MANOD

At the start of the war most of the National Gallery collection was evacuated to the relative safety of North Wales, many of the largest and most valuable pictures finding refuge at Penrhyn Castle. By the Spring of 1940 Lord Penrhyn, who was universally loathed by all the National Gallery staff that accompanied the pictures to the castle, was making the gallery's presence at the castle untenable. Writing to Kenneth Clarke, his director in London, Martin Davies, the National Gallery's supervisor in North Wales wrote:

> *"For your most secret ear: One of our troubles at Penrhyn is that the owner is celebrating the war by being fairly constantly drunk. He stumbled with a dog into the Dining Room [where 200 pictures were stored] a few days ago; this will not happen again. Yesterday he smashed up his car, and, I believe, himself a little, so perhaps the problem has solved itself for the moment."*

These problems, coupled with the risk of aerial bombing following the Fall of France, led Brigadier Temple-Richards of HM Office of Works Defence Architects' Department to initiate a search for alternative underground storage nearby. A slate quarry at Manod was subsequently acquired and steps taken to adapt it to accept the pictures from Penrhyn. Work was scheduled for completion by Christmas, 1940, but was impeded by winter weather and completion was not expected before February, 1941. Further delays were experienced during construction of the four-mile approach road, due to the low height of a railway bridge near the village of Ffestiniog. The railway company agreed to lower the road below the bridge, a task which was expected to involve simply cutting away a certain amount of solid rock. They discovered, however, that the bridge was founded on compressed shale and deep concrete footings were thus required to support the abutments. As a result of all the delays it was impossible to move the pictures out of Penrhyn Castle and the other country houses in North Wales until 18 August, 1941.

Below: One of a fleet of railway-owned lorries on the four-mile private road, heading up through the Snowdon mountains to Manod Quarry, loaded with pictures from the National Gallery.

Left: Van Dyck's 'Charles I on Horseback', stuck under the railway bridge at Ffestiniog en route for Manod Quarry. Three attempts were required before the picture – at thirteen-foot six inches high the largest in the National Gallery collection and, even without its frame, weighing over half-a-ton – could be safely transported under the arch.

Below left: A GWR container lorry loaded with pictures approaching the quarry entrance.

Below: Inside the main entrance tunnel. Headroom in the tunnel was increased to allow vehicles of this size to traverse its entire quarter-mile length right up to a transit shed deep inside the quarry. The brick building on the left of this photograph is the quarry's emergency generating station.

Above: Transferring pictures between buildings on the narrow-gauge railway system. One of the lightly constructed storage buildings can be seen in the background.

Left: Unloading a lorry container in the reception building. There are approximately forty paintings of medium size jostling for space in this container and their value today would probably amount to many tens of millions of pounds.

Below: Manoeuvring a loaded 'dark-box' on the railway behind storage chamber No.3.

Chambers within the quarry were much too large (some were in excess of 100 feet high) and far too wet for the storage of pictures, so a series of lightweight, airtight and moisture-proof brick storage sheds were built within the chambers. All the buildings were connected by a narrow-gauge railway system and each building was fitted with double air-lock doors. One of these brick structures was adapted as a reception building and constructed so that laden lorries could enter it through an air-lock. Inside the sealed reception building pictures were loaded into air-tight packing cases or 'dark-boxes' and placed on railway wagons for transfer to their designated storage building.

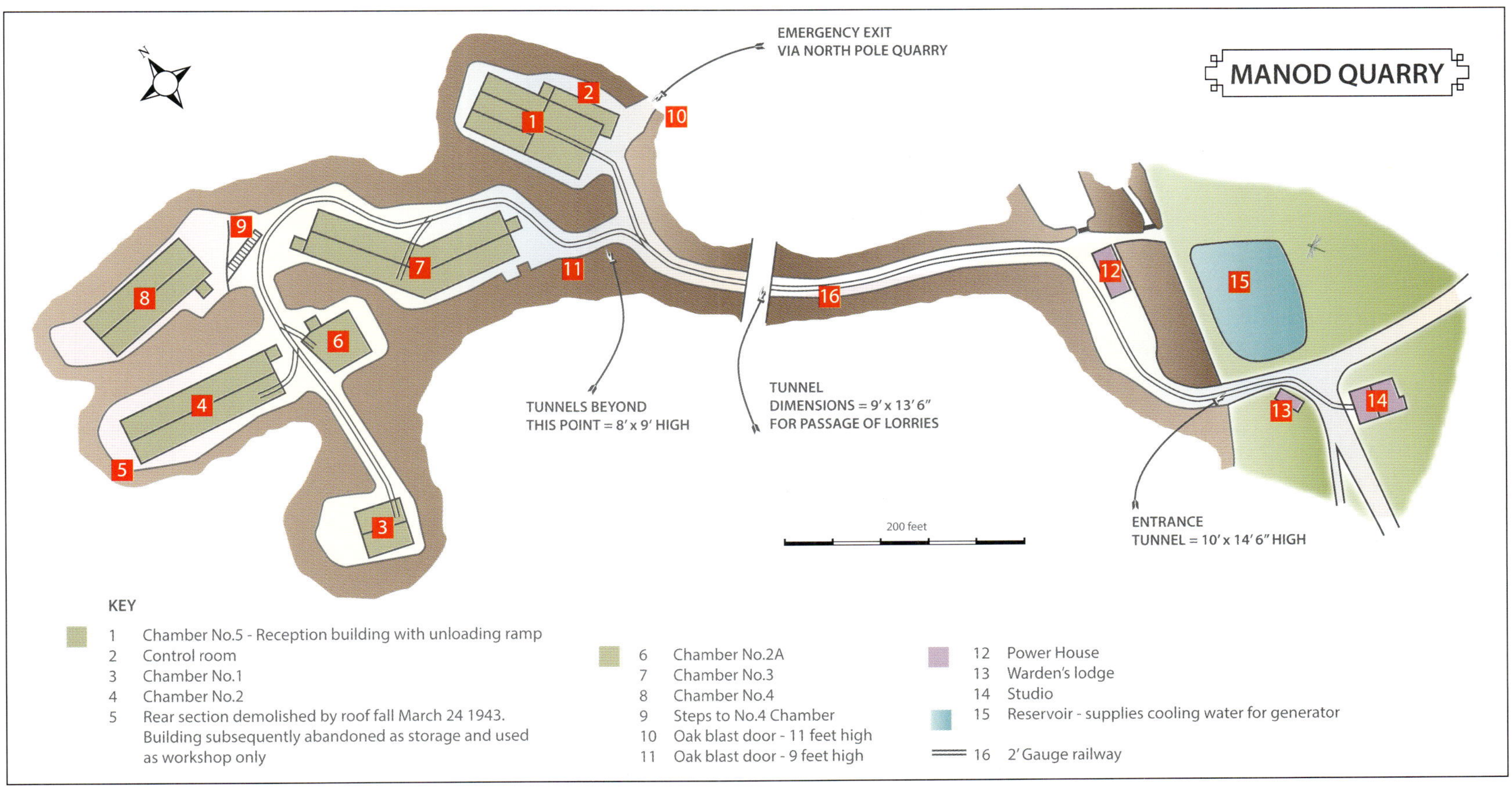

Below: Chamber No.3 in 1986, stripped of all salvageable material after the quarry reverted to it previous owner.

Below: The gated entrance to the quarry in 1986 when the entrance tunnel was being used as an explosives store by a nearby slate quarrying company.

Above: Bradley Wyatt making preparations, with ropes and a wire ladder, for the first attempt to gain access to the quarry for forty-six years. The hurricane lamp is to test that there is sufficient oxygen underground.

Above: Inside the concrete cap, a wire ladder is suspended down the eighty-foot vertical shaft through a hole in the security grille. The lights are from Bradley's twin headlamps as he descends the ladder.

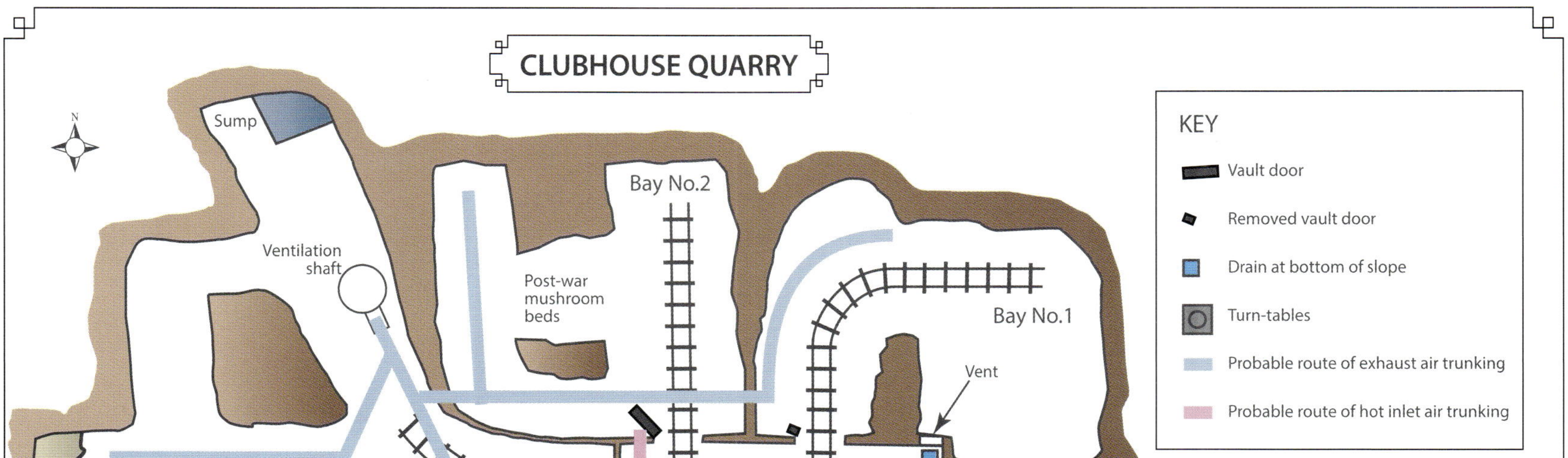

CLUBHOUSE QUARRY

Shortly before the first edition of this book was published in 2010 evidence of the continued existence of a small quarry long thought to have been lost below a residential development at Neston near Corsham, was discovered. For decades it was rumoured that Clubhouse Quarry, a small and apparently unsuccessful quarry which had started work in the years immediately preceding the First World War and ceased operation in the inter-war years, had been used by the De La Rue printing company to store bank-notes it had printed under contract with a number of mid European and eastern European countries. Following the declaration of war in September 1939 the company had been unable to deliver these bank-notes due the German occupation of those countries, but felt itself honour-bound to ensure their safe keeping.

Documentary research both at the National Archives and De La Rue's company archives substantiated these rumours. By a complex series of legal agreements the mine had been leased from the Neston Estate in March 1943 by the Bath & Portland Stone Company who then immediately sub-let it to the Ministry of Works who did a certain amount of conversion work before itself leasing the quarry to De La Rue as a secure storage facility. Thereafter, the story became somewhat murky. The exact date of De La Rue's departure is unknown but at some time soon after the war the quarry was offered to a Corsham quarryman, Bert Hiscocks. But the offer was declined because in his opinion it could not be worked profitably due to the thinness of the beds of stone. It was thought that for a brief period the quarry was used on a very small scale for mushroom growing although there was little evidence to support this. By 1963 all trace of the quarry was apparently lost when the shaft was infilled and a small estate of council houses built above it.

Since that time a degree of mystery has enshrouded the site. Many suggested that it had been abandoned by De La Rue and the shaft sealed with the money, which after the war was practically worthless, entombed within. Another local legend claimed that the quarry was prone to flooding and that the money had long ago turned to sodden pulp.

Days before the first edition of this book went to press a small, conical, very heavily bomb-proofed structure was discovered in an overgrown corner of a garden in Neston. Preliminary investigations and research indicated that this must be the fortified cap above the ventilation shaft for Clubhouse Quarry which, unlike the main entrance shaft, appeared not to have been infilled. Access via the tiny ventilation apertures did not seem feasible, but it was possible to position a camera above the shaft and the resultant images indicated that, indeed, the quarry appeared to be flooded. A constant stream of water poured from a rift on the side of the shaft and at the bottom water seemed to have risen to roof level. At much the same time it was discovered that a Corsham quarryman, Jack Dancey, had recorded in his memoirs that shortly after the war he had helped remove the money from Clubhouse. Jack, who had been born in 1897, worked at Hartham Park Quarry before and after the war, before moving finally to Monks Park Quarry. During the war he had been employed as an ammunition handler at the underground Royal Navy store at Pickwick, helping out at Brocklease and Elm Park quarries when required. At some date which, unfortunately, he does not specify, he was employed removing the money from Clubhouse by the Bath & Portland Stone Company which had been contracted to do the work on behalf of the Ministry of Works.

These discoveries took the edge off of the intrigue surrounding Clubhouse Quarry, but in July 2014, just a week before the second edition of this book was due to go to press, access was gained to the quarry under extraordinarily difficult conditions and the myths were finally laid to rest. As the photographs that follow will show, the quarry was not flooded but had, indeed, survived in remarkably good condition. Huge vault doors divide the quarry into three storage chambers each served by a narrow-gauge railway. There are substantial remains of a fairly complex air handling system and arrangements to dispose of the influx of seepage water from the airshaft. Of the money once stored there, there is no trace.

Below: The inconspicuous airshaft for Clubhouse Quarry, discovered buried in undergrowth in the corner of a Neston garden in September 2010.

Above: Initially, the rumour that the quarry was prone to flooding appeared to be substantiated when access was gained via the airshaft, as this photograph illustrates. Rather unexpectedly, the bottom of the shaft terminated in a large, conical-bottomed iron tank bolted to the ceiling with a four-inch pipe outlet at the bottom and a slightly larger circular duct near the roof on the side. This was part of a system designed to drain the copious amount of seepage water that poured from a spring half-way up the air-shaft: water collected in the tank and drained via the pipework into a sump, fitted with a pump, at the innermost end of the heading

Above left & right: Close-up views of the tank, the presence of which came as a surprise to our explorers, who first found themselves knee-deep in water, then had to wriggle through a narrow tube only to find themselves emerging at ceiling height with a twelve-foot drop to quarry floor level.

Left: The primary slope shaft entrance, securely blocked near the top by a steel door. The upper section above the door is filled with rubble and has a house built on top of it.

Above: A panoramic view of the quarry showing, from left to right, the door to No.3 Bay, the entrance to No.2 Bay, then No.1 Bay and the bottom of the slope shaft. Notice the louvres above the doors which once were connected to overhead ventilation trunking.

Left: To the left is the baseplate of a railway turntable. Originally there were turntables at the entrances to Bays 1 and 2. The one at No.1 Bay was removed to Monks Park Quarry by the Bath & Portland Stone Company in the 1950s. The bay on the right was the location of the quarry's heating and ventilating plant.

Right: A long view of No.3 Bay with the air shaft passage to the left in the middle distance.

Above: One of three massive Chubb vault doors used to seal each of the storage bays. The small doors within the main doors are locked with a key; once opened they give access to a lever on the inside which releases the bolts on the main door.

Above left: A view inside No.2 Bay which was used briefly in the early 1950s for mushroom cultivation.

Above right: The ruined remains of a heavy-duty narrow-gauge truck which it is supposed was used to transport heavy strong-boxes full of banknotes.

Left: The main access roadway through No.1 Bay. Like all the other areas of the quarry, this has survived in remarkably good condition with its railway track intact. Most of the plant, including the heating and ventilation equipment, drainage pumps and overhead trunking, however, and much of the electrical system has been removed for scrap. The louvred grille in the left-hand wall seems to have been an inlet for heated air from the lobby area.

Chapter 7

PORTLAND COMMAND BUNKER

PORTLAND COMMAND BUNKER

Following its development in the last quarter of the nineteenth century, Portland became the largest deep-water harbour in Europe. From the outset it was of pivotal strategic importance to the Royal Navy, but during the Second World War, after the fall of France, its vulnerability to enemy air attack became apparent. To mitigate this threat, during the summer of 1940 it was decided to construct a protected underground headquarters in the steeply rising hillside to the south of the harbour to provide a secure communications centre and sub-command headquarters for the Commander-in-Chief Portsmouth and Fort Southwick.

The underground complex consists of two parallel pairs of entrance tunnels which enter the hillside, each pair joining to form single tunnels after approximately sixty feet. After a further 150 feet the tunnels pass through air-locks before entering the main bunker which consists of a 'ring' of offices and other accommodation (actually an enclosed rectangular system of passages with the entrance tunnels joining at the north-east and north-west corners). Plans to extend the underground accommodation to the west of the original bunker, effectively doubling the size of the headquarters, were abandoned before any work was started, although a smaller extension to the east was built to house a standby generator and ventilation plant.

The complex appears to have fallen into disuse at the end of the war although it was kept under a care and maintenance regime until 1952 when it was refurbished as a nuclear war headquarters for the dockyard. All the existing concrete-block partitioned offices and most of the surviving plant date from that period. Records of its operation through the Cold War years are sparse, and the functions of the numerous offices constructed during that period are unknown. It would appear that the bunker was disused by 1968, the communications centre having been moved by that time to newly built surface accommodation adjacent to the Rotor radar site on the Verne.

Below left: Location plan of the Portland bunker.
Below right: Plan showing the wartime configuration of offices within the bunker.

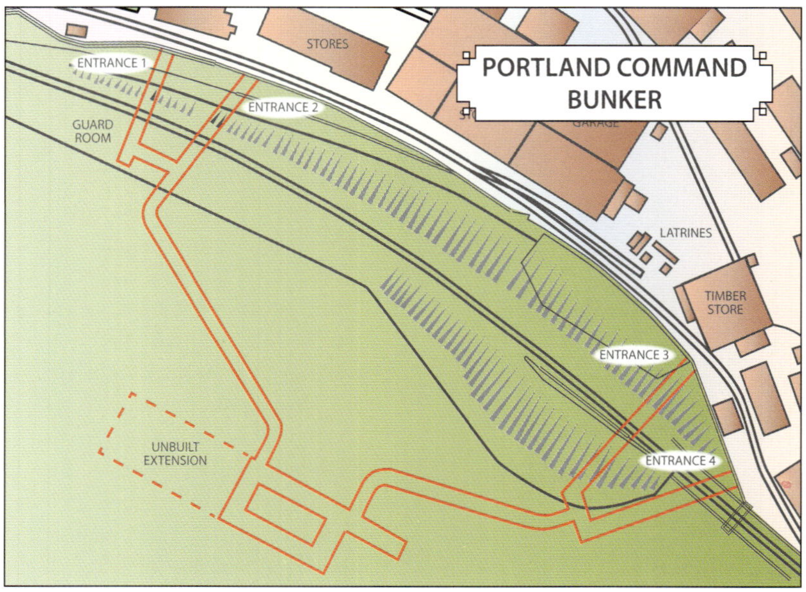

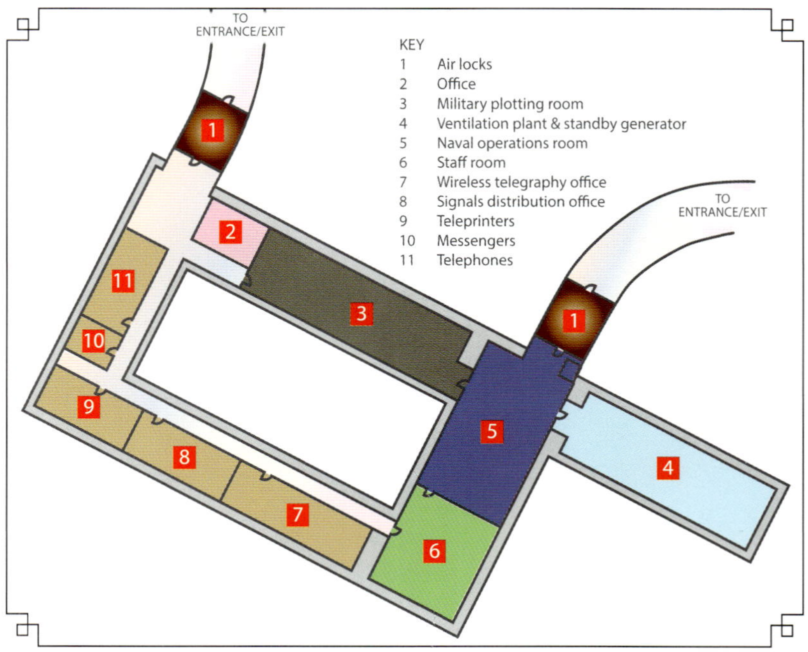

Above & below: Two of the four entrances to the bunker; one from each pair. The example below seems to be in its original wartime form while the one above may have been partially reconstructed for its Cold War role.

Above: A view looking out through the east air-lock with the curved approach tunnel in the background.
Below: Looking in through the airlock into what was, during the Second World War, the Naval Operations Room.

Above: One of the limited number of toilets in the bunker. The fittings appear to be wartime in style but are attached to concrete-block walls which are probably part of the Cold War reconstruction.

Above left: The offices on the left are from the Cold War era but the curved asbestos cladding to the tunnel girders was part of the Second World War specification.

Left: This view of the southern spine corridor illustrates the form of construction employed at Portland, using standard London Transport style cast-iron ring girders.

Opposite: The rusting remains of the bunker's air filtration and ventilation plant.

BIBLIOGRAPHY

The post-war use of Spring Quarry as the Central Government War Headquarters in the event of a nuclear war is described in:
Nick Catford, 2012, *Burlington, The Central Government War Headquarters at Corsham*, Folly Books, ISBN: 978-0-9564405-6-3

For a full description of all the underground wartime locations in London (both Second World War and Cold War) see:
Nick Catford, 2013, *Secret Underground London*, Folly Books, ISBN: 978-0-9564405-7-0

Additions and alterations to the British railway system frequently give clues to nearby wartime military and industrial installations. A chronology of these changes can be found in:
R A Cooke, 1988, *Track Layout Diagrams of the GWR and BR WR*

For a detailed, definitive account of the construction and operation of all the underground factories and storage facilities in the Corsham area, see:
N J McCamley, 2014, *Secret Underground Cities*, Folly Books, ISBN: 978-0-9928554-0-6

The complete story of the evacuation of Britain's art treasures from London and the provincial cities are detailed in:
N J McCamley, 2002 *Saving Britain's Art Treasures*, Pen & Sword, ISBN: 978-0-8505291-8-0

The full story of the Fauld disaster and the subsequent Court of Enquiry is told in:
N J McCamley, 2014 *The Fauld Disaster, 27 November 1944*, Folly Books, ISBN: 978-0-9928554-3-7

For a detailed account of the construction and operation of the Royal Enfield underground factory at Westwood, see:
Nick McCamley, 2004, *Avoncliff: The Secret History of an Industrial Hamlet in War and Peace,* Ex Libris, ISBN: 978-0-19033412-3-0

The complete history of chemical warfare, with special reference to the UK mustard gas factories and underground storage facilities, can be found in:
N J McCamley, 2006, *The Secret History of Chemical Warfare*, Pen & Sword, ISBN: 978-1-8441534-1-1

The history of the Drakelow engine factory and its subsequent cold-war roles, is told in:
Paul Stokes, 1996, *Drakelow Unearthed: The secret history of an underground complex*, BCS/Paul Stokes, ISBN: 978-0-9040157-6-9